D0887040

The Apache Indians

970,3
I

C·)

# The Apache Indians
## In Search of the Missing Tribe

### Helge Ingstad

Translated by
Janine K. Stenehjem
With a preface by
Benedicte Ingstad and
an introduction
by Thomas J. Nevins

University of Nebraska Press : Lincoln & London

DISCARD

STAUNTON PUBLIC LIBRARY

Copyright © 1945 by Gyldendal Norsk Forlad A/S.
Translation copyright 2004 by the Board of
Regents of the University of Nebraska. All rights
reserved.
Typeset in Fred Smeijers' Quadraat by
Kim Essman. Book designed by Richard Eckersley.
Printed by Thomson-Shore, Inc. Manufactured
in the United States of America.
⊛

Library of Congress Cataloging-in-Publication Data
Ingstad, Helge, 1899–2001
[Apache-indianerne. English]
The Apache Indians : in search of the missing tribe
/ Helge Ingstad ; translated by Janine K. Stenehjem;
with a preface by Benedicte Ingstad and an intro-
duction by Thomas J. Nevins.
p. cm.   Includes bibliographical references.
ISBN 0-8032-2504-0 (cloth : alkaline paper) –
ISBN 0-8032-0481-7 (electronic)
1. Apache Indians.  I. Title.
E99.A61613 2004  979.004'9725–dc22  2004011775

# Contents

# Illustrations *following page 86*

# Preface

BENEDICTE INGSTAD

When my father, Helge Ingstad, died on March 29, 2001, he was 101 years old. Born on the day before New Year's, 1899, he had lived in three centuries. But that was only one of his achievements.

He grew up in the Norwegian town of Bergen, from the Middle Ages an old Hanseatic seaport located between high mountains. His father, Olav Ingstad, was an engineer, and his mother, Olga, was the daughter of a school principal from Tromsø, in northern Norway. Together with his elder sister, Gunvor, and his younger brother, Kaare, he grew up in a home with plenty of love and few worries in spite of a World War brewing farther south in Europe. Outdoor activities, especially skiing, played an important role in the life of this family, and when the children needed new skis the father would cut down a tree in the garden and make them himself.

As a teenager Helge spent his summer holidays on the mountain plateau Hardangervidda together with a friend. They would take off for weeks with a tent and a fishing rod and live on what they were able to fish from the many lakes, where trout were plentiful. Here he would also encounter large herds of wild reindeer. This is where his dreams about exploring the wilderness were born.

After finishing high school he told his father that he would like to travel. But his father, whom he held in high regard, managed to convince him to get an education first, so he went off to Oslo to enroll in the university, which was at that time the only one in the country. His grandfather was a professor of law, and Helge decided to follow in his footsteps. After finishing his law degree he established a law practice in Levanger, a town in the middle part of Norway. However, after a few years he got restless. He sold his practice, bought a boat ticket to Canada, and set off to explore what were then unknown patches on a map. In later life when people asked him what made him give up a prosperous law practice for such an insecure future, he would answer, "I was afraid of getting rich and getting stuck."

He spent a total of four years in Canada, in the area around the Great Slave Lake. Here he lived by hunting and fur trapping, the life he had dreamed about as a boy at Hardangervidda. First he teamed up with another Norwegian, the older and more experienced trapper Hjalmar Dale. For some time he lived as the only white man with a group of the Chipewyan Indians, and for a whole year he lived all alone with his dog team on the tundra. The adventures of these years were written down in his first book, *Pelsjegerliv blandt Nord-Kanadas indianerne* (Gyldendal, 1931; *Land of Feast and Famine*, McGill-Queen's University Press, 1992), for many years a bestseller in Norway.

Sitting around the campfire with the Chipewyans – or the "Caribou-eaters" as they were called – he listened attentively to the tales they told. Helge was not only an adventurous young man, fond of nature and rough living, he also had the mind of a scientist. He was fascinated by the life of people who lived in – and from – nature and who, in his opinion, had preserved qualities in life that had been lost in "civilization." He took it upon himself to experience the way of life of these people and to write down as much as possible of what they told him. He was particularly interested in hearing the stories about Chipewyans who had wandered south many years ago, never to come back. These, he later learned, were the people now called the Navajos and the Apaches, people who even today speak languages that are related to the Chipewyan. These tales raised his curiosity, and he made up his mind to investigate them. His interest peaked when he was told that a group of Apaches led by Chief Geronimo had escaped some years before from a reservation and made their way south to the Sierra Madre, never to be found. He felt that if he could find these Apaches they would still be in possession of traditions and knowledge that might have been lost to the Indians living on the reservation. He was interested in doing a piece of what we today would call ethnographic work by writing down and preserving such knowledge, and he was particularly interested in comparing this knowledge with the information he had gathered among the

Chipewyans. Thus, a dream about an expedition to meet the Apache Indians and explore the Sierra Madre was born.

It would, however, take some years before this dream was realized. In the meantime he was sidetracked by happenings on the international scene. In 1931 the Norwegian government occupied the northern part of East Greenland, a land that had for years been utilized by Norwegian trappers. Previously all of Greenland had been considered part of Norway, but it was kept by Denmark when the Danish lost Norway to Sweden in the Peace of Kiel in 1814. In 1932, Norway, by then an independent country, decided to send a governor to what they had named Eirik the Red Land after the Norseman who, according to the sagas, sailed from Greenland and discovered the North American continent some five hundred years before Columbus.

Being well known as a fur trapper from his best-selling book, and as a lawyer who had expressed strong opinions about preserving and strengthening Norwegian interests in the Arctic, Helge was asked to go to Greenland as a governor to preserve Norwegian interests. He immediately went off with an expedition of experienced men, sled dogs, and equipment. They established a base in Antarctichavn and went about inspecting and restoring old Norwegian trapper stations along the coast. Denmark, however, brought the case to the International Court in The Hague, and in 1933 Norway lost on all points, a great disappointment for many Norwegians, including my father. He did, however, write a book about his experiences in East Greenland, Øst for den storbre (Gyldendal, 1935; East of the Great Glacier, Knopf, 1937).

Shortly after his return from East Greenland he was asked to take up a position as a governor in Svalbard (Spitsbergen), and once again he took off to the North. He stayed for two years in Svalbard, looking after Norwegian mining interests, patrolling this beautiful land with his dog team, and visiting fur trappers at remote places. These years resulted in the book Landet med de kalde kyster (Gyldendal, 1948).

Perhaps he needed a break from the cold climate – who knows? On leaving Svalbard he started to make serious plans for an expedition to Arizona to realize his old dream of meeting the Apache Indians. Actually, this was the only trip he ever made to a warm climate. On arriving in Phoenix he soon found a good friend in Vic Householder, who helped him get a job as a cowboy (although he had never been on horseback before) and later introduced him to the Guenther family at the White River Mission on the Apache reservation. He spent some time getting to know the Apaches, in particular talking with old people who still had memories of Geronimo, the war with the American soldiers, and the people who left the reservation to go south. Eventually he got a group of men together and set off for the Sierra Madre.

Although he never managed to find the Apaches in the Sierra Madre, he did write this book, *Apache indianerne: jakten på den tapte stamme* (Gyldendal, 1939; *The Apache Indians: In Search of the Missing Tribe*), a unique document from a time gone by. It was first published in Norway in 1939 and has been translated into many languages, but it is now published for the first time in English. My father always believed that he was very close to the "runaway" Apaches, finding still-warm fireplaces he believed they had used. Many years later he got a letter from a scholar of Apache origin who claimed to have grown up in the Sierra Madre, having been captured and raised by Mexican farmers and later educated and sent to college. This man claimed that as a child he had been hiding with his Apache relatives when they saw my father and his group passing by in a valley, but they did not dare to make themselves known because one man in this group had a reputation for having killed Apaches. The authenticity of this claim has never been verified, and so far the letter has not reemerged among the papers my father left behind.

When he returned to Norway he thought of going to Siberia to study Native people there and had started to negotiate with the Soviet authorities, but once more his plans were disrupted by international happenings – this time the Second World War. Norway was invaded and occupied by the Germans in April 1940. At forty, being somewhat old to become a regular soldier, he dedicated his time to working for the Red Cross, driving along the front, bringing medicines and other emergency equipment to wounded soldiers and communities that had been isolated by the battles. As the regular fighting subsided he continued working for the Red Cross on various assignments throughout the war but was also in close contact with the Norwegian underground opposition. He had settled with my mother, Anne Stine, (whom he married in 1942) on a farm near Lillehammer, and during the war years he managed to complete one novel and a play, showing the variety of his literary talents.

After the war, in 1949, he brought me (age four) and my mother back to visit his friends at the Apache reservation on the way to seeing his brother, Kaare, who was at the time Norwegian consul in Los Angeles. Somehow during the stay in Los Angeles he heard about a small group of Eskimos who lived in the great mountains of the Brooks Range in Alaska. This group was unique in two ways: they lived solely from caribou and not the sea mammals that other Eskimos depended upon, and they had only very recently had their first contacts with the outside world, thus still living a very "traditional" life. This became an irresistible temptation, and my mother and I had to take the long way back to Norway by car and boat alone, while he set off for a year with the Nunamiut people in the Brooks Range.

This became the experience he had always dreamed of, and in many ways it was similar to his years among the "Caribou eaters" in northern Canada. The Nunamiut greeted him with great friendliness and hospitality, although they must have found it strange in the beginning that this white man wanted to settle among them. They helped him prepare for the winter, with clothes and a tent of caribou skin. He lived by hunting as they did, but all the time taking film and photographs, tape-recording their songs and music, and writing down their tales. When he left Anaktuvuk the people there named a mountain after him so that he would always be known to the Nunamiut. Back in Norway my father wrote Nunamiut, a book about his experiences in Alaska, and later published the book Nunamiut Stories (The North Slope Borough Commission on Inupiat History, Language and Culture, Barrow, 1987) and a CD of their music (Songs of the Nunamiut, Tano Aschehoug, Oslo, 1998).

More than thirty years after his stay with the Nunamiut he got a long-distance call: "This is from Anaktuvuk, Alaska." Imagine his surprise! He had memories of a remote place between high Arctic mountains where people lived from caribou hunting, and all of a sudden this long-distance call! The explanation was simple. The discovery of oil on the North Slope of Alaska had led to a rapid development where even places like Anaktuvuk had become part of the modern world. The call was from the curator of a local museum,

Mr. Grant Spearman, who in cooperation with the local people was putting up an exhibition of Nunamiut cultural heritage. They were calling to find out if he had anything that might be useful for the museum. After having received a positive reply to this question, a delegation from Anaktuvuk arrived in Norway a few months later and were highly surprised to find more than they could ever have dreamed of. In this way my father became instrumental in saving a large part of the cultural heritage of a people who had come to mean so much to him. When the Simon Paneak Museum, named after his old friend and translator, was opened a few years later, he, at the age of eighty-nine, set off for Alaska and joined in a celebration in which he was the guest of honor and where he was able to meet some of his old friends who were still alive and the small children, now adults, who had been his interested spectators when he sat with candles and typewriter in his tent in the evenings, putting the knowledge he had gained down on paper.

I believe this was somewhat the role he had hoped to have among the Apaches of the Sierra Madre, if he had found them: the recorder of an oral cultural heritage before it became (too much) influenced by the modern world.

Back again in Norway he soon turned to new challenges. Combining his interest in the Arctic with his interest in history he decided to take a closer look at the old Norse sagas, especially the stories about the Viking discovery of North America. This brought him back to Greenland, this time the western coast, where immigrants from Norway and Iceland had settled around the year 930 and lived for almost 500 years until they mysteriously vanished, leaving no trace of what had happened to them. It was from this colony that a man named Leif Eirikson around year 1000 sailed toward the west and discovered Vinland, which was believed to be North America. Scientists had for years been wondering where on the American continent Vinland might be. Most of them thought it must have been relatively far to the south, in areas were wild grapes – or vines – may be found. My father, however, thought differently. He believed that the syllable *vin* did not refer to grapes, but to the old Norse word for "meadows," the way it is found in many Scandinavian place names. He also believed that one should take seriously the indications of wind directions and sailing distances given in the old Icelandic sagas about the discovery of Vinland. If there was anything that seagoing people would be sure to hand down correctly throughout the generations it would be such information, he thought, and by following the directions in the sagas one would end up much farther north than the grape-growing areas of North America.

In 1960 we set off on an expedition, the two of us – I was just a teenager at the time – trying to find traces of Viking settlements. His theory was that they would be somewhere along the northern coast of Newfoundland or southern Labrador.

It would have been like looking for a needle in a haystack if not for the indications of landmarks and distances given in the sagas. There was also a medieval map that indicated Vinland at the northern tip of Newfoundland. We set off by boat and small plane, going into every little bay and harbor and asking the same question – "Are there any old ruins around here?" One day, in a tiny fishing port called Lance aux Meadows on the very northern point of Newfoundland, we met an old fisherman by the name of Gorge Decker who answered, "Yes, come with me." I remember it clearly. My father was very excited when he saw the shape of the ruins and how they were placed in the terrain. He said, "This must be it. It all fits so well. This must be where Leif Eiriksson landed." Eight years of archaeological excavations led by my mother, who was an archaeologist, proved him to be right. A total of eight houses of Norse type, including a smithy, were excavated, and the final proof came when they found a spinning wheel and a bronze pin of undisputable Nordic type. The houses have been dated close to the year 1000, which fits well with the time of Leif Eiriksson's sailing. The ruins have now been made into a UNESCO World Heritage Site and receive more than thirty thousand visitors per year.

The Vinland discovery was the last in a long life of adventures. My father stayed alert and active almost until the end. He went to China and climbed the Great Wall at the age of ninety-three, read several newspapers every day, and kept up a large correspondence with people from all over the world who had read his books. After my mother died in 1997 he became more housebound, but he still enjoyed the many visits from young admirers who had read his books and wanted to travel in his footsteps.

The *Apache Indians* has been an inspiration for many young Norwegians to take interest in American Indian history and even to travel to the Sierra Madre. I hope that an American audience, and in particular the Apache people, will be interested in reading this historical document. It is written by a man who was not only an adventurous traveler but also had the mind of a scientist and a genuine respect and interest in the way of life of people who lived in a close relationship with nature.

Oslo, June 2002

Benedicte Ingstad

# Introduction

THOMAS J. NEVINS

Helge Ingstad traveled to Arizona in the late 1930s to visit the White Mountain Apache Indians, a Native American people who are linguistically and culturally related to the Chipewyan people Ingstad had met on an earlier trip to Canada. Ingstad's account of his adventures is invaluable for the picture it paints of the Apaches and the other peoples of the region he visited. This account must be placed, however, in the context of some of the research that has since been done on the prehistory, history, society, and culture of the White Mountain Apaches, and the Apache people as a whole.

## The Apaches

Ingstad spent most of his time with a particular subset of the Apaches, the White Mountain people, who together with the Cibecue, Tonto, and San Carlos peoples constitute a larger ethnolinguistic grouping known to researchers as the Western Apaches. There are six other ethnolinguistically distinct Apache groups, some of whom Ingstad mentions in passing in his narrative. These are the Chiricahua, Jicarilla, Kiowa-Apaches, Lipan, Mescaleros, and Navajos. These seven groups are known collectively as the Apacheans.

These seven Apache groups have been known by a variety of names. The first possible mention of the Apaches is in the records of the Coronado expedition, which encountered a group they called the Querechos. Contemporary scholars still debate whether this group, or other groups variously named the Vaqueros, Chicimecas, Jocomes, and Janos in sixteenth- and seventeenth-century Spanish records, were actually Apachean peoples.[1] The name "Apache" was first used by Spanish colonial officials in the late sixteenth century. The name is thought to be derived from the Zuni word for "enemy," *aapachu*, although there have been attempts to find its source in the language of the Yavapai Indians, or more improbably, from the Spanish language.[2]

Other names used to designate particular groups of Apache people include Apache Mansos, Apache de Xila, Gilenos, Coconinos, Tejua, Coyotero, Arivaipa, Mibrenos, Faorones, Warm Springs, and Pinaleno, to name just a few.[3] Some of these names are now obsolete, but several referred to what were actually subtribal bands of one of the seven major Apachean groups that have been subsumed within the modern, ethnologically informed system of nomenclature. For example, the Mimbre, or Mimbres Apaches, who Ingstad mentions several times in his history of the Apache Wars, are now considered to be a subgroup of the Chiricahua.

Whatever its origin, it is important to note that "Apache" is not the name the Apaches use for themselves, at least when they are speaking their own language. For example, the White Mountain Apaches call themselves *ndee*, which means something like "the people." The San Carlos people, who speak a slightly different dialect of the Western Apache language, call themselves *nnee*. Both names are linguistic cognates of *dene*, which is the name many Northern Athabaskan people use for themselves, and *dine*, which is the term used by the Navajos.

The seven Apachean peoples are divided into eastern and western groups. The eastern group, also known as the Plains Apaches, includes the Jicarilla, Lipan, and Kiowa-Apaches. The Kiowa-Apaches did not settle in the Southwest with the other Apachean people, but instead settled an area near the Kiowa Indians in the central Great Plains. The Jicarilla and Lipan lived on the western and southwestern edge of the Great Plains. The western group includes the Chiricahua, Mescalero, Navajos, and Western Apaches (somewhat confusingly, the Western Apaches are a distinct ethnolinguistic division of the western Apachean grouping). Members of the western group tended to settle in the mountainous areas of the Southwest.[4]

Today there are four major Apache reservations in the Southwest: White Mountain, San Carlos, Jicarilla, and Mescalero. Prior to the creation of the reservations in the 1880s, Apache territory, called by the

Spanish and Mexicans Apacheria, extended from Flagstaff to Tucson in the west and from southeastern Colorado to northwestern Texas. At times their territory may have extended as far south as Sonora and the northern Sierra Madre, where Ingstad went looking for the allegedly "lost" Apaches. Today it is considerably more circumscribed, although still large as compared to that of other contemporary Native groups.

The languages of the seven Apachean peoples are closely related to one another and constitute a single language family. The Apachean language family is sometimes called Southern Athabaskan, a term which identifies it with the Pacific Coast and Northern Athabaskan families of languages. With Tlingit and Eyak, two more distantly related languages, the Apachean and Athabaskan languages together constitute the Athabaskan–Eyak–Tlingit macrofamily.[5] Some authorities go further and lump the Athabaskan languages together with yet another language, Haida, into an even larger grouping called Na-Dene. As with most things having to do with the study of Athabaskans, the status of Na-Dene is controversial, and only a few authorities recognize it.[6]

## Origins

Ingstad was familiar with much of the research that had been done on Apache culture and history before the late 1930s. He correctly acknowledges that the Apaches were related to the Northern Athabaskan – speaking peoples – although their closest linguistic relatives are not the Chipewyans but more likely the Sarcees.[7] As he notes, the ancestors of the Apachean peoples lived in what is today western Canada or the northwestern Great Plains of the United States alongside many other Athabaskan peoples. The cold prairie and steppe where they lived afforded few opportunities for agriculture or horticulture, and like the other indigenous peoples of the region they were nomadic hunter-gatherers who lived on big and small game hunting and traveled between different campsites with the changing seasons. This way of life is practiced in a somewhat modified form by many Northern Athabaskan peoples today.

Linguistic and archaeological research conducted since Ingstad's visit to Arizona has greatly expanded our understanding of the place of the Apaches in the prehistory of North America. Using a technique known as glottochronology, linguists have estimated that the ancestors of the Apacheans separated from the Northern Athabaskans roughly one thousand years ago.[8] Reasons for the split remain unclear. One theory holds that a continent-wide warming trend in the first several centuries AD encouraged the proto-Apacheans to slowly colonize the Rocky Mountain foothills in the southern parts of their territory. This pattern gradually led to their separation from the other Athabaskan peoples, while later fluctuations in climate impelled them to move south in search of a warmer region.[9]

Not all Apaches agree with the scientific accounts of their origins. Some Apache people believe that the Southwest is their place of origin, and they cite as evidence of this stories that recount how they came into being on lands near to where they presently live. However, many do acknowledge their people's beginning in the north and tell stories that describe a long, hazardous journey through cold, dark lands and forbidding places.[10] There are also a few stories that describe the circumstances of the Apaches' ancestors' departure from the north. According to one of these, the mischievous behavior of one family's dog brought about the split. This story is particularly interesting because it is similar to a story still being told by some Northern Athabaskan people.

While scholars agree that the ancestors of today's Apaches once lived in the north, archaeological evidence of their journey south is scanty. Despite this lack of evidence, most authorities agree that they migrated south along the eastern edge of the Rocky Mountains over a period of several hundred years. Some archaeologists claim to have found evidence of early Apache occupations at sites in Wyoming and Colorado, but these attributions are not certain. However, based on what we know of their way of life, it seems likely that the ancestors of the Apaches did reside in territories near these sites for some time before they entered the Southwest.[11]

Most authorities agree that the Apaches did not enter the Southwest before 1400, and some argue that they may not have entered the area until after 1500. Most debates on this issue draw on the records of the Spanish expeditions sent to the area in the sixteenth century. Frequently cited are the records of the Coronado expedition of 1540. In Ingstad's day the prevalent view among historians was that the people members of the expedition called the Querechos were an Apachean group. Contemporary scholars disagree with this interpretation, however, arguing that the description given of the Querechos in the expedition's records also fits any one of several nomadic peoples.[12] What is known is that when Coronado and his party passed through the region of the Southwest historically associated with the Apaches they reported the area to be unpopulated.[13] Of course, any Apaches who lived there may have been present but stayed out of sight while the conquistadors passed through their territory.

## Contact and History

Ingstad himself went on an expedition into the Sierra Madre region of Mexico in order to find a group of people he thought might afford him a window into what Apache culture had been in a time when it was less influenced by contact with Western culture. However, it is important to note that since they first entered the Southwest the Apaches have been influenced by contact with Western culture and society. Of course, contact was a two-way street: encounters with the Apache had significant effects on the colonizers as well. Both the Spanish and Apaches were fairly recent immigrants to the Southwest, and their interactions shaped the geopolitics of the region for over two hundred years.

Spanish colonial policy was directed to assimilating indigenous peoples into the empire and converting them into loyal Christian subjects of the Spanish crown. They attempted this through the establishment of mission churches and policies designed to remold the societies of the indigenous peoples in the image of European peasant life.[14] While this was somewhat successful in Mexico, it was much less so in the New Mexico and Arizona territories. The Spanish attempted to extend this policy into the Southwest when they established Santa Fe in 1610. There, Spanish colonial authorities managed to bring the numerous Rio Grande Pueblo peoples under their sway, until a general revolt in 1680. For a time it seemed their expansion was checked, but they eventually reestablished control of the Pueblos and the Santa Fe area in the late 1690s.[15]

At around the same time the Pueblo revolt was taking place, the Apaches were settling into their respective historic territories. A hypothetical ethnographer working with the Apaches a century earlier, in the sixteenth century, probably would have noted different and perhaps less distinct divisions among the Apacheans than we do today. As they moved south, they gradually transformed into the groups we currently recognize. Contact with Europeans and other Native American societies played an important part in this process.

The eastern groups were, to varying extents, seminomadic bison hunters. The Jicarilla and Lipan settled the area between New Mexico and Texas. The Kiowa-Apaches settled farther east and formed close ties with the Kiowa Indians. Two of the main western Apachean groups, the Mescaleros and Chiricahua, moved into the mountainous areas of New Mexico, southeastern Arizona, and northern Mexico. Here they developed a way of life that combined big-game hunting with foraging and a seminomadic pattern of residence.[16] The Navajos settled in the southern reaches of present-day Colorado and Utah, just to the north of the Hopis, from whom they picked up a number of practices and traits. The Hopis taught the Navajos pottery and weaving, as well as agriculture based on maize. Contact with Hopis and other Pueblo peoples also influenced the development of Navajo religion and ceremonialism.[17]

The Western Apaches occupied a territory that extended across much of central and eastern Arizona. It was centered on the southern edge of the Colorado Plateau region, along an escarpment known as the Mogollon Rim, essentially a thousand-foot-tall wall of rock that runs through east-central Arizona. On the eastern edge of the Rim were the White Mountains. South of the Rim and White Mountains was the Salt River Canyon, which was where many Western Apache families lived during the winter months.

Western Apache social organization is similar to that of the Navajos, who live north of them, across the Painted Desert. These two

groups are unique among the Apaches for having what some anthropologists have described as matrilineal clans. Interestingly, several Western Apache clans trace their origin from the Navajos.[18] In
addition, the languages of these two groups are closely related, to
the point where someone speaking Navajo can usually make themselves understood to Western Apache speakers, and vice versa. Like
the Navajos, the Western Apaches also acquired agriculture through
contact with Pueblo culture, although some practices, like weaving
and pottery, they did not adopt.[19] But despite cultural, linguistic, and
social ties, relations between the Navajos and Western Apaches were
sometimes hostile.

Living in the eastern section of Western Apache territory were the
'Dził Gą'a, or White Mountain people. Save for the Navajos, they were
probably the most agriculturally oriented of the Apacheans.[20] To the
west were the Tontos, who lived in a similar manner as the Chiricahua
and were generally the most nomadic of the Western Apaches. In
between these two groups lived the Cibecue people, and to the south
of them were the San Carlos people. These two groups probably fell
somewhere between the Tontos and the White Mountain people with
regards to their social organization and the amount of agriculture
they practiced.

The areas that the Navajos and Western Apaches settled had once
been occupied by other Native peoples, such as the Anasazi, architects
of the ruins for which the Southwest is so famous and ancestors of
today's Pueblo Indians. This has led to the widespread notion that
Apaches drove the Anasazi into extinction. However, there is little
archaeological evidence to support this idea. Most evidence suggests
that during the twelfth and thirteenth centuries, while the Apacheans
were still on their way from Canada, Anasazi society was transform-
ing in response to the same environmental forces that impelled the
Apacheans to migrate south. Anthropologists and archaeologists
agree that the Anasazi did not actually disappear, but instead became
the Hopi, Zuni, Acoma, and the other Pueblo Indian peoples who
now live along the Rio Grande River.[21]

The intensive raiding with which the Apaches have become associated probably did not begin until after their encounter with the

Spanish military in the sixteenth and seventeenth centuries. As Ingstad points out, relations between the Spanish and Apaches were not initially hostile. It was not until the 1650s that Spanish records mention what may have been Apache raiding activities in northeastern Sonora and northwestern Chihuahua.[22] The Apaches were fairly marginal to early Spanish mission efforts, which were primarily directed at the Pueblo Indians. The Apaches did not have anything to do with the Pueblo revolt of 1680, nor did they resist the reestablishment of Spanish colonial control of the Rio Grande valley in 1690s.[23]

Beginning in 1680s the Spanish attempted to tie Native American groups such as the Chiricahua and Mescalero Apaches more securely to their sphere of colonial and political control. To curtail the growing threat of raids the Spanish built a string of presidios – essentially fortified residential compounds – in northern Sonora and Chihuahua. There they attempted to resettle the local Indian groups, convert them to Catholicism, and persuade them to adopt a European-based style of small-scale farming. Some Apaches took to the presidio way of life, but the majority fled from it, and when the Spanish later attempted to resettle and "pacify" these people by force, hostilities quickly erupted.[24]

These and other attempts to directly or indirectly impose Spanish authority on the Apaches backfired. The Spanish were unable to induce many Apaches to voluntarily give up their way of life and join their empire or intimidate them into surrendering. The Spanish were never able to subdue the Apaches, who raided their settlements with impunity. The Apaches relied on small-scale hit-and-run fighting techniques, rarely allowing the Spanish to draw them into the kind of large-scale, set-piece battles the Spanish preferred. Even in the few cases when they did win on the battlefield the Spanish were unable to translate their successes into political control over Apache society and territory.

Part of the reason the Spanish had such difficulty in establishing control and dominion over Apaches had to do with the dispersed, decentralized nature of Apache social organization. Apaches lived in seminomadic settlements spread out over a vast landscape and did not invest political power in a single government or ruling body. Their chiefs, or *nant'án*, had no coercive authority and did not rule as much as lead by persuasion and example.[25] Consequently, the Spanish were contending with a loose confederation of people connected to one another through language, culture, trade, and, in some cases, kinship, and who possessed great knowledge of the complex terrain in which they lived.

Contact with the presidios alerted the Apaches to the dangers the Spanish posed. As the western Apacheans were coming into contact with the Spanish, the eastern Apacheans were beginning to deal with attacks from other Indian groups, particularly the Comanches. The Comanches forced the Lipan into east-central New Mexico and central Texas, eventually dispersing them. Some Lipan joined with Mescaleros and Chiricahua, or with other, non-Apachean people. Comanche raids also pushed the Jicarilla from the Plains into northern New Mexico.[26]

The Apaches did not wage war in the same manner or for the same purposes as the Spanish or other Europeans. For the Apaches raiding was not about conquest but instead about subsistence.[27] They engaged in raiding to acquire materials they deemed necessary to their survival and well-being. They did not attempt to seize land from the Spanish and their subjects. Instead, they sought resources, primarily horses, but sometimes cattle.[28] They also seized weapons and occasionally durable goods such as metal tools and cookware, although they usually acquired these items through trade.

The most common targets of Apache raiding were settlements in Sonora and Chihuahua. Most of this raiding was done by the Chiricahua, Mescaleros, and Western Apaches, although the Jicarilla and what was left of the Lipan also engaged in raiding on a smaller scale. Raids were also occasionally directed at Pueblo and Tohono Odham (Pima and Papago) settlements, but the Spanish and later the Mexicans were their primary targets.[29] The Utes and Pueblo Indians were usually the main targets of Navajo and Jicarilla raiding.

By the late seventeenth century the Spanish had lost effective control of northern Sonora and Chihuahua to the Apaches, and several of the presidios they had built as a bulwark against Apache raiding had been abandoned. Occasionally a governor or military leader would attempt to mount retaliatory counterraids into Apache territory, but these had little lasting effects on the ability of the Apaches to mount raids into Mexico. A strip of territory that ran along the border of Arizona and Sonora became known as the Apache Corridor, and Apache raiding parties moved through this zone with impunity. Although it was never their aim to do so, the Apaches essentially wrested effective control of northwestern Mexico from the Spanish. [30]

In 1786 the Spanish began another push to pacify the Apaches. Under the leadership of newly appointed Viceroy Bernardo de Galvez, they combined military raids with policies designed to attract the Apaches and other hostile Native peoples to live on agricultural presidios in exchange for rations and domestic goods. This strategy began to have some success, but it was abandoned in the 1810s when Spanish rule in Mexico began to crumble. By the time of the Mexican Revolution in 1821 Apache raiding had resumed, and quickly thereafter the Spanish once again lost control of Sonora and Chihuahua. [31]

After the Revolution the Mexican government policies toward the Apaches were similar to those of the Spanish. They sought to incorporate the Apaches, along with other Indian groups, into mainstream Mexican society, usually as farmers but sometimes as laborers in other industries. They also saw missionization was an important tool in this process. [32] In this and other policies the Mexicans were just as deluded as the Spanish. At a certain point in the battles for control of the Sonoran territories the Mexicans became so desperate that they began to issue bounties for the scalps of Apache men, women, and children, which initiated a period of increasingly violent conflict in the region. [33]

## The Americans Arrive

The Arizona and New Mexico territories were seized by the Americans after their war with Mexico in 1848. The first official contacts between the U.S. government and the Apaches took place shortly thereafter in 1850, when General Kearney and Colonel Kit Carson led an expedition to survey the Arizona and New Mexico territories. As had been the case with the Spanish, relations between the Apaches and the U.S. forces in the southwest were initially amicable, and after some negotiations the former allowed the Army to build a string of forts and garrisons throughout the Arizona territory.[34]

According to the peace treaty they had signed with the Mexicans, the Americans were obligated to keep the Apaches from crossing the border to attack settlements in Sonora and Chihuahua.[35] The Apaches resented this, as well as the U.S. government's claim to have legal sovereignty over Apache territory. Other obvious sources of tension were the growing demands of white settlers, ranchers, and miners for access to Apache land and resources.

Contrary to popular accounts in film and fiction, the events precipitating war between the Americans and the Apaches were not raids by the Apaches but instead a series of provocative actions on the part of whites, miners, and army officers, particularly events such as the 1871 Camp Grant Massacre discussed by Ingstad. In fact, most Apache leaders relied on diplomacy and negotiation in their dealings with the Americans whenever possible. Because of this, relations between the Apaches and Americans remained mostly peaceful through the 1850s. The primary catalyst for open conflict came in 1861 when a U.S. cavalry lieutenant named Bascom took Cochise and several other Chiricahua leaders hostage while looking for a Mexican captive. Cochise escaped, but Bascom killed the other hostages, setting in motion a cycle of conflict between the U.S. Army and the Apaches that would last for over twenty years.[36]

With the exception of the Tontos, most of the Western Apaches, in particular the White Mountain and San Carlos Apaches, did manage to maintain a kind of tense peace with the U.S. Army. After a series of Army raids into their territory, the White Mountain Apaches agreed to allow the Army to build a base on their land.[37] In 1870 Fort Apache was built on a bluff overlooking the confluence of the eastern and northern forks of the White River. It eventually became General Crook's main base of operation in his actions against the Chiricahua. While relations between the Army and the White Mountain people were generally peaceful, some Cibecues and other Western Apaches did take up arms against them in response to the killing of the religious leader Nock-ay-del-klinne at Cibecue Creek in 1881 by a cavalry patrol. This revolt led to a siege of Fort Apache, which was relieved only when Army reinforcements arrived from New Mexico.[38]

General Crook, who took over Army operations in the Arizona territories in 1872, succeeded in persuading many White Mountain, Cibecue, and San Carlos warriors to join his forces as scouts. More than a few Chiricahua Apaches also served as Indian scouts, and all were vital to the Army's war efforts. But despite their accomplishments, the federal government treated the scouts very poorly. The Chiricahua scouts, who were particularly important in actions against Geronimo, were unceremoniously and involuntarily discharged from the army after the wars and shipped to Florida with the other Chiricahua.[39]

In contrast with Spanish and later Mexican policies, early U.S. policy involved the relocation of Native peoples away from places of white settlement. Unlike the Spanish, who typically recognized the territorial claims of the Indians but not their political independence, the Americans regarded the Native American societies as politically distinct from themselves and, at least in the early years of their expansion west, did not attempt to incorporate them into their own social and political system. They also did not recognize the territorial claims of Native peoples.[40] Instead, Americans often viewed these claims as obstacles to their expansion.

Signs of an evolution in the U.S. government's thinking about their dealings with Natives appeared in the 1830s. Weighing in on the debate over Jackson's relocation of the Cherokee Nation, U.S. Supreme Court Chief Justice John Marshall described Native groups living inside the territory of the United States as "domestic dependent nations," which could be construed as meaning that they were in some way a part of the larger, encompassing non-Indian society. The reservation system was a product of this rethinking. Rather than simply remove the Indians from the path of American expansion, the reservations were intended to contain and isolate them.[41] The idea was to manage conflict between Indians and settlers by forcing tribes onto the most remote, and from a white perspective, least desirable sections of the respective territories, thereby keeping the two groups from contact with one another. This change in policy came into being as the U.S. government began to realize that it was impractical to relocate all of the Indian groups to Indian Territory in Oklahoma.

## The Reservation Years

The formation of the reservations often married aspects of the older and newer policies, as many Indian groups were forcibly moved to reservations not located on their original ranges. In 1873 the U.S. government began to consolidate the various Apache groups at San Carlos in eastern Arizona. The relocations proceeded gradually, and over the next five years the Chiricahua and most Western Apaches had been moved there. [42]

While at San Carlos the Apaches were forced to live near the army outposts, and their movements were severely restricted. This policy was designed to keep the Apaches from leaving the reservation, eliminating the problems associated with contact between them and white settlers. But it also created overcrowded living conditions and put stress on the limited local subsistence resources. What food people could gather locally was quickly exhausted, and as a result many people could not feed themselves. The Army attempted to deal with this by distributing rations. In the best of times these were barely adequate, and on many occasions rations didn't reach the people at all. Conditions were abysmal, and many people died as the result of starvation and communicable diseases.

The conditions at San Carlos are often cited as the cause of the Chiricahua outbreaks and revolts of 1880s. Eventually the policy of concentrating the Apaches on one reservation was abandoned. The White Mountain and Cibecue people were allowed back to their lands to the north in the early 1880s, although some White Mountain people stayed on in the San Carlos community of Bylas. [43] Many of the Chiricahua were shipped to Florida, especially those who had actively resisted the Americans. Some Chiricahua were dispersed among the remaining Apache reservation lands; some moved north and settled with the White Mountain people, while others either stayed on the San Carlos reserve or were relocated to the Mescalero reservation in New Mexico. [44]

Conditions on the White Mountain reservation were considerably better than they had been at San Carlos. However, even here the people were still forced to exist under the watchful eye and of the Army and the Indian Affairs superintendent. As at San Carlos, the ability of people to move about on or off the reservation was tightly controlled.[45] Ingstad observes that the Army went so far as to issue identifying "tags" to Apache men in order to better keep track of movements. As he notes, most of the people resented this, although records from this period show that more than a few Apaches adopted these tag-names as personal monikers.[46] In fact, some are still in use today.

## White Mountain Apaches

The White Mountain Apache culture that Ingstad observed in the late 1930s was the product of a long history that had reached a turning point when the reservation was established in the 1880s. Perhaps most immediately altered at the beginning of the reservation period were certain aspects of Apache social organization, particularly those having to do with seasonal patterns of migration. However, the prereservation culture was not overthrown completely, but instead modified and adapted by Apaches to fit the changing circumstances of their relations with American society.

Prior to their internment on the reservation, the White Mountain and other Western Apache people were fairly nomadic, typically moving between winter camps located in riverine lowlands located near the Salt River Canyon and summer camps in the highlands of the Mogollon Rim and White Mountains.[47] The summer campsites were connected to an aspect of their social organization described by anthropologists as the clan system. Each of the summer campsites were "owned" in the sense that specific groups of women, all related to each other through their mothers and mother's sisters, had broadly recognized use-rights to them. These women cooperated in farming arable plots of land located near the campsites and in performing a variety of domestic and subsistence activities. These women and their daughters formed associations that constituted the cores of the clans, and because of this anthropologists sometimes describe the clans as matrilineal. When the reservation was established there were sixty active clans. Men related to the associations of women were, of course, also important to the clans, and groups of brothers and male cousins cooperated in hunting, trading, and building residences and other structures, as well as in raiding and warfare.

Western Apache families lived in what are commonly called "wickiups," or what they called *gową*. The exact shape of the wickiup varied somewhat from one subgroup to another, but generally they were either domed or conical structures built from a framework of long, slender branches onto which were plaited heavy grasses. After the turn of the century, when the Apaches began to have access to finished lumber and building materials, the design of the wickiups began to change. It is possible that when he visited in the late 1930s Ingstad saw wickiups built with framed doors, windows, and internal wood stoves.[48] Wickiups were usually inhabited by married couples and their children. In most cases they would be located in the camp, or *gotah*, of the wife's mother. In these circumstances the husband would be expected to perform a variety of tasks for his wife's family. However, a husband would always maintain close ties with his own family and clan, and it was not unusual for young couples to periodically move their residences between the husband's and wife's family's campsites.[49]

Different family groups who lived in close proximity were loosely associated in local groups and larger, regional confederations known by anthropologists as bands, which facilitated cooperation in gathering foodstuffs, working agricultural lands, performing ceremonies, maintaining communication, and, in prereservation times, organizing raiding parties.[50] As in the case of the San Carlos reserve, Army restrictions sharply curtailed the movements of White Mountain Apaches, and for the most part they were restricted to their summer campsites. This restriction had a profound and negative effect on the local economy and society. People were no longer able to hunt or gather many of the materials they depended on, and as a result they were forced to rely on rations dispensed by the Army. The White Mountain Apaches were thus forced to adopt a more sedentary way of life. Over time, the relative significance of the local groups and bands as forms of social organization was attenuated, while that of the clans increased.[51]

There were other threats to White Mountain Apache culture in the early years of the reservation as well. As Ingstad notes, the Apaches at one point came into conflict with Mormon settlers. In the latter half of the 1870s the Mormons established a string of communities on the northern edge of the Mogollon Rim. [52] Many of these still exist, such as Snowflake, Show Low, Pinetop, Lakeside, and Greer, to name a few. A few adventurous Mormon families decided to build ranches at a site they called Forestdale, located in the north-central area of the Apache reservation, just south of Show Low. Accounts of what happened to this first settlement are unclear, but it appears that some Apaches managed to pressure the Mormon families into leaving. The Mormons made another attempt to settle the Forestdale territory in 1881. This understandably irked the Apaches, and in order to placate them, and possibly forestall another outbreak of hostilities, the Army forced the settlers off the reservation in 1882. After being ejected a second time the Mormon settlers abandoned the project. [53]

The concept of reservations as lands that belonged inviolably and in perpetuity to the Native American people who lived on them was an idea that the U.S. government did not take seriously until the passage of the Indian Reorganization Act of 1934. Up until this time many people both inside and outside the Indian Bureau pushed to integrate the reservations with the mainstream society and open up their lands to outside commercial interests. The Dawes Act of 1887 divided Indian reservation land into allotments that were to be distributed to individual tribal members as their personal property. This had a disastrous effect on many reservations, as white land speculators took advantage of this system to offer small sums of money to impoverished and frequently malnourished people in exchange for ownership of their land. As a result, many Indian communities were essentially wiped out. [54] The relative isolation of the White Mountain reservation and the general hostility of Apaches to selling land helped to forestall or at least mitigate this policy to some extent.

The years between the formation of the Apache reservations in the 1880s and the mid-1930s were a period of indecision in U.S. government policies toward the Apaches. Occasionally the Indian Affairs Bureau would devise policies to provide Apaches with some limited degree of economic and political autonomy. In furtherance of these goals the bureau attempted teach the people of San Carlos and White Mountain American-style ranching and farming. The farming program was somewhat successful in the moderate climate of the White Mountains, which receive most of Arizona's precipitation. On the hotter, more arid San Carlos reserve these farming programs did not fare as well.[55] Cattle ranching was not initially successful on either reservation, and eventually the bureau leased a sizable portion of Apache rangelands to white ranchers. The real heyday of white ranching on the reservation was during the First World War, when there were beef shortages because of the war effort. In the years after the war, Apache-run ranches began to perform better, and the number of leases issued to white ranchers began to drop until the practice was done away with in the 1930s.[56]

In the years immediately after the establishment of the reservation, the U.S. government decided that perhaps the best way to "civilize" the Native Americans would be to convert them to Christianity. The government divided the reservations between the denominations interested in establishing missions. The franchise for the White Mountain Apache reservation was awarded to the Lutherans, who in 1896 established a mission at Eastfork, not far from the site of Fort Apache.[57] In time both Catholics and Mormons also made inroads on the White Mountain and San Carlos reservations. However, under the auspices of the capable Reverend Guenther, who took over as the local leader of the Church in 1911, the Lutherans remained the dominant Christian sect on the White Mountain reservation throughout the first half of the twentieth century.

Based presumably on information from Reverend Guenther, with whom he stayed at White River, Ingstad comments that few Apaches had converted to Christianity and that Apache religious practices continued to be observed. On the last score he is certainly correct, and in fact they continue to be observed to this day. However, it is possible that Ingstad's interest in the surviving Apache religion led him to overlook the influence the missionaries were having on the religious life of the White Mountain Apaches. For instance, although contemporary Apaches continue to observe aspects of indigenous religious practice, many if not most of these people also consider themselves to be Christians. However, even though many Apaches adopted Christianity they did not necessarily abandon their Apache identities. In the 1930s a faction of White Mountain and San Carlos

Apaches broke away from the main branch of the Lutheran Church and established their own independent church based on the Lutheran rite but administered by Apaches.[58] Among other things, all of this suggests that missionaries such as Reverend Guenther had at least some impact on the religious life of the reservation, although perhaps not the impact they intended.

At the turn of the century the authority of the traditional religious leaders was increasingly threatened by a number of forces, not the least of which were the efforts of Lutheran missionaries and government administrators to convert the Apaches to Western social and religious values. During this time there were many apocalyptic movements, some of which prophesied the return of the land to the Apaches, and some of which promised the disappearance of the whites. Most of these, such as the Na'ilde' movement started by Nockay-del-klinne (who was killed in the 1881 Cibecue Creek Massacre), were short-lived. Others, in particular the later Daagodighį́ movement between 1903 and 1908, were longer-lived and had a greater impact on Apache religious life.[59]

A religious movement ongoing at the time of Ingstad's visit to the White Mountains was created by a man named Silas John Edwards.[60] His religious teachings blended aspects of Christian and Apache religious practices. Silas John was instructed in the arts of Apache religious practice by his father and grandfather and was also employed as an aide and translator by Reverend Guenther, who taught him Christian liturgy and theology. He was held in high esteem by Christian missionaries and Apache people alike and was noted for his ability to translate Christian religious concepts into the Apache language and Apache concepts into English. In the 1920s Silas John began to develop a theology and a set of ceremonial practices that combined aspects of both religions. Over time he became a prominent religious leader in his own right, developing a following that extended beyond White Mountain to the San Carlos and Mescalero reservations. He even invented a special writing system for recording his liturgy and ritual procedures.[61] Silas John eventually ran afoul of the Bureau of Indian Affairs and Christian missionaries. In 1933 he was framed for killing his wife and imprisoned, although he was exonerated and released in 1954. His teachings became the inspiration for what is today called the Holy Ground Movement.

## The "Lost" Apaches

Ingstad visited the reservation during a time when there was a great deal of anthropological interest in the Apaches. An American ethnographer named Grenville Goodwin (whom Ingstad talked to on the telephone but never met, according to Ingstad's daughter, Benedicte Ingstad) performed fieldwork on the White Mountain and San Carlos reservations from 1931 to 1937, and, like Ingstad, was also a self-taught ethnographer and anthropologist. He worked closely with a number of professional anthropologists and published a number of technical articles. A monograph he was working on before his untimely death was published posthumously by his wife under the title *Social Organization of the Western Apache Indians*. Goodwin had himself mounted an unsuccessful expedition into the Sierra Madre in the early 1930s in search of the "lost" Apaches. He recorded some interesting sites that might have been inhabited by a small group of Apaches, but the sites had obviously been abandoned by the time he found them, and despite a few leads, he never found conclusive proof of the existence of the "lost" group.

Despite the fact that both Goodwin and Ingstad failed to find the "lost" Apaches, it is certainly possible that a small band of Apaches had managed to eke out a fugitive existence in the Sierra Madre until the 1920s or even later. What is less certain is who they may have been, what their relations were to other Apache groups, and how they ended up in the Sierra Madre. In 1974 Goodwin's son Neil led an expedition to revisit some of the areas in the Sierra Madre noted by his father as possible sites of Apache habitation in the late nineteenth and early twentieth centuries.[62] His findings were no more conclusive than his father's, but he and his fellow searchers did suspect that the materials they did find were from a small band of Apaches who had fled to the region in order to escape conflicts with American and Mexican forces. What happened to these people, if they in fact existed, is unclear. Definitive answers to the questions about the Sierra Madre Apaches may never be known.

# Notes

1. Edward H. Spicer, *Cycles of Conquest: The Impact of Spain, Mexico and the United States on the Indians of the Southwest, 1533–1960* (Tucson: University of Arizona Press, 1989); Morris Opler, "The Apachean Culture Pattern and Its Origins," in Alfonso Ortiz, ed., *Handbook of North American Indians, Southwest v.* 10 (Washington, DC: Smithsonian Institution, 1983), 368–92.

2. Opler, "Apachean Culture Pattern."

3. Opler, "Apachean Culture Pattern."

4. The distinction between the eastern and western Apacheans is based partly on geography and related subsistence practices, and partly on the linguistic analysis in Harry Hoijer, "The Chronology of the Athapaskan Languages," *International Journal of American Linguistics* 22 (1956): 219–32. However, both Opler, "Apachean Culture Pattern," and Charles R. Kaut, *The Western Apache Clan System: Its Origins and Developments*, University of New Mexico Publications in Anthropology 9 (Albuquerque: University of New Mexico Press, 1957), propose more complex and detailed analyses. The division of the Apacheans into eastern and western groups has been retained for the sake of simplicity.

5. Marianne Mithun, *The Languages of Native North America* (Cambridge: Cambridge University Press, 1999).

6. Mithun, *Languages of Native North America*. Na-Dene was first proposed in Edward Sapir, "The Na-Dene Language: A Preliminary Report," *American Anthropologist* 17 (1915): 105–31.

7. Michael E. Krauss, "Na-Dene and Eskimo," in Lyle Campell and Marianne Mithun, eds., *The Languages of Native North America: An Historical and Comparative Account* (Austin: University of Texas Press, 1979), 803–901; and Harry Hoijer, "The Position of the Apachean Languages in the Athapaskan Stock," in Keith Basso and Morris Opler, eds., *Anthropological Papers of the University of Arizona* 21 (Tucson: University of Arizona Press, 1971), 3–6.

8. Hoijer, "Chronology of the Athapaskan Languages."

9. Richard J. Perry, *The Western Apache: People of the Mountain Corridor* (Austin: University of Texas Press, 1991), 122–25.

10. Two good collections of Western Apache stories are Pliny E. Goddard, "Myths and Tales of the White Mountain Apache," *Anthropological*

*Papers of the American Museum of Natural History* 24 (New York, 1920); and Grenville Goodwin, *Myths and Tales of the White Mountain Apache,* (1939; reprint, Tucson: University of Arizona Press, 1994).

11. Perry, *Western Apache.* For an overview of the archaeological and physical anthropological research into this topic, see J. Loring Haskell, *Southern Athapaskan Migration A.D. 200–1750* (Tsaile, AZ: Navajo Community College Press, 1987).

12. Opler, "Apachean Culture Pattern."

13. Spicer, *Cycles of Conquest,* 229.

14. Spicer, *Cycles of Conquest,* chap. 11.

15. Spicer, *Cycles of Conquest,* 230. For a more complete discussion of Pueblo history see Edward P. Dozier, *The Pueblo Indians of North America* (1970; reprint, Prospect Heights IL: Waveland Press, 1983).

16. Opler, "Apachean Culture Pattern."

17. Perry, *Western Apache,* 152–53.

18. Grenville Goodwin, *The Social Organization of the Western Apache* (Chicago: University of Chicago Press, 1942), 109–10.

19. Perry, *Western Apache,* 153.

20. But even so, according to Grenville Goodwin, "The Social Divisions and Economic Life of the Western Apache," *American Anthropologist* 37 (1935): 55–64, agriculture supplied only about twenty-five percent of their subsistence needs. Both Navajo and White Mountain social organization retained most elements of the Apacheans' nomadic, hunter-gatherer way of life.

21. Dozier, *Pueblo Indians of North America,* 31–43.

22. Spicer, *Cycles of Conquest,* 230–31.

23. Spicer, *Cycles of Conquest,* 231.

24. Spicer, *Cycles of Conquest,* 232–36.

25. Goodwin, *Social Organization of Western Apache,* 164–92.

26. Spicer, *Cycles of Conquest,* 230.

27. The Apache distinguished between raiding and forms of warfare based on vengeance. See Grenville Goodwin and Keith Basso, ed., *Western Apache Raiding and Warfare* (Tucson: University of Arizona Press, 1971).

28. Goodwin, *Social Organization of Western Apache,* chap. 2.

29. Goodwin, *Social Organization of Western Apache,* chap. 2.

30. Spicer, *Cycles of Conquest,* 236.

31. Basso, "The Western Apache," 465; Spicer, *Cycles of Conquest*, 239–40.

32. Spicer, *Cycles of Conquest*, 334–42.

33. Spicer, *Cycles of Conquest*, 240–41.

34. Spicer, *Cycles of Conquest*, 245–48.

35. The Treaty of Guadalupe Hildalgo.

36. Spicer, *Cycles of Conquest*, 245–50.

37. Maj. John Green, from his 1869 report, "Interesting Scout Among the White Mountain Apache Some of Whom Sue for Peace and a Reservation," reprinted in Peter Cozzens, ed., *Eyewitnesses to the Indian Wars 1865–1890: The Struggle for Apacheria* (Mechanicsburg PA: Stackpole Books, 2001), 40–48. According to Goodwin's account, the negotiations that led to the construction of Fort Apache were underway one or two years prior to Green's raid. See Goodwin, *Social Organization of Western Apache*, 13–15.

38. Spicer, *Cycles of Conquest*, 254.

39. Opler, "Apachean Culture Pattern," 401–18.

40. Spicer, *Cycles of Conquest*, 343–45.

41. Spicer, *Cycles of Conquest*, 345–47.

42. Spicer, *Cycles of Conquest*, 251–52.

43. Goodwin, *Social Organization of Western Apache*, 9.

44. Spicer, *Cycles of Conquest*, 255–56.

45. Opler, "Apachean Culture Pattern."

46. See Goodwin, *Social Organization of Western Apache*, appendix C, for a more complete examination of the tag-names and their place in Western Apache society.

47. In developing this discussion of Western Apache social organization I have relied on Goodwin, *Social Organization of Western Apache*, and Kaut, *Western Apache Clan System*.

48. See Winfred Buskirk, *The Western Apache: Living with the Land Before 1950* (Norman: University of Oklahoma Press, 1986), 13, for a picture of a wickiup with a framed door.

49. Goodwin, *Social Organization of Western Apache*, 127.

50. Goodwin, *Social Organization of Western Apache*, 147–60.

51. Kaut, *Western Apache Clan System*, 72–73.

52. Thomas R. McGuire, *Mixed Bloods and Cattle Barons: Documents for a History of the Livestock Economy on the White Mountain Apache Reservation, Ari-*

zona, Arizona State Museum Archaeological Series 142 (Tucson, 1980), 34–36.

53. McGuire, *Mixed Bloods and Cattle Barons*, 38; see also Spicer, *Cycles of Conquest*, 255.

54. Spicer, *Cycles of Conquest*, 347–48.

55. Spicer, *Cycles of Conquest*, 256.

56. McGuire, *Mixed Bloods and Cattle Barons*, chap. 5.

57. For a brief biography of Reverend Guenther and history of the Lutheran Mission on the White Mountain Reservation, see William B. Kessel, "Edgar and Minnie Guenther," in Alan Ferg, ed. *Western Apache Material Culture: The Goodwin and Guenther Collections* (Tucson: University of Arizona Press, 1987), 9–26; Spicer, *Cycles of Conquest*, 257.

58. Spicer, *Cycles of Conquest*, 260.

59. Grenville Goodwin and Charles R. Kaut, "A Native Religious Movement Among the White Mountain and Cibeque Apache," *Southwestern Journal of Anthropology* 10 (1954): 385–404.

60. Goodwin and Kaut, "Native Religious Movement;" Alan Ferg and William B. Kessel, "Ritual," in Alan Ferg, ed., *Western Apache Material Culture*, 109–52; Kessel, "Edgar and Minnie Guenther,"

61. A description of Silas John's writing system can be found in Basso, *Western Apache Language and Culture*, 25–52.

62. Grenville Goodwin's record of his hunt for the Sierra Madre Apaches has been collected in Grenville Goodwin and Neil Goodwin, *Apache Diaries: A Father-Son Journey* (Lincoln: University of Nebraska Press, 2000). See also Morris E. Opler, "Grenville Goodwin," in Alan Ferg, ed., *Western Apache Material Culture*, 27–40.

The Apache Indians

Southwest Territories, ca. 1945

I

# The Long Migration

A trail of dog sleds and men wearing pelts and snowshoes wind their way across the white tundra of northern Canada. It's slow going. The dogs suffer from hunger and trudge along with their tails hanging low. The twelve Indians and one white man who straggle behind their sleds aren't that much better off. Glaring sunshine floods down upon the white-covered earth, but that low-hanging, glowing ball on the horizon is a bit of a farce. The air is so bitterly cold that even through the smallest slits in the caribou coats the snow blows in and stings like needle pricks, and misty billows of steam waft around the faces of both man and animal as they breathe into the icy air.

It was toward the end of my journey with the "caribou-eaters," a group of Chipewyan Indians who brave the hard life in the forest and tundra west of the Hudson Bay. For nearly a year we had been following the caribou, creatures that play a vital role in these people's existence. There are millions of these animals here, but the land is so vast that relying on hunting them day after day can be risky. Sometimes we were lucky and lived high on the hog, other times it was a race against hunger. Midwinter we had to push north right up to the Northwest Passage in hopeful search of the caribou, but no sign of life was discovered. Food had to be found, and quickly. There was nothing else we could do but travel south and try our luck there. So we headed for the forests.

We keep looking ahead longing to reach the green, sheltering pine forests that we haven't seen for quite some time. The caribou must be somewhere down there. At least there will be plenty of wood to build a flaming fire to warm our frozen bodies. That thought in itself impels us and we push the dogs on across the seemingly endless, rolling snowy hills.

We come upon a fairly fresh caribou carcass that wolves have chased down. It helps our hungry bunch but it doesn't last long, and a short time after we're back in the same situation. Then one day, around noon, we reach a small crest where Chief Tietchan suddenly stops his leading pack of dogs. He flings back his fur hood to see better, seemingly unbothered by the biting wind that stings his face and tangles his long, black hair. He stares off into the distance then points to the south and impassively says, "The forest."

Sure enough, way off in the distance we can see a faint strip of green. The sight of it raises our spirits and we hurry along. By late afternoon we reach the outermost areas of the forest, which are clusters of windblown spruce trees. A large, frozen white lake appears nearby, and close to that we catch sight of something dark – caribou! We hop into our sleds, crack our whips, and shout commands at the dogs, who strain in their harnesses with every last bit of their energy. We race across the frozen water at incredible speed.

There appears to be about a couple hundred caribou. Wary of danger, they quickly rise to their feet. A buck jumps in alarm and throws back its magnificent head of antlers, which sets the rest of the flock running, their grayish-brown bodies moving en masse. Our sleds follow after and then scatter. One of them quickly cuts in front of the animals' path and closes in. An Indian sitting on his knees in the sled raises his rifle and fires two or three shots that shatter the stillness. Two caribou fall to the ground.

It is evening now and we have settled down onto a layer of spruce boughs in front of a roaring fire that rises like a pillar between the trees. Skewers of caribou joints, intestines, stomachs, livers, and kidneys lean against the flames. The smell of grilling meat drifts our way and once more our lives are good again.

After our meal a new feeling sweeps over us as we sit there cross-legged, puffing away on our pipes and staring into the flames. The bad is forgotten and the Indians laugh and joke and talk about this and that. All that we have been through together during this past year has closely bonded us, and the Indians talk about things they seldom would in the presence of a white person.

Tijon, the old chief, starts to talk and eventually speaks about the forgotten greatness of these people and says, "Once the caribou-eaters ruled all of the northern country, the forests and plains were theirs. There were so many of them that when their tents were raised in The Land Without Trees (the tundra) it was like an entire forest. They fought against many tribes and defeated them. Many men were killed and women captured. All of the caribou passes and waterholes belonged to them. The country was full of caribou and musk ox, which were killed with arrows and spears. Food was plenty. They were a mighty people."

"What was the tribe called then," I ask.

"The same as it is now, Dinnéh (The People)," he replies.

"But as your forefathers were so numerous and mighty, how did the tribe lose its power?" I continued.

"Long ago," he said, "many Indians traveled away. This was before the white people came to the country. It was a very long time ago."

"Where did they go?"

"South," answers Tijon and points the direction with a quick wave of his hand.

"How do you know this?"

"The old ones say so."

Later in the evening the Indians make a rough version of a drum by stretching caribou skin over some bent twigs. Then they begin to sing to the rhythm of the beating drum, and strange music drifts across the moonlit wilderness where trees cast dark shadows over the bluish-white snow.

The fire dies down and I crawl into my sleeping bag. Out of a small, open flap, I lie there looking up at the stars. It takes a long time before I fall asleep because my thoughts keep wandering back to what Tijon said, "In the old days many Indians traveled away – to the south." Whatever happened to them? Someday, when I am finished here in the snow country, I will have to explore this.

It is eight years later in the sunny land of Arizona, far to the south in the United States. I am riding around the great forests of the White Mountains together with a group of Apache Indians. Far below us lies the desert with its scorched plains and strange, bristly giant cactus. The hot air is sweltering and I would give anything for a clump of snow to quench my thirst.

The Indians don't seem to be bothered by the heat. They sit there on their horses quite expressionless but carefully scanning the area. They are average-sized, wiry fellows with raven black hair and features that in every way remind me of my Indian friends from the snow country.

As we ride toward a clearing in the woods, one of the Apaches suddenly jerks his horse around and gallops off. The others follow. Far off in the distance I catch a glimpse of a white-tailed deer leaping away over the high bracken. We tear off through the forest lying flat against our horses' necks as we break through the branches and brush. Then we're out again onto an open plain and I hear two shots ring out in front of me. I see the deer sprawled on the ground kicking in its last throes of death.

We throw the animal on the back of one of the horses and head down the mountain toward the Apache camp by the White River. By early evening we reach the beautiful small valley, where leafy, green woods grow along a rippling river and where Indian tents are scattered in small clusters across the green fields. Close to the tent of my good friend, the old medicine man, we settle down, get comfortable, and then kindle a big fire. Skewers of deer joints, intestines, stomachs, livers and kidneys lean up against the flames or are laid on top of the coals. We eat to our heart's content.

Afterward we sit around and talk about the hunt and the forests, about the Indians' lives and battles of long ago. It is strange to listen to their voices because they sound so familiar. Their tones rekindle memories of such words I often heard while sitting around the fire at our camps far up north. It strikes me how this language doesn't really characterize a people who stem from this sunny, southern area.[1] There is a feeling of snowstorms over tundra, gushing waterfalls, and blustering wind blowing through northern forests.

Later in the evening, the old medicine man begins to tell stories from the old days. "We were always at war," he says, "killed many men and captured several women. We were stronger than other tribes and all of the land in the south became ours. Deer were everywhere back then and in some places there were large herds of buffalo. We hunted with arrows and spears. There were many of us and we were strong."

"What did the Apaches call themselves?" I ask.

"Dinnéh (The People)," replies the medicine man.

"Have the Apaches always lived here in the south?" I continue.

"We come from a cold country in the north. That was a long time ago."

"How do you know this?" I ask.

"The old ones say so."

Darkness descends and we can only barely make out the big mountain in the distance from where we hear the roar of the river. The fire burns low, flickers and casts dancing shadows across the fine-featured brown faces. There is a gentle wind and it smells of the Southwest.

One of the Apaches begins to beat the drum. All the others join in singing, a bit muddled at first but then in unison, powerful and focused as the beat of the drum rises and falls. They gaze off into the distance, absorbed in the rhythm.

My thoughts also drift, for this music sounds so incredibly similar to that of the polar Indians! It has that same driving rhythm, that equally strange singsong dissonance that begins with a shrill and ends in a gentle hum. I feel that I am again back on the northern tundra together with the "caribou-eaters," chasing away on our dog sleds and then sitting around the fire on a cold winter's evening listening to distant howls of a wolf.

I think of what Tijon said that time we sat together in front of the fire: "Long ago, many Indians traveled away – to the south . . ."

Long ago, the Indians of the northern country were in turmoil and feeling restless. This might have been because more powerful tribes had found their way across the Bering Strait and had taken control of the caribou passes and waterholes, or because the caribou themselves had dwindled. Life had always been hard up there in the snow and cold, but now it was more severe than ever. And so some of the northern Indians decide to leave their homelands and head off on a great adventure – a journey south to search for new land. They paddle away in their birch-bark canoes down the big rivers that break the way through vast forests and marshes. After a hard day's toil, the tired travelers sit around their evening fires along the riverbanks. They grill their meat on sticks and make herbal drinks in small birch-bark bowls where heated stones bring the water to a boil. Light from the campfires dances across their half-naked bodies.

They seldom can rest. On such a long journey it is vitally important to keep everything in order, and that requires hard work. Some of the women sit there hunched over mending moccasins and others are busy repairing the canoes with threads of sinew and resin. The men make arrows and chisel flint tips as they talk about the journey and the great unknown that lies ahead of them. Only the children sleep, lying in bundles around the fire.

The years pass and the people continue to move southward. They carefully and vigilantly push on, never knowing what to expect behind the next bend in the river. Once a moose appears on the riverbank but is startled and jumps into the water to swim away. The Indians arch their backs and drive the paddles into the water, propelling the canoes forward so hard that foam gushes around the bows, while the entire time they screech and shout. Arrows go whistling by, the river water turns blood red and the moose grows weaker. The head with its mighty antlers finally droops and in the end the animal drifts downstream in the current.

The Indians live in continual fear of foreign tribes and they never let their guard down. Scouts follow along on land and warn the others with smoke signals or other signs, and runners are often sent ahead before they break camp. Yet sometimes the enemy still surprises them, and then they have to fight for their lives using their bows and arrows, spears and clubs, or even their bare fists and sharp teeth. They fight like animals for what is theirs.

Their losses can often be bitter, but when the opportunity arises the warriors fight back and delight in taking revenge, which includes stealing food and equipment. They capture women and children and assimilate them into the tribe, for this helps their small group grow in number and strength. Fighting like this encourages more of the same, and in difficult times attacking and raiding is how they usually procure what they need.

During the course of time, these wanderers often find a favorable region with few signs of other humans and think, "Here is our land, here we can live." They erect their tents and adapt their lives to the new conditions. But again they encounter mightier tribes and are forced to flee, farther and farther south.

The great river routes come to an end and the canoes are left behind. Now they must continue on foot through the forests. Much differs here from what they are used to, but still they are familiar with the spruce and aspen forests, beaver, moose, and bear. Winters also continue to come as they did in the north with heavy snowfall and bitter cold. During these seasons they rely on their traditional means of survival, but without their dogs. Now the Indians pull their own sleds as they tramp along on snowshoes.

Time passes, years, centuries. Those who first took off from the polar country have long since died. Their offspring, however, live on and continue to wander in search of a country for their families. The main leaders are still together but a few groups have separated along the way and now are gone. Having to struggle so hard to survive has toughened the Indians, eliminated the weak and created a hardy and vigilant race who are now used to persevering in even the most difficult conditions. They have developed a warfare based on craftiness and their ability to endure hardship and suffering.

The forests begin to thin and one day the migrating people stand utterly amazed looking out across endless stretches of prairie where lush grass waves in the wind and countless herds of buffalo graze. There is something very familiar about this; their forefathers' home in the north, which they often heard stories about, was also supposed to be a tree-barren plain with heavy, shaggy animals. Somehow they feel at home here.

They live a long time on the prairies. It's possible to scout the area in all directions from every encampment, which therefore protects them against attacks, and food is plenty. They soon learn how to hunt the buffalo. There is something instinctive about this, something passed on to them from their forefathers who hunted musk ox and caribou on the tundra. A shower of arrows shoot out and thousands of animals thunder off en masse, shaking the earth beneath them. A few of the wounded giants lag behind, stomp the ground to charge, then lunge toward these naked people who bolt ahead with their spears held high.

Masses of meat and hides! Here is everything they have dreamed about during their long travels. Large tents are raised and covered with buffalo hides and strong tools are made of bone. Stray dogs from other tribes are taken in and used to pull tent poles and other things when camp is moved. The people are still hunters and nomads, but their lives are in many ways more stable in this plentiful land, and the tribe grows.

In the evenings, the Indians gather to feast and celebrate. They play their drums, women and men dance, and the old songs from the tundra region resonate across the prairie. Every morning when the sun rises above the horizon, the people bow and praise the great spirit that has followed the tribe and provided them with a land so rich with meat.

Centuries drift by and the polar people continue to roam the prairie. They now feel at home in this country. However, more powerful tribes appear in numbers paralleling the buffalo herds. The polar people are forced to move on and once again they travel southward.

Enduring hardship, deprivation, and bitter fights they slowly make their way through the mountains. The sun grows hotter and hotter and they travel across a new land with strange flowers, trees, and animals. Finally, a remarkable, sunny region appears with vast deserts overgrown with bristly vegetation, fertile tracts along the rivers, flat mesas, and mighty forest-covered mountains scattered across the lowlands. Deer, antelope, beaver, bear, birds, and in some places even buffalo abound here. The heat is stifling and the aridity worse. The land gasps for water. The wandering people have reached what we know today as New Mexico and Arizona.

They also encounter other foreign tribes here. Some of them live in the mountains in caves or stone huts, others have settled along the rivers in the lowlands, where they have built small villages using mortar and clay to create places just like fortresses. The inhabitants cultivate the earth and irrigate their fields and crops with water carried through a network of canals. They are masters in making clay items and woven baskets. They are called the Pueblo Indians.

These permanent-dwelling people are no match against the warring nomads, and wherever the Pueblo Indians' settlements lay scattered and poorly defended they are forced to retreat. Once the invaders get a foothold in the mountain areas, most of them make their homes here. They face unfamiliar and unknown conditions in this southern country, but the hard life of migration has honed their abilities to adapt and taught them many things along the way. The culture that began on the tundra had now been gradually transformed. The Indians migrated slowly enough through the ages and stayed for long periods in between so that when they did make a leap to a new life, the change wasn't too drastic.

The newcomers take on the land and make it their home. They roam the area and learn the ways of the wild animals, what fruits, roots, and berries they can use, and where materials for tools and household goods can be found. They often try to apply their own methods, but equally rely on the Pueblo Indians' experience. During the many skirmishes with the Pueblos, the newcomers capture several women, who teach them well.

During their long and perilous migration, it has been vital for the polar people to stick together. But after the worst difficulties and dangers of the journey are over and life has become easier in the new country, opportunity arises for conflicting dispositions. The young, bold warriors have their own ideas about things, and in the end they separate from the tribe and travel even farther south. Those who stay behind were later called the Navajo Indians, and the restless characters who left became known as the Apaches, or the Enemies.

The antagonistic Apaches evolve to become a strong people who scatter across a great area and later divide into many tribes: Jicarilla, Mescalero, Chiricahua, Tonto, White Mountain, Cibecue, and San Carlos Apaches. Each tribe establishes their own hunting grounds across large regions.

Living as hunters and warriors means that the tribes must divide up. Family groups combine to become larger or smaller bands who roam certain areas they consider to be their own. The distance between these bands is often great, which causes the Apaches to no longer be a collective people.

Their societies, though, are arranged along the same democratic lines as before. Each individual is entitled to his say and included in deciding the group's affairs. A chief acquires leadership only after showing that he is the most skilled warrior, and his power rests upon his character. Tyrants are not tolerated by these individualistic people who have no words in their language for the command, "You will!"

Up in the mountains or in certain spots in the lowlands where the buffalo move, the Apaches erect their dome-shaped grass huts or their tepees, or tents, and continue to be the same wandering nomads as they always have been. Summer and winter they wear nothing but their breechcloths and knee-high moccasins. They survive mainly on their catch and on wild plants. Some of them also grow a little corn where the women stay for longer periods. Their weapons are by and large the same as those their forefathers used on the tundra: bows and arrows, flint-tipped spears, axes, slings, flint knives, and stone clubs.

Their culture is in many ways to be admired. They are very musical and enjoy reciting songs. During the long winter evenings, the young gather around the elders, who with their clever talent for telling stories talk about the Apaches' history, legends, and supernatural world. In their own way these Indians are very religious. Their beliefs are deeply rooted in nature, and they worship the spirits of the sun, stars, clouds, plants, and mountains. The medicine man has great influence over the people, for it is he who connects them to the spirits and in times of war and peace calls upon these powers for assistance. The Apaches have strong morals: the young girls are chaste, adultery is not tolerated, and those who lie are banned. They are cruel to their enemies but love their children and will fight to their deaths for their family.

The urge to fight lies deep within them, and they wander far and wide on raiding parties, the terror of the permanent-dwelling Indians. The Apaches are always ready to fight. From when they are young they are trained to endure severe hardship and depravation. Their strategic plans are laid out with the utmost care, and in battle they know no mercy.

In time, the Apaches grow in strength and power and in the end rule over the areas now known as Arizona, New Mexico, and large parts of western Texas and northern Mexico, an area as large as Germany and France put together.

The polar people's unwavering will to survive has triumphed. They have succeeded in acquiring a land of their own after centuries of migrating from the great Arctic plains to the sunny regions of the Southwest.

## 2
# San Carlos

The heat of the early summer sun swells across the San Carlos Reservation. The air is so crystal clear that the distant, slender-leafed yucca plants with their tall, white blossoms reaching toward the sky seem to be closer than they are. A rider appears over on the bone-dry sand dunes, where giant cacti stand with outstretched arms. Moving at a steady trot he heads for the gully, where large cotton trees unfold their massive leafy tops like a cool, green blessing over clusters of Indian tents and herds of horses wandering loose.

The rider is quite close now, and I can see that it is an old Indian who is easily and comfortably slung in his saddle. He stops by one of the tents, dismounts, and walks about the women and children, and then takes a seat under a leafy awning. I approach him and say hello, but he doesn't greet me in return. He just looks at me as if to say, "What are you doing here?"

He has a typical, strong, slightly broad Apache face. It is rough and wrinkled, yet defiance still shines in his eyes. He is probably in his seventies, a warrior who has survived the desperate Apache fights for freedom under the leadership of Geronimo and others, one who so many times galloped off on his horse from San Carlos to Sierra Madre, one who has killed. Within his soul lives not only the memory of past times when Apaches controlled the land and were free to roam, but also the memory of all that his people have suffered under the white man's yoke. The tribe's might has been broken, and now he lives under sufferance of the subjugator. Yet within him there is something that still survives – his defiance. With the help of a boy who can speak a little English, I try to talk to him. But he gets up, turns his back, and walks inside the tent. I have no business being here.

It's certainly not easy to win the trust of these proud Apaches, for their wounds still bleed. While other Indian tribes in America have been subjugated for one or more generations, there are still some Apaches who are living testimonies of days gone by, and their spirits prevail. The American government has provided for these people and has tried to teach them farming and cattle ranching, but they have the restless blood of the nomad in them and do not do well with such routines. Schools have been provided, but in the camp they live in their own world in which the children gather around the old men who tell of their battles and their forefathers' legends and tales. They have acquired missionaries and doctors, but down by the river the medicine man beats his drum and his word is law. They have received everything, except that which they love – freedom.

One evening at sunset I ride across the hills above the Indian camp, and at the top I can see forever. Beneath a flaming crimson sky, the desert and all its bristly growth and flat mesas gradually converges with the dark blue mountains. Over on a nearby ridge, I catch sight of a man. As I cautiously ride closer it appears to be the same old Indian whom I had tried to talk to earlier. He sits there motionless as if made of stone, staring off into the distance, across his forefathers' country.

My horse is called K'a-o-nih, Flying Arrow, and there's probably not a faster horse in San Carlos. It is a young, shiny-brown animal with such fervor to chase across the hills that I have to continually rein back so it won't take off. I ride from camp to camp attempting to win the Apaches' friendship so that I can learn a little of their world. I am especially eager to discover traits that might attest to their migration from the north and their relation to the snow country people, the Chipewyan Indians.

There are about three thousand Indians at San Carlos, many coming from various tribes who were thrown together here during the time of the Apache Wars. Most live as they did before in wickiups, dome-shaped huts constructed of saplings and covered with grass, and others live in tepees. Some have small patches of land where they grow a little corn, melons, and so on, others work at ranching or road construction, and then there are those who don't do anything but sit by their tents and watch the sun shine.

After a while, I have a change of luck. Apache friendship, as with most Native peoples, is gradually won if a person speaks to them as an equal and doesn't exaggerate or let it appear that one thinks oneself higher. They are incredibly quick to pick up on anything that isn't true, and I know no other people capable of assessing another person as well as they. As for me, I have invaluable help from the missionary F. Uplegger and his two daughters, who have lived with the Apaches for years and who are among the few who have gained their trust and can speak their language.

One evening I pay a visit to the Apache man Mull, one of the Indians' best storytellers and singers. Mull speaks only his own language, so I take along Bullock, a stocky fellow and son of a well-known chief, to interpret. It is dark when we arrive and the sky is full of its own wildness: lagoons of stars in between fleeting dark clouds.

Sitting beneath a canopy of twigs and leaves, the Apache Mull looms above the old women and children. He is a pleasant middle-aged fellow with a broad face and strong but friendly eyes. His upper torso is bare and there is something very ancient about him as he sits sprawled over a stump with the light from the small fire dancing across his bronzed skin.

I greet him and then take a seat on the ground, proceeding to do what I usually do to quickly gain trust. Rather than ask him to tell a story, I begin talking about the Indians whom I have lived with in northern Canada. The listeners eagerly follow along and the children's eyes light up when I recount the stories that the "caribou eaters" often told in front of a crackling fire while camped under snow-covered pine trees after a strenuous day's dog-sled journey. When I unfold the tale about "He who lassoed the sun," all the Indians break out in laughter. The northern Indians' legends clearly and strongly resonate in the souls of these people.

The ice has been broken and Mull naturally reciprocates by telling something of the Apaches' wonderful collection of sagas and legends. He begins by telling about the tribe's oldest times:

*Nobody knows where we came from to this country. It is as if awakening in the shadow of a tree and not knowing where you are. In the beginning, the Apaches were poor. They dressed in coyote hides. Coyotes were caught* in traps made of stone. The Apaches dug a hole in the earth and laid bait there. Then they would position a flat stone so that it would fall over the hole when the animal moved the bait. Coyotes were caught alive and killed later.

The Indians walked around naked, only wearing leather breechcloths. They had poor weapons and few deer hides. They wore moccasins on their feet. The upper portion of the moccasins were made of buckskin and the soles were braided yucca fibers. Their huts were also made from the yucca plant.

They had small gardens with corn and they collected grass, roots, seeds, and mescal. It was important that they always had enough mescal. This was the women's work. They had to go high into the mountains to find mescal, then they chopped the tops off with a flint knife and fried them on the ground over stones heated on a fire. The pieces were covered with grass and dirt and would lay there for two days before they could be eaten.

There were many gophers during that time. The Indians set up traps, at times a hundred traps a night. Afterward they gathered the rodents and cooked them. They ate the meat and drank the soup. They used salt that they pried from the mountains at a place where the Indians had long found salt. One of these places was by the Salt River. Salt could be found way up on the face of the cliff and the Indians would reach this by using ladders made of yucca plants. They would knock the salt down with sticks.

The Indians in time got better weapons. They killed many deer and made bow strings of stronger sinew. Their moccasins were also now made of buckskin. They used the thicker hide from the legs and jowl of the deer and tanned it with the help of the animal's brain matter.

They learned how to make better weapons and other things by studying what they had found in all the ruins that were there when they first arrived. They also found blue stones in the ruins, which had power and were used by the Indians' medicine men, and are still used today. But only the blue stones from the ruins have powers. The Apaches called the people who lived where the ruins lie "the people who came before us."

The Indians now had good weapons and roamed and hunted in the mountains. They had quivers made of coyote hide, and one quiver could hold fifty arrows. When they hunted deer, the best archers would hide *along a deer path. The other hunters would drive the game toward the Indians who lay waiting.*

*Before they set out on a hunt, they would dance and the medicine man would use his power to pacify the animals they were to hunt. In this way it was easy to slay them. But no Indian was ever to kill a snake.*

*This was before the white people came to the country. There were no horses and no tamed animals. The Apaches seldom fought and mostly lived in peace with other Indians. Then came the whites who wanted to take the land, and turbulence began. The Indians rose up against the whites and stole horses and cattle, which they then used to make moccasins with.*

*The whites took the land and sent many Indians to prison. Many terrible things have happened and nothing is the same. When you look at us today you think that perhaps we are few. But in the old days, there were thousands of tents in the valleys. Then the men had stronger spirits and greater strength and the women had more children. We were free.*

*What I have told you now is what the old ones have said. Nobody is alive today who has seen these things I have talked about. It is a long time ago.*

When Mull finished his story, he just sat there with his hands on his knees staring ahead, and for a while nobody spoke. The moon appeared from behind the drifting clouds and cast its light through the branches of the flowering peach tree and upon the small Indian children who lay there on the ground with their hands cupping their cheeks. Mull eventually snapped out of his daze, shook off the gloom, and with a merry gleam in his eye he began telling about Coyote, the scapegoat in Apache tales:

*One time Coyote was out walking and met the Great Black Insect. Coyote wanted to eat it but the insect said, "Wait a minute, I have something to tell you."*

*"Now, then," said Coyote, "you can tell me while I hold you between my teeth."*

*"But then I'll be so frightened that I won't be able to speak," said the insect.*

*"OK, then, tell me now," said Coyote.*

Then the insect walked along the ground with its head bent as if trying to listen to something under the earth. And then it said, "The people down there underneath the ground say they will catch anyone who has done something wrong and beat them with an iron whip."

Coyote said, "A while ago, I may have done something that wasn't very good to do. I will go and sort it out and then afterward I will come back and eat you up." After he had gone, the insect crawled in-between two rocks and when Coyote came back he couldn't find the insect.

Coyote walked farther and after while he met a grasshopper. The grasshopper asked if he wanted to race him. Coyote said, "Who are you who wants to race against me! No one can run as fast as I and least of all you, who are only a pile of skinny legs."

The grasshopper replied, "We'll run from here over to where the grass is tall." They drew a line, counted to three, and away they went. Just as they took off, the grasshopper leapt and landed right behind Coyote's ear. Coyote ran as hard as he could but when he neared the finish the grasshopper took another jump and landed in the grass in front of Coyote.

Coyote was very disgruntled and said, "This is the first time that someone has ever beaten me in a race. Now all my cousins and sweethearts will laugh at me and I don't dare go back. The only thing I can do now is to run myself to death." And Coyote began running. After a while he met a toad. The toad asked him what was the matter and Coyote explained the shame that he had suffered. "Come and race me and then you'll feel better," said the toad. "Well, all right," said Coyote, and they got ready and took off. But ahead of him the toad had placed two other toads. When they started, the first toad took a great leap, then the second toad jumped and at the end the third toad hopped across the finish line before Coyote.

Coyote continued on his journey. After a time he met a crane that was standing by the river and fishing. They began discussing in which direction the sun rose in the morning. Coyote said it was in the east, while the crane said that the sun first could be seen in the west. They then made a wager on a pile of fish that lay by the riverbank. Both of them would now look in the direction they thought the sun would rise and whoever saw the sun first could eat the fish. Coyote looked toward the east, the crane looked toward the west. But toward the east there was a large mountain and when the sun rose, its rays stretched across this peak and toward the mountains in the west. The crane won all the fish.

When Mull finished this story, all the Indians had a good laugh. He continued then with a tale of how the Indians first acquired fire. In the beginning, it was only the squirrel who had fire, but once when all the animals were gathered together Coyote's tail got too close to the fire and lighted up. He took off running but was chased so closely by the flames he had to throw the fire to the hawk. The hawk gave it to the hummingbird, who flew around bringing fire to all the people.

Then came the long and fantastic tale of Coyote, who was out wandering and caught sight of *nagon-a-ha* (some small birds) who were in the midst of playing a game. They had picked wild hyacinths, which they threw way up into the air and then caught again by the bulb. When Coyote asked them what they were doing the birds answered that they were throwing their eyes up into the air. Coyote wanted to join in the fun and asked them to take his eyes out. So they did and Coyote began playing like the birds had done. He threw his eyes into the air and let them drop into his eye sockets again. Then Mull began singing:

Alch-gísh-da mba – í ye djí-ní
ñ'í bí-na ya-yílq-tílq-go bí-na-g'ae na-dílq
hí ya hí ya ae ng ya.[1]

Just as Coyote was doing this, however, his eyes got stuck up in a large sycamore tree, and no matter how hard he jumped and struggled he couldn't get hold of them. Coyote had to leave his eyes in the tree. Then he found a cane and continued to wander around in the world. Sly as he was, though, he managed to get hold of a young girl, who accompanied him on his long journey from one adventure to the next.

There was something so magnificent about the Apache who sat there half-naked and broad-shouldered telling his forefather's tales and legends. And oh, how he could tell a story! His whole face lit up with delight when he told his tales and it was as if he became part of every word he spoke, actually giving the listeners bits of himself. The strange language wavered up and down like the sound of a foreign instrument. It rose to something harsh and grating, then to a sound like a solemn hum, and so down to something gentle as the cool evening breeze that softly blew in from the dim land around us.

Shi-go-sh-k'anni-sidja, or "here lies my yucca fruit," was Mull's last line of the story, and then he began rolling a cigarette. This was how every Apache story ended. I wanted so much for him to talk about the Indians' wars and religion. Mull said that the Apaches had so many stories that he could keep on telling them for two months and still not finish. But there were things that could only be told during the winter evenings, otherwise he might have misfortune.

In the light of the moon, I wandered home with my head full of Apache tales and adventurous folklore. Walking along in this shadowy-dark, southern land made it all seem so real that almost anything could happen.

My horse, Flying Arrow, races across the parched hills, throwing up billows of sand with its hooves. On top of a hill I rein the horse back because in such intense heat we must carry on carefully. With quivering nostrils and pointed ears, the horse stands and gazes intently. It belongs in this scene.

Below lies an exotic desert country with rolling hills and glinting red gravel between strange vegetation. Mesas rise from farther away, so flat on top they look as if they have been leveled off. Beyond them lies another range of rugged mountains capped with green forests and almost indistinguishable dark canyons.

Apache country is as colorful as a fairy tale, but it is also hard and precarious. The low country around me is so dry that it almost steams under the blazing sun and the air shimmers and pulsates across the hills. There are no lakes, and in the wide river bed to the west there isn't a drop of moisture. This is the land where people have walked until collapsing of thirst, where Pueblo Indians starved to death because of sun-scorched cornfields, where Apache medicine men sought mercy from the rain gods: Water!

And still, a variety of plants and animals have found habitable conditions here in these low lands. In a small hollow just below me I see a green forest of giant cacti that protrude thirty feet into the air. They stand there side by side like huge candelabra stretching their arms into the blue sky. Many other varieties also exist out here, ranging from that strange barrel cactus to the prickly pear cactus that spreads out in rich clusters of juicy heart-shaped bulbs. These plants thrive and are full of sweetness despite drought and the scorching sun. In this legendary world of cacti, flowers bloom in red, yellow, and white and their fruit are as sweet as dates.

Down there on the flatlands I catch sight of the olive-green creosote bush and an occasional friendly mesquite tree. But on the ridge behind me stands a tall row of sharply silhouetted century plants bearing yellow clusters of flowers up toward the sun.

I ride farther along and everywhere there is something happening. A lizard scurries over the scorching sand, and then farther on I frighten a rattlesnake who quickly slithers away between the bushes. Now and then one of these funny birds called a road runner darts with an outstretched neck in front of the horse. Besides these creatures, all other life seems to have taken refuge from the stifling heat, which can be very well over 100 degrees Fahrenheit in the shade. The owl is hiding in the giant cactus, where it has made its nest in holes pecked by the woodpecker, the long-eared jackrabbit has crawled under cover in the thick underbrush, and other peculiar animals the desert land has fostered such as the pack rat, coyote, joker, horned toad, poisonous spider, and equally poisonous Gila monster, are nowhere to be seen. But what is that? Something shiny like a jewel with red and blue hues – a hummingbird that shoots toward the sun with lightning-fast wings.

It is almost hard to believe that plants and animals can thrive in this water-starved country, but nature has provided means to fight off drought just as life in the polar regions is equipped to deal with the cold. The plants have long roots that spread across a large surface and absorb every bit of moisture, hoarding it for further use. Leaves, stems, and bark allow as little evaporation as possible. But it is not enough that the plants can handle the drought. In desert country, plants must also be able to defend themselves from the greedy animal world. Unlike fertile regions, the vegetation cannot tolerate wear and tear because it regenerates so slowly; the giant cactus first blossoms and bares fruit between its fiftieth and seventieth year. The plants have several means of defense, the most important being their needles. Everywhere in the desert there are needles. Some are as long and stiff as darning needles, others are like spikes, and still others are shaped like fishhooks and work well enough to land a decent trout. Then there are plants that are protected by their odors, such as the creosote bush, while the poison from the loco weed can create a kind a madness in animals and people.

The animals, like the plants, are distinctively equipped to attack or defend, whether by poison, scales, or spines. Life in the desert is a perpetual and exasperating struggle.

Only by first understanding this land and life is it possible to know the Apaches. They too have been shaped by the natural environment, the same as the cacti and desert animals. Survival in these harsh areas have conditioned them to endure deprivation and thrive where others would have failed. It has hardened within them the will to fight.

Way off in the distance, the sun turns into a crimson blaze and sinks behind the forest-covered mountains. Up there at higher elevations it is a very different and fertile world that is also very much a part of Apache life. They are not only people of the desert but also, to a greater extent, of the mountains. Only a day's journey away lies the beautiful White Mountain, where many Apaches have lived since olden times. I would like to go there, away from the scorching lowlands to a cooler region where streams trickle and the wind whistles through pine forests. And I want to stay there for a good while.

It is dusk and wonderfully cool as I head Flying Arrow over the hills and back toward the Indian camps. I can see a campfire burning down there in the valley between large cottonwood trees, and in the ring of light I see shadows moving to a rhythmic beat. I halt my horse and listen. The sound of the drum drifts toward me and the Indians sing:

> Ní ya ní ya na í ya na í yu-u,
> ní ya na ya na í yu-u, ní ya na ya na í yu-u,
> hí hí hí e-ya,
> Ty ís Ka-go í-na-go dzí-í, na na ya í-na-go dzí
> nyí, ní ya na ya na í yu-u, hí hí hí e-ya.[2]

The Apaches are absorbed in their own world now. The music still stirs the same longing as it did in their forefathers, those who soared like eagles across the country and ruled the land. But then over on the highway, a car horn toots.

# 3
# White Mountain

Just below the big mountain, the river winds like a glistening ribbon between the woods and green hills. A young Indian girl using a wide tumpline across her forehead to carry a clay jug on her back appears at the edge of the river, just where a deep pool forms and where bits of foam swirl around in an eddy. She stands there a while, absorbed in her own thoughts, gazing toward the rippling river, which pleasantly splashes along over smooth, polished stones. Then she kneels, brushes her long black hair to one side, and begins to fill the jug. As she rises to stand, she catches sight of me. She jumps back, startled, slings the jug over her back, and hurries toward the path so quickly that her broad skirts reel around her.

Slowly I follow her and come to a beautiful clearing with a little cornfield and a cluster of Indian tents. As I wade through a mass of man-high sunflowers some of the large, dark flowers slap me in the face. All of a sudden I come upon an Indian family sitting by a fire eating roasted cobs of corn. Everyone looks up. There is more curiosity in their eyes than hostility, so I venture to take a seat on the ground. I eventually offer tobacco and try to talk to them by using some gestures and an occasional Apache expression. But after making a fool of myself long enough, I give up. Everything becomes very quiet and I silently sit there puffing on my pipe and staring into the fire. Suddenly one of the men pleasantly says in fluent English: "Perhaps it would be better if you spoke the white man's language."

This was how I met Chester Gatewood, who later became my good friend and invaluable interpreter during my stay with the White Mountain Apaches. I couldn't have found a better helper. Not only was he an excellent interpreter but he also had a good understanding of how to approach the difficult older Apache men. He was also a wise fellow with a cunning sense of humor.

A short time after this chance meeting, my friend and I were in full swing traveling from one Indian camp to another. About twenty-eight hundred Apaches dwell up on the rolling high plateau of White Mountain. They have set up their tents in scattered clusters around the various small gullies where the people have sought shelter since olden times, and because they have been able to continue to live isolated from the white man they have retained more of their native life-ways than Apaches in other places. They are protective of their old ways, and strangers are generally not very well liked in their country: they want to live in peace by themselves.

Their land is some of the most beautiful anywhere. Arriving there from the desert is like entering a new world because in the mountains the rain gods are gracious and the grass and forest are made green and lush. Here the juniper grows to be thousands of years old and its bark is like the scales on an alligator. The evergreen oak thrives in the red sand hills and woods grow thick along the rippling river, where small trout scurry about like black shadows. New kinds of cactus shoot up and vibrant-colored flowers grow in every direction. It is so luxuriant here, with warm, shady nooks radiating such a peace and beauty that you could be tempted to set up your tent and stay.

The majority of the Apaches have their permanent camps at about forty-five hundred feet high. The large mountain looms above where the forests begin in earnest; first the pine forest, and then the spruce. Up there roam mountain lions, bears, deer, wild turkeys, beaver, mink, bobcats, lynx, fox, and yes even some elk.[1] But at the mountain's naked summit lie snowdrifts that never melt and dangling flowers that are indigenous to Arctic regions.

Several of the old men who were part of the hostile Apache Wars, some as renegades but most of them as scouts for the soldiers, still live on the White Mountain Reservation. Many significant places in Apache history are also located here. On a plateau by the White River lies the famous Fort Apache, a beautiful settlement of long, low log houses shaded by enormous leafy trees. The log cabin where General Crook used to stay still stands there. Farther west is Cibicu, where Nock-ay-del-klinne, the powerful medicine man, started the perilous uprising in 1881. At Turkey Creek stretches the beautiful area where the wild Chiricahua Apaches lived and from where Geronimo and his small band broke out in 1885 and fled to the Sierra Madre in Mexico to fight their last desperate fight for freedom.

One of the most powerful Apaches on the White River Reservation is the old medicine man A2, William Gushonay. [2] Unlike anyone else, he can drive out disease and cure people from one thing or another. But first and foremost, he is an expert on how to conjure up rain. Not so long ago, the San Carlos Indians sent for him during a long period of drought. They gave him three hundred dollars to make it rain, and soon. In the course of three days, A2 did just that, and then it poured down with such velocity that no one had ever seen anything quite like it. He was undoubtedly one of the greatest of all medicine men.

A2 was also a famous warrior and had a reputation for knowing more about the Apaches' religion and history than most. At the same time, he was supposedly so difficult and stubborn that it was almost hopeless for a white man to get anything out of him. However, I decided to take the bull by the horns, and one evening I rode down to his camp together with Chester. We found the great medicine man at some tents in the woods by the White River, along with his closest kin. An awning of leaves was set up outside the tent under which the people were sitting when we arrived.

The medicine man was in his shorts, which he outwardly considered to be a fine garment. On his head he wore a wide-brimmed hat with eagle feathers, and around his neck he wore a chain of amulets from which also hung a pair of tweezers, which Apaches use to pull out beard stubble. He was a medium-sized, strong fellow with graying hair that hung down to his shoulders. He carried himself with a dignity fitting for a famous medicine man.

I seat myself in the circle and begin to talk about the Apaches' northern relatives from the snow country. Everyone is very interested, and not the least is their surprise when I begin to utter several words from the Chipewyan Indians' language. [3] At once they appear to understand a good deal of them. I then talk about various customs of the Northern Canadian Indians. Among other things, I talk about when young hunters are initiated into the adult ranks. First, they must venture alone out into the forest, remain awake, and continue to fast for several days until they fall asleep from pure exhaustion. The first animal they see in a dream will be their guardian animal throughout their life.[4] The medicine man smiles and says that the Apaches also had this custom in the old days. He sternly stares ahead and adds that he has heard from the elders that the Apaches were said to have come from a country with much snow far in the north, but it must have happened so long ago that no one can say for certain. We speak for a while about *ndnae-nza-yu-nahokossai-biyayu*, "the people who live far away under the whirling" (The Big Bear). When we finish A2 says:

> You have told us many things and we have listened with eager ears. It was almost like we could see the Indians in that cold country. It is my word to you that you can come to my tent when you like and the women say the same. Now I would like to tell you a story. I will tell you how the world and the Apaches came into being.

> At one time, many relatives ago, everything was a large darkness. There was no sun, no stars, no moon. So the sun, the stars and the moon were born, and they kept watch. Then the wind, the thunder, the lightning, and other powers came together; all in all, thirty-two of the mighty forces. They created earth. At first, it was small, but it grew larger and larger in a spiral. Bolts of colored iron were driven into the center of the earth to keep it together. Afterward, everything was jumbled together, and that is why we find iron everywhere on earth. Now the sun brought great warmth. The sun made heat waves that quivered in the air and from these the Apaches were created.

When the great medicine man was finished, he gave his shorts a lift to stand, turned his back, and shuffled into the tent. His audience with us was over.

A short time later, I received another story from R23, Kosen, about how the Apaches were created. He explained:

> A long time ago, there were no people living on earth. In the north there was a mountain, "the mountain that looked the same from all directions." At this mountain, People originated. The Dancing People began there. One night they saw a fire far off in the distance. They walked toward the fire

until the break of day but found nothing. For several nights they saw the fire, and each time they tried to find it. But they did not find it. They cleaved a staff, stuck it in the ground, and aimed it toward the fire, but still they could not find it. They could not find the people who had lit the fire and who must have lived in one place or another. Then the hummingbird flew off and found the strange people and their land. The Dancing People then received a message to come there, for in that land there was no illness and no death.

The Dancing People lived scattered about, and the chief sent a message for everyone to meet at an agreed spot. When the sun set, they gathered together and sat in a circle. The chief said that he had received an offer from a people who lived in some other country where there was no illness or death.

"We want to go there," said the Dancing People, "but we must let one girl stay behind. We must also let one boy remain." They then made a bow and arrows for the boy and a basket for the girl. But it was difficult to find two to leave behind. When parents were asked, they answered that they loved their children and that they did not have in mind to be separated from them. One of the fathers then agreed to let his son remain and another father gave his daughter. These children were to remain in this world, and the others were to depart to the other world where there was neither illness nor death.

Everyone left the camp and after a while they came to a large river and stopped. Now the parents of the two children pretended that the bow and arrows and the basket had been forgotten at the camp. "Go and fetch them!" they said to the boy and the girl, who went back. The people's chief had a small black ring. He now rolled this ring toward the river and the water lifted. He had three other rings, a blue, a yellow, and a white. He also rolled these rings toward the river. The water lifted so high up into the air that the Indians could walk under without bending over. This is how it is said that they got across the river and to the people who lived in the strange country where there was neither illness nor death.

Ten years later, the two fathers returned to the place where they had left behind the boy and the girl. They wanted to see how their children were doing. When they got there, they saw a large teepee. The boy and the girl had set it up and they had many children. This is how the Apaches began. They later scattered across a large country.

The following story was told by the medicine man A89, David Dahkoskay:

> The big flood came and covered the earth. But some Indians saved themselves. They lived in the north in a land where it was cold and had lots of snow. They had a tree trunk that they had hollowed out with fire, and in this they drifted about. When the big flood subsided, they were stranded here.

The most incredible genesis myth of the Apaches was told to me by the medicine man D42, Thomas Tenijieth, who is probably one of the best storytellers on the reservation:

> Nobody knows when the heavens were made. When the earth was created, there were no people anywhere. It was flooded throughout with water. The Creator of all Life drained the water from the earth and made oceans from it. Water seeped out from dirt and stones. The Creator made small, yellow people. They were the same type of people who lived in the houses that are now ruins. Their land was shaped like a star and they lived in the west of this land. There were many of them, as many as ants, but no one has ever seen them. People like this are still living somewhere or another. The Creator of all Life did not like them because they were small and yellow. He made a new people. He made them from dirt. Just as Apache children make dolls from dirt, so too were the Apache people made out of dirt. After the Creator had made these people, he moved them to the east. They spoke one language. Later, the people were divided up and then had several languages. Then the Creator of all Life made the first horse. It was thin and red and stood turned toward the north. It stood in the land where the first people, the yellow people, had been made.

"Tonight I would like to hear about war," I said to Chester. "The white people have their own way of talking about the Apache Wars, now I want to know what the Indians themselves think about these." Chester looked dubious and answered that it is difficult with such "intense" stories during summertime. Winter is when the elders tell these kinds of tales. Then we go and visit v46, John Taipa. He is the oldest Indian on the reservation, and according to what he and others say, he must be about a hundred years old. He is a bit shaky on his feet but there is a sparkle in his eyes and nothing indicates that this old warrior's spirit is weak. He tells us:

> I never saw a white man until I was a grown warrior. I had heard that white men had entered our land, but I had never seen them. The Indians wanted to stay away from the whites. When they did meet, they wanted to kill each other straight away. Before the Indians encountered the whites, they were happy. They had a large and rich country. In the forests there was plenty of elk and that was enough to live on.
>
> The first time I saw a white person was at Fort Thomas. I was a scout for the soldiers there. Later, I was along in many battles, so many that I cannot remember them all.

I ask if he has killed many people. He begins to count his fingers, looks up smiling and says: "Not enough fingers." He continues:

> Many great chiefs lived in my time, such as Mangas Coloradas and Cochise. But Be-da-jo was the greatest of them all.[5] I was there when Be-da-jo was killed. It was on a mountain in the south, where there are many rocks. The mountain was white. A few trees grew on the mountain, but not many. On top of the mountain lived Be-da-jo and his people, and they had built a wall of rock around themselves. The scouts and one soldier were sent up to capture them. It wasn't easy. Then we took stones and shoved them in front of us like shields. This is how we got into Be-da-jo and his men. Many white soldiers were killed as they crept up, but only one Indian scout. The whole time we heard Be-da-jo and his warriors singing. They sang and fought. When we got close to the stone wall, the soldiers took out bags that were filled with dynamite. They put fuses in, lit them, and threw the bags over the wall. Be-da-jo and all his people were killed. They had all been blown apart and burned when we stormed in. This is the way the great Be-da-jo was killed.

We then went to see my good friend D42, Thomas Tenijieth, medicine man and one of the elders. He tells us:

> The sun god's son, Nayenaezghani, "the dragon slayer," taught the Indians everything. He chose twelve Indians and made them medicine men. They made a pipe out of dirt. The pipe had four sides, black, blue, yellow, and white. The twelve medicine men gathered together four times. They

lifted the pipe toward the sun and the fourth time it began to burn. Now they had power over everything. They could speak to animals and tame them. They could see as in a dream where the enemy was. They knew prayers that helped so no arrows could penetrate their bodies. Even if they were hit, the arrows only struck and fell. Other times the arrows just grazed their bodies as if against a rock. They were not hurt.

The sun god's son taught the twelve medicine men how to fight. He showed them how they should use their spears. He placed a flint rock facing the east and sang four songs. The medicine men danced toward the rock and angled their spears into it. The spears pierced through the rock as if it were meat. Then the sun god's son said: "If any of you go on the warpath, sing these four songs and run the spear into the rock. If the spear bends or does not enter, do not go farther, turn around. There are also different things that you must not pass when you are about to go on the path of war. If you find a dead rabbit, do not go past it, turn around. If a bird falls down dead, do not go farther, turn around. All of these signs say that you will be killed if you continue on the warpath."

The sun god's son spoke to the twelve medicine men: "You have now seen how I have completed all things, go now among the Indians and do as I have taught you." When the twelve medicine men thought it was time to go on the warpath, they called the Indians together. Everyone gathered their war clothes and prepared arrows, bows, and spears. The night before they were to fight, they danced.

While the people were on the warpath, they found a large trail in the white man's land. They stopped at the track and sent three warriors up to the top of a hill to scout. They saw the white men and the scouts on the hill gave a sign. The Indians prepared to fight. They painted themselves with charcoal and some white color. They tied leaves and grass in their hair. They had their bows and arrows and spears prepared and were ready to fight. They spread out along the path and waited. The white men had sixty pack mules with them. There were soldiers in front of the mules, along the side, and in the back. Among the Indians who lay waiting, there was one who had a shotgun. When the soldiers were near, he raised his gun and shot a white man, that was the signal. Then all the other Indians stormed ahead and killed the white men with spears and arrows.

The white men grew very frightened because the Indians were painted black and white, had grass in their hair, and screamed the whole time.

All the white men were killed except five of them. The Indians gathered everything they could find in the packs, clothes, fabric, brown sugar, rifles, ammunition, and much more. Before, only a few of the Indians had shotguns. Afterward, everything was taken into the mountains where their old men lived. There they divided everything up.

What the Indians wanted more than anything were rifles, ammunition, saddles, and horses. So they rode out, killed men, and took these things. On the raids to the white men's towns, they also sometimes captured Mexican women. The brought them home to the camp, gave them grilled meat, and danced with them. Many white women were also taken. They were not killed. The Indians married them, provided well for them, and treated them fairly. They are now dead but their children are alive. They brought us many children.

Things went very different though for the men who were captured. When one of them was brought to camp, his ankles were tied together with rope so that he could not walk or run, only hop. He was kept tied all night while they danced. When morning came, he was given to the women whose friends he had killed. The women chased the tied-up men with spears and stabbed and killed them as they hopped around.

The Apache women – they are seldom talked about, yet they played such an important role in the nomadic people's lives that their help to the tribe is difficult to overstate. The Northern Canadian Indian Chief Manitoba once said to the famous researcher Samuel Hearne (who in the 1700s traveled from the Hudson Bay to the Northwest Passage and on his first unsuccessful attempt didn't take any Indian women along to assist): "Without women, one could not survive here in this land." This was especially true for the Apaches.

The Apache women's contributions meant a great deal to the life of the tribe. They were the fertile mothers who deeply loved their children. They provided food, clothes, and tents for the people, and there was no end to the work that they had to carry out. When needed, they rode out into the wildest battles and fought like a fury; yes, they fought with such wildness that they were feared more than men. They were cruel avengers who in unspeakable ways tortured those who had killed their husbands or relatives. For years when the whites pursued the Apaches from one place to another, the women faithfully followed. Month after month they rode over scorching deserts and rugged mountains. They thirsted, starved, fought, bore children along the way, slung their bloody bodies onto a horse again and continued the wild ride. At times, when the warriors were pressed the hardest, the women were left in the mountains and abandoned to their fate for long periods of time. But they held out, and they and their children courageously survived on their own. If anyone threatened them or theirs, they defended themselves to the end. Like wild tigresses they defended themselves, even after their limbs were slashed with fatal wounds. They saw their children killed, their tribe driven away from the Indians' land, and witnessed their people's slow annihilation. Despite this, everything female about them arose within; for them, kin was an even deeper sense than for the men. Kin, one's own flesh and blood, was what they protected with their nurturing, their wildness, their cruelty.

I meet one of these women, Anna Palmer is her name now. She is over eighty years old and is one of the few Chiricahua Apaches who live on the White Mountain Reservation. Throughout her life she has followed her people in war. The last time was with Geronimo's band on their bloody trek across the country when thousands of soldiers were after them.

She is sitting in front of her tepee, staring off into the distance. The sun is setting in a dazzle of white, down behind the tents on the plain, across the river, which glimmers between gravel hills and green woods, and over yonder big mountain. When she notices us, she quickly gets up with more suppleness than I have ever seen in an eighty-year-old. She is small, her skin is wrinkled, and her clothes are wildly flung over her in such a way that her brown body shines through here and there. It's almost as if she'd like to tear the whole thing off and run around half-naked and free like the time she roamed the wilderness. Her gray hair hangs in disarray around her wrinkled face, but there is an alert and fierce look in her eyes. I expect this is how she has had to be. It's as if I can see the old woman chasing away on her horse with a shotgun in her hand, throwing herself into battle. She tells me:

*I have lived during a difficult time. Now when I think back, it is as if a dream. I was always roaming. I always had to duck for bullets (she stoops and ducks her head). There were always battles with the white men. There were three big chiefs in my time: Cochise, Victorio, and Geronimo. They were all good men to their people. Geronimo was the last I followed. Then we were like wolves being hunted down by many. Once there was a big battle in Mexico. The whites surrounded us and nearly all the Indians were killed. They were going to kill me too but I crawled between the fires and ran to the woods.*

I ask her if she has even been taken prisoner. She obstinately tosses back her head and replies, "I always got away." I then ask where the women were when Geronimo and the other warriors went to fight. She says, "We fought alongside them. We hid the children in the mountains. Sometimes we had rifles and sometimes we had clubs. Many men were killed. But our own people went against us, that is why we lost."

There was a deep bitterness in her last words, which were directed toward the Apaches who helped the American troops fight against the rebellious Indians. And true enough, without help from the Apache scouts the wars would have continued for another quarter, if not half, of a century longer. The United States is greatly indebted to their helpers, but then the most loyal were rewarded with prison sentences. One can wonder why the Apaches would fight against their own, but at times tribe stood against tribe. The Apaches also never quite understood what a victory for the whites would actually lead to.

I pay a visit to the most typical of the few remaining Apache scouts, A100, or Taipa.[6] He is also known to be one of the roughest men on the reservation. He has been married to three sisters, and has killed two of them and is now living with the third. A while ago, soldiers tried to lay their hands on him and went to his tent. As soon as Taipa understood what they wanted, he quickly grabbed one of his own children by the leg, held him over a steaming pot of home brew, and threatened to drop him if the soldiers came a step closer.

In order to get an understanding of this man, I asked one of the missionaries about him. He said, "Taipa is a real rough type, and he has such a strong personality that it is disturbing to meet him. It's best to let him be." I understood this to a degree because I too had sensed a dynamic force in some Apaches, an almost fanatic intensity in their temperaments. But whatever the risk, I *wanted* to see Taipa.

I like him at first sight. He is a small, sturdy fellow who seems to be immensely self-assured, stands straight as an arrow, and has long hair.

There is a reckless flair about him and a flashing vitality. He gets up from the ground, takes a few steps toward me, and looks me straight in the eyes as if to say, "I am Taipa, as good as anyone else, who are you and what do you want!" Gradually, his look turns friendlier, and suddenly he shakes my hand and we are friends. Neither of us has said a word.

We seat ourselves under the awning, where we have a view of the forest, green fields, and a skinny yellow horse. Taipa tells me about his life. There is dramatic force in his story, and his singsong voice rises and falls like strange music. Simply and with vivid details about grass, animals, tracks, stones, mountains, and forests, he depicts pictures from war time in such a way that I can almost see it as it has happened. Through his words he takes me to the top of high mountains where heated battles against the Tonto Apaches took place, then to deep canyons where Cochise and his people struck like eagles down upon the troops, then far away to the Sierra Madre in pursuit of Geronimo. I hear about Be-da-jo's second in command, who was scalped and whose finger was chopped off because there was a gold ring on it. He adds that he knows of only one other incident in which the Apaches scalped their enemies. I also learn more about how he could have become a scout for the American troops and fight against his own people. He doesn't hide his bitter feelings toward Geronimo and the Chiricahua Apaches. At the same time, he gives them full credit for being so clever and says, "The Chiricahua Apaches were more cunning than anybody. As sly as the prairie wolf they were." He says about Geronimo, "He was the slyest of them all. Nobody could find his trail because he left in one direction, turned completely around, and zigzagged over the mountains. He was a great medicine man, but mean. When soldiers approached and Indian children screamed, he twisted their necks."

In the end, Taipa says, "It was the Apache scouts who straightened everything out. We made good peace for the whites, but they took our land. Now, most of the warriors are dead. Just myself and a few others are alive. We are growing old, but everyone knows what we have done. Everyone knows me. When they see me they say, "There is A100, Taipa."

# 4
# Glimpse of the Old and the New

One of the first things that strikes me during my stay with the White Mountain Apaches is how clever they are. They are quick to perceive, have a keen sense of logic, and are able to express their thoughts clearly and concisely. Our self-righteous race can often be quite condescending regarding Native peoples' understanding. In truth, the capabilities of the Apaches, as well as many others, are no lesser than those of the white race. They are highly intelligent and within their cultural framework they have achieved the utmost in warfare, hunting, and other pursuits. There are many examples of them now achieving comparable deeds under modern conditions. In 1872 nearly one hundred Apaches were slaughtered by American troops in a cave in the Salt River Canyon, Arizona. Furthest inside the cave, a one-year-old boy was found lying under the body of his mother. The child was later adopted by an American family, sent to school, educated in medicine, and later became a distinguished doctor in Chicago.[1] One person's leap from a thousand-year-old stone age culture to the twentieth century.

One day, I'm walking around the Indian tents together with a reservation employee. A small Indian lad runs smack into his legs and is rudely pushed aside. The boy flies into a raging fit and as quick as lightning grabs a stone and hurls it at the man. This is his Apache pride, a hostility and lust for revenge, prevalent even in the children.

Revenge is a burning issue for the Apaches and it haunts his every thought until it has been fulfilled. Blood vengeance was the family's right, as it was for the Vikings. In earlier times, revenge was most likely taken during warring raids. Now, however, it is taken whenever, sometimes in complete disregard of all consequences. Once an Apache who was under the influence was walking along the road when a woman snapped her fingers and called him a louse. He killed her on the spot with a stone.

Such incidents don't often occur, but they do happen. They are very serious, but don't forget they concern a people who were only recently brought in from the warpath and who not until adulthood have seen white people. Their search for revenge grew from always having to fight bitterly for their survival. They were a minority nomadic people who had to struggle to win respect – or die.

But this is only one side of the picture. The Apache is also a member of a very morality-based society. I meet an old Apache who tells me, "When I was young, the chief said to me, 'Wake up early in the morning, walk up a hill, and behold the sun's face as it rises above the mountain. In the sun you will see the one who will be your wife. Live your life as pure as you see it then so that you are worthy of her.' "

In the old days, it was very important for the Apaches to live a proper life. A man who lied was considered a disgrace, and theft never occurred except from the enemy. The women were virtuous, and adultery was punishable by cutting off the nose of the woman and by death for the man who had come between the marriage. Intercourse between unmarried people was punishable by having the man hang by his thumbs or wrists in a tree for half a day. More recently, several of these things have changed. An Apache is now about equal with his white tutor when it comes to lying, and as for the new moralities in marriage, he isn't slow to follow suit. Just a few elderly noseless women still remain. Only a decade ago, young girls went around with "maiden flowers" in their hair. Now, however, the era of wearing maiden flowers has come to an end, as it has elsewhere.

One day I am sitting with my interpreter, Chester, and his family talking about this and that and enjoying ourselves. When Apaches are together or with people they know well, they really relax and joke around. Half-naked Indian children are playing around us and have so much fun with the simplest toys that it is a delight to watch them. Over by the tent, a woman is sitting weaving a basket that has some beautiful symbolic patterns. Apache women are masters in making flat and jar-shaped baskets as well as nice carrying baskets. But unfortunately, this is an art that is about to die out.

As we sit here chatting, I suggest that we go see Chester's father-in-law and talk with him. Chester hesitantly agrees and we stroll over to his tent, which is close by. But what in the world is wrong with Chester? He is walking along sideways with his head half-tilted. I ask him if he is ill. Chester replies, "Mother-in-law!" Then I understand. The Apaches still follow the old rule of not looking at your mother-in-law. Strangely enough, this custom shows the son-in-law's respect for her.

It certainly can't be easy to continue this practice. Today, as in the old days, the man moves near to his wife's family when he marries and usually has his tent quite close to his mother-in-law's. He is in continual contact with her because being married to her daughter obliges him to help care for her and her closest family. Chester, though, doesn't think it causes too many problems and says, "It only means that you have to turn your head quickly."

Now, as earlier, parents often have the deciding say concerning marriage. From what an old Apache woman told me, the old ceremonies that initiated a marriage were fairly straightforward: "The boy and his family would go out into the woods to hunt for deer. The slain animal and other gifts would be placed in front of the tent of the girl's parents. Then this family would go out hunting and place their catch in front of the tent of the boy's parents. Festivities and a dance were held and afterward the young couple would move in together."

This custom is no longer practiced. Now when White Mountain Apaches initiate a marriage it turns out to be more like buying and selling.[2] The suitor who pays the most often gets the girl, even if he is both old and ugly. There is some tradition in this because before it was the warrior with the best catch who was regarded as the best suitor.

If a man's wife dies, he is obliged to marry her sister or cousin if no other serious reasons stand in the way. Similar rules apply to the widow. Polygamy was also practiced but has now dwindled away. And love? It undoubtedly exists, perhaps somewhat different than what we are used to and even if it is hardly mentioned.

The woman's role in Apache marriages has never been easy. She has always had a tremendous workload, and her quick-tempered husband doesn't always treat her with silk gloves. But she has never been suppressed, and often there is deep harmony between husband and wife. Most likely these forthright women have also had an important say in issues of war and diplomacy even though it seems to be the mighty man who decides all. This is also apparent today and can especially be seen with elderly women, particularly with grandmothers, who have a great influence on their community.

Much of the White Mountain Apache social system still exists, although certain elements have begun to dwindle. The system is based on a division of bands and local family groups. Within all of this lies the clan system. Family means a great deal to the White Mountain Indians, as well as to other Apaches. Blood relations have a special duty to help each other, take revenge for each other, avoid marriage with each other, and address each other with language that shows respect. Overall, the Apache social system is anything but simple, indeed, it is based upon a tangle of many rules.

One morning two Indians brush past me and I notice that their cheeks and foreheads are streaked in yellow. It is flower pollen; they have just come from prayers, which they learned from their forefathers. It's not easy to tell which spirit they have prayed to. The Apaches' spiritual world is like an entangled weaving in which the threads are difficult to find. It is grounded in the fear of the unknown and a sensitive understanding of nature, which infers that in every little flower, every tree, every stone, every mountain, in the stars, moon, and sun, and thunder and lightning are living spirits that are willing to help the Apaches whenever needed. But the highest of all spirits is Ihidna-nohhaineh'hn, "he who has given us life," or as also expressed, Ihidna-yae-bik'eh-hn, "Lord of Life." These and other words have not been derived from Christianity's influence, such as Jus-n, which is equivalent to the Spanish word *dios*. The earlier Apaches independently reached a belief in a supreme God.

In some cases, as for prayers for a long life, the Apache individual can direct his prayers to one of the spirits. In most other situations, however, prayers or invocations are mediated by the medicine man, who has had strict training in this craft. His help is often sought when illnesses need healing, when wild animals need pacifying to ensure a good hunt, when missing items need to be found. During times of war, he played an important role because he held visionary powers to see where the enemy was and could predict the outcome of a battle. Rituals and ceremonies, especially with dancing and chanting, are part of the medicine man's craft. Certain colors such as black, blue, yellow, and white, the number four, which represents the directions of the wind and sun, the snake, flower pollen, blue stone, and much more all have important roles. The Apaches are not just religious, they weave religion into their daily lives.

I haven't been able to find any clear White Mountain Apache concepts of life after death even though their mythology does deal with the question.[3] The people who are searching for the land "where there is neither illness, old age, or death" is often discussed. Christianity, though, has had comparatively little affect on the Apaches' deeply ingrained superstitious beliefs, despite the self-sacrificing efforts of missionaries such as Pastor Guenther and his wife, who for a generation have been with the White Mountain Apaches.

From one of the tents down by the river, monotone chanting has carried on now hour after hour. It is the medicine man tending the sickbed of a young Indian girl. Some days later I go down and look in on her. She is lying on the dirt floor with some rags over her and is as still and patient as a sick dog. Her face looks drained and she appears to be almost nothing but wide, feverish eyes under bluish-black hair. Outside the tent some of her family are sitting, sewing death robes. When they go inside the tent, they walk around the patient, who doesn't receive any care other than a little water and corn now and then, which she is too weak to consume. This is how she has it until she dies.

The Apaches have a fear of illness and death. When they become ill, they give up. Other than calling the medicine man, they almost do nothing else for the sick, who they practically avoid. In certain cases, they will seek help from the reservation's hospital.

However, if the illness is obviously very grave, they can't get the patient into the ground fast enough, sometimes too fast. Pastor Guenther, who is sometimes sent for when an Indian is to be buried, told me about a time that he once was called to administer a funeral. He came to the place where the hole was dug in the ground and the coffin stood ready with the corpse inside. He finished the ceremony and then lifted the coffin lid so the family could have one last glimpse of the body. Suddenly, the "deceased" sat right up from the coffin and protested, and ended up living for seven more years. Another time something similar happened with a small child, who began to cry when the coffin was about to be lowered into the ground. Perhaps not everyone has been so lucky to wake up in time.

The Apaches still follow old rituals concerning death: they burn the deceased's tent and belongings except for the very personal items such as his saddle, rifle, and so on, which are laid in the grave together with water and food. Ashes taken from the deceased's home are scattered over the grave site, and the name of the dead relative is never mentioned again.

In recent times, diseases have seriously debilitated the Apaches. An ancient nomadic and warring people who through thousands of years developed to be some of the fittest humans known, have in only half a century physically deteriorated. John Taipa, nearly a hundred years old, describes the old times:

> The chief always had to be up before sunrise. From time to time, he would go to the top of a hill and stand there in the first rays of sun and speak to his people. He told the Indians how they should live properly. He talked about hunting and when the time was right for gathering nuts from the oak and walnut. Before they ate anything, the men trained. They ran long distances to strengthen their legs and lungs. They wrestled and practiced shooting with bows and spears. They bathed in the river, even if there was ice. They just chopped a hole in the ice and swam. All of them knew how to swim. They stood under trees that were covered with snow and let the snow come tumbling over their naked bodies. This was how they built stamina. After their meal, they hunted for deer. They ate very much meat as well as many wild plants such as mescal, mesquite beans, sunflower seeds, bark from the aspen tree, cactus fruit, nuts, berries, wild potatoes, onions, grass sprouts, and many other things that grew in the forest and mountains. The food often tasted a little bitter but it was a healthy diet that provided strength. There were no diseases back then. People grew big and strong and lived to become old.

Training and diet were two of the most important factors that shaped the Apaches' fantastic physique, but other factors also played an important role. There were unwritten laws in the society that were geared to increasing the people's strength. Weak children were killed and the decrepit were abandoned to their fate when it was for the tribe's best interests. Intermarriage was forbidden, but captured women and children who later were integrated into the tribe ensured fresh blood into the lineage.

Capturing people wasn't coincidental; it happened often enough to indicate some kind of plan. Strict rules governing relations between the two genders was also a plus for the family. In addition, their requirements for cleanliness were upheld by religious inclinations, and it was therefore more imperative to follow them. The Apache's sweat baths – steam baths in grass huts where water was thrown onto heated rocks – were at times part of a ritual.

Diseases that may have emerged in olden times seldom had any effect on these healthy people. If illness did strike, it was taken care of by the medicine man, who typically specialized in various types of ailments. They had many types of medicine, most of which were collected from plants. There is every reason to believe that many of them were very effective, as several of them have even been adopted into modern medical science. Other healing methods also played an important role, such as the sweat baths, massage, etc. The medicine man's craft often went hand-in-hand with these methods and included dancing, chanting, and invoking spirits as well. This had a suggestive influence on the patient and surely affected the healing in many cases. All in all, the Apaches were well-prepared to fight diseases of that period and keep them at bay.

The people flourished and became a model of health and strength – then came Western civilization. In just a short period of time, the Indians' health and bodies radically deteriorated. Tuberculosis, trachoma (an eye disease), and other illnesses became as devastating as a plague. In 1922, it was estimated that three-fourths of the population in San Carlos suffered from trachoma and a third from tuberculosis.[4] At the White Mountain Reservation, conditions have been somewhat better because people are living in a more isolated way. No better survey of the spread of these diseases exists since most of the sufferers avoid hospitals and instead seek treatment from the tribal medicine men.

It should also be mentioned that the Apaches' teeth are similarly affected as white people's. Likewise, Apache women now experience the same pain and possibility of complications during childbirth as white women. Earlier, births were easier and without excessive pain. Interestingly enough, though, cancer and diabetes have not been detected among the San Carlos or the White Mountain Apaches.

There are probably many other deeper reasons for the Apaches' decline in health and physical strength. Lack of immunity against new diseases is one factor, a change in diet is another, as well as the fact that they don't follow the same hygienic practices as before. Concerning the Apaches' health as a whole, the abrupt transition from a roving, nomadic lifestyle to the restricted existence on the reservation has also surely had a great influence. Experience shows that nomads are those who suffer the most when encountering social changes. They are so thoroughly conditioned, physically and mentally, to live a life of wandering that the transition to a stationary lifestyle is much more of a shock to their systems than it is for permanent-dwelling tribes. It is almost like strapping a full-blooded racehorse to the front of a cart.

The Apaches have lost their land and their freedom, and now they watch as the world their forefathers created collapses, piece by piece. Such a blow can't help but physically affect the people the same way that despair hinders the healing of a patient. The Apaches no longer have any goals, and they have lost that which gave them happiness. They feel the same as if an Anglo-American, a Frenchman, or a Norwegian might have felt if their land had been conquered, they themselves displaced and put under guardianship, and their entire culture trampled upon.

Despite all of this, the Apache's *collective* population has increased by 2,605 people during the last forty-eight years. In 1938 they numbered 8,274.[5] This shows the vitality of this people. These tough nomads who struggled down from the northern snowy tundra to the South's sunny regions haven't been defeated by their newest enemy – diseases of civilization.

And the future of the Apaches? In recent years, the American government has done much for the tribes. The Indians have acquired decent land where cattle-raising yields good returns, and schools, hospitals, missionary stations, and churches have been established on the reservations. The Indians are being trained in agriculture, ranching, and handicrafts and are assisted in various ways. This has helped change the Apaches' lives and their financial condition. Over-all, external conditions exist to aid these people's progress, but what good does that do when the Apaches are not inclined to give in to the new? They have little desire for the modern routines and are rather lukewarm about carrying them out. There is still too much bitterness, and the past has too great of a hold on them. There is also too great a lack of trust and human understanding, which are so necessary for anything at all to be achieved with this proud, wise, and pugnacious people.

It would be too shortsighted, though, to judge the situation as it is today because just now an intense conflict rages between the Apache and Anglo-American cultures. It is as if two mighty waves have broken against each other and have become a churning chaos. It will take a long time for the waters to calm, but one day it will happen. Then the strength and rich capabilities of the Apaches will rise and find their rightful place among the best.

# 5
## Dance and Prayer

The same intense sunshine and the same clear, blue sky above the red hills and green forests. Donkeys doze motionlessly in the shade of a large, leafy tree, and the Indians retreat under their sunshades while the children splash around in the river. Sunlight shimmers in through the trees and dances over their plump, bronzed bodies. As I'm walking along, I suddenly startle them. Like a brood of frightened animals the children take off running toward the shore and disappear into a tangle of overgrown sunflowers. Golden blossoms swing back and forth where the naked bodies darted through.

The air is getting hotter, the drought worse. Is it ever going to rain soon?

Then one day in July a cloud forms. It's as if it came from nowhere and suddenly hangs there up against all that blue. Then more clouds drift out from behind the big mountain, wonderful, billowing clouds high in the sky. Later in the afternoon rain finally begins to fall in light showers over the forest and hills, dousing every living thing. The people turn their faces toward the wet drops and breathe in the marvelous smell of damp grass and earth.

For a time the rain falls quite regularly now, every afternoon. Heavy clouds gather, thunder rumbles over the forests, and bolts of lightning flash across the sky. Other times though, good weather returns and seems to be appreciated more.

"This evening many Indians in Day Canyon," Chester says, and so we go there. Some big event is about to begin, a sunrise dance (puberty ceremony) for three young girls who are to be ushered into the ranks of womanhood. Indians are streaming into Day Canyon from near and far. Over on the hills, I can see a few riders wearing vibrant red shirts and groups of women walking beside them with their colorful dresses looking like varicolored clusters of flowers in the open fields.

It is beautiful down there in Day Canyon. The Indians have pitched their tents in the wooded area along the sunny, glimmering White River. In between the trees I can see a lot of activity, red and yellow dresses glaring against the green leaves and smoke from several campfires rising high into the blue sky. Several canvas-covered wagons from afar have been left at the edge of the woods, and unharnessed horses and mules graze in small herds over on the hills.

We move close to the old medicine man, who is preparing a dress for one of the sunrise girls who is to be initiated the following morning. It's going to be quite some dress: a voluminous, ankle-length, yellow garment decorated with eagle feathers, bells, and colorful ribbon. The medicine man works intently and lays the dress out on the ground, arranges the decorations, then takes a few steps back to scrutinize his work. Next to the dress lies the girl's staff, her knee-high moccasins, and a tanned buckskin. Nothing must be left out. Everything has to be arranged according to the old rituals if the sunrise dance is to bring luck and fertility to the young girls.

I wander around the woods and greet the Indians that I know. They all seem to be in good spirits and ready for the festivities. Next to the river, I notice a low, dome-shaped hut covered with blankets. Around it sit about a dozen Indians who are completely naked except for their breechcloths. A fire burns close by beneath a pile of round stones. The men are getting ready to take a steam bath. This signifies a physical and spiritual cleansing and since olden times has been a ceremonial part of the sunrise dance.

Three Indians are splashing about in the river and dousing themselves with water, which is also part of the ceremony. They wade up to the shore and crawl into the low lodge, where a pile of the glowing-hot stones and a jar of water have been brought in. The opening is closed and an Indian on the outside begins to beat his drum. Those inside begin chanting and their muffled, wild, monotonous sounds rise out of the steam bath.

I stand there thinking what an incredible steam bath this is. Then I ask the ceremony master if it is possible for a white man to participate. Of course, he says, that can be arranged. You'll have to get ready to

go in with the next group. I throw off my clothes and in nothing but a
pair of shorts I wade out into the river together with two warriors of an
older generation, fellows who could well be about sixty-five years old.
They have streaks of gray in their hair and wrinkles on their faces, but
their bodies are still handsome, with their broad chests and muscular
arms and legs. We stride up onto the shore while the people stand and
stare at us. I don't feel very representative in my soaking wet shorts
and I glance over with envy at my breechcloth-clad companions who
look really wonderful and manly.

We crawl into the steam bath and a blanket is hung over the opening, which makes it pitch dark inside. I squeeze between the two men,
sit with my legs pulled up under my chin, and wait to see what happens. The Indians begin to throw water onto the hot stones and steam
hisses into the air. Soon that small space turns into a real oven. Sweat
pours down me and I feel the Indians' soaking-wet limbs leaning
against mine. The drum begins beating outside and at once the two
on each side of me start chanting. At full volume, they start singing
a "snake song." It depicts how the snake moves, how big it is, how
powerful and poisonous it is, but it also explains that the Indians have
medicine against its power. The chanting sounds wild and haunting.

I am at a bit of a loss here because snake songs aren't a part of my
repertoire of childhood tunes, and there are some rather difficult and
indeterminable quarter notes and so forth. But I listen a while and
then jump in and sing along on the chorus while I keep beat with my
big toe. I can't manage the words, but it turns out that a snake song
sounds just fine using *hei – hei – heia – hei*. We sing four snake songs
as the sweat pours off of us in steady streams.

As I sit there between those Indians singing my heart out in that
snake song and really having a wonderful experience, it strikes me
how far we white people lag behind in creating the same spirit in
our steam baths. I remember how back in Norway the men would
slither in through the steam bath door glancing fiendishly at each
other, and then sit there all to themselves. The socially influential
men, those with big stomachs and double-chins, would try to hide
away on the uppermost benches, avoiding eye contact with anyone,
while the skinny and straggly ones would attempt to take cover behind them. Others who weren't of any influence but were athletic

and had muscular bodies to show off would arrogantly strut across the floor, clapping themselves on the chest and doing knee-bends. Silence reigned and there was an overall feeling of animosity. We should really try something different and follow the Indians' example: sit together and let loose a few snake songs. Toleration would rule and the steam bath would be inspiring, something to look forward to.

It is dawn the next day. In the large open area just by the woods in Day Canyon, a crowd of Indians has gathered. The sunrise dance is about to begin, the ceremony that will initiate the young girls into womanhood. There are three sunrise girls this time, but two of them have already had their first initiations on previous mornings and so will be acting more as assistants now. For the third girl, this is her true initiation.

It is a promising morning, with dew covering the fields and a distinctive chill in the air. The sky is clear, but farther in the east there is a faint tinge of red over the mountains. It's time to begin the dance. Within the circle of people, the three sunrise girls step forward and stand side by side behind each of their own buckskins, which are spread out on the ground. Just in front of them are twelve baskets filled to the brim with fruit, tobacco, and much more, which will later be distributed among the people by those holding the dance. Behind the girls stand a closely packed group of drummers and singers, knowledgeable old men.

The three girls are probably about seventeen winters old and have the usual Native slenderness, gracefulness, and stature. I catch a glimpse of their lovely, solemn faces that are framed by their flowing, dark hair, which hangs down their backs and over their shoulders. They are a marvelous sight in their long, wide, yellow dresses that the old medicine man has decorated. A fringed Mexican shawl hung with eagle feathers and colored ribbon drapes over their shoulders and small bells dangle from the hems of their dresses. A shiny shell glimmers from their narrow headband. They are wearing knee-high moccasins and carry a curved staff with bells and blue, white, yellow, and black ribbon. Everything has its symbolic meaning, from the staff, which represents age, to the shell on the forehead, which catches the sun god's own power when the first rays shine over the mountain.

Suddenly, the drums begin to sound and the singers start in with a strange melody that resonates to the beat and fills the air. Everyone is instantly energized. The sunrise girls begin dancing in place behind their buckskins and tap their staffs on the ground, ringing the bells. All of the onlooking women are holding each other under their arms, shuffling back and forth, moving en masse like a wave.

The two sunrise girls who have had their dance the previous morning step to the side, leaving only the new initiate there. She dances and dances and dances, always in the same spot and never stopping. The people dance with her and all the while the reddish tinge over the mountains in the east grows brighter. Then the first golden rays of sunlight wash over the land and people and glimmer in the shell on the girl's headband. She kneels on her buckskin, stretches her palms toward the sun, and begins swaying rhythmically from side to side.

It is such a beautiful, marvelous sight that really only a paint brush could do it justice: that young girl kneeling there, dark hair flowing down over her yellow dress, so childlike and so deeply serious. The crowd of people rhythmically rocking back and forth with their multicolored clothing looks like a swaying bed of flowers in the green forest. Across all of it, the first rays of sunlight shine through the dew-fresh morning and cast a golden glimmer from beyond the distant ridges.

The sunrise girl eventually stands and continues to dance as before. An older woman steps forward and then the girl lays down sprawled on her stomach on the buckskin with her head lifted toward the sun. The woman moves skillful hands over her, straightens out her back, draws her shoulders back and pats her loins and chest and in the end steps on her.

The girl stands and goes on dancing. With a quick stroke of her hand, she wipes the sweat off her brow. She is very tired but sluggishly continues because this is the most important ceremony in her life.

Then the old woman goes forward a short distance and sticks the girl's staff into the ground facing the sun. The girl runs out and goes around the staff and back again. Three times the staff is moved farther back and each time she runs around it. Finally, it is positioned toward the south, then to the west, and to the north, and the girl runs around it again but this time she is followed by the group of people.

Then comes the last act of the dance: The girl stands there with bowed head behind the buckskin while a long line of men walk by her. Each one of them tosses a handful of flower pollen over her head, in the end completely covering her black hair in yellow. The somber mood suddenly ends; with uproar and laughter several young boys rush forward and grab the twelve gift baskets, sling them up onto their heads, and storm into the crowd, who happily help themselves to their heart's delight.

The sunrise dance is over but the drumming continues along with the rhythmic sway of the crowd, which makes its last swell.

But the girls are not yet finished with their initiation. The morning after they will all participate in the big concluding ceremony. Then they will dance opposite three boys who will stand holding eagle feathers in front of a symbolic tent marked with four attached poles. When that dance ends, the sunrise girls will be grown women and ready for marriage.

In the evening, there is a dance for everyone in Day Canyon, and all the sunrise girls are there. A large campfire burns in an open area in the woods sending flames high into the sky like a red sword in the darkness casting a large circle of light. This flickering light dances over the dense crowd of Indians in their colorful clothing and sheds a fine glow across the shiny leaves on the nearest trees. The women and children have settled farthest away in the ring, where the trees are dense, dark columns, while the men sit and stand closer to the flames on the other side of the fire.

A young boy comes racing in with a huge staff that he drives into the fire, making sparks fly. Then Tenijieth, the old medicine man and my good friend, walks up a small hill and begins speaking to the people, something that is usually done before the dance begins. He speaks well and long and makes it clear that now there is going to be dancing and fun and no roughhousing. He says it humorously and is a wonderful master of ceremony standing there affably and confidently with his funny, squinty eyes and a small tuft of a billy-goat beard hanging on the end of his chin.

The drums begin beating and the singers get under way. The three sunrise girls dance arm in arm in all their finery and staffs ringing with bells. Taking small, short steps, they dance toward the group of men. Then they begin dancing back and forth in front of those they would like to dance with, inviting them with a light tap on the shoulder. Three men stand, lock arms with each other, and then begin to dance around the fire. The girls dance backward and the men dance toward them. They all take small steps as in a kind of foxtrot. All the other women suddenly rush forward in groups of twos, threes, and fours and do as the sunrise girls. This gradually forms a tight circle of dancers who slowly and rhythmically move around the fire.

As soon as one dance ends, another begins, similar to the last. It is always the women who ask for a dance. The singers' rich, deep voices keep time to the rhythm of the drums, and sounds of laughter and fun echo from the dancers. It is a wonderful forest festivity for all of them.

I, as the only white person here, have taken a seat on a tree stump together with the Apache Pailzote, a young, practical fellow who speaks reasonable English. We are not very lucky. Dance after dance goes by and the women rush forward laughing and giggling and choosing their victims; to the right, then to the left, always near us – but never directly at us. We just keep sitting there on that tree stump all alone.

We try to be dignified about it and say to each other that it is jolly good that we can sit in peace and don't have to go stomping around the fire like the others. However, I can't deny that I feel a little out of sorts, since being rejected for every single dance is a little too much to take. Now and then, a bunch of girls swing in close to me and I tense up a bit. But no, it's always those sitting next to us who win the beauties' attention.

As I sit there brooding, for the first time I clearly understand the white girls' world, in which they delight in dressing up in their prettiest dresses and eagerly go off to a ball – only to sit as I am sitting now. Oh well, at least I'm not wearing my finest, although I have donned a newly-washed blue shirt. My shoes, though, are so full of holes that I'm nearly walking around barefoot, not that anyone can see. There, they're starting to dance again. I light my pipe, try to show indifference and decide that the ladies' dance doesn't suit me.

The three sunrise girls dance out, arm in arm, with swaying eagle feathers and ringing staffs. They come closer, dance right next to me now but I don't look up. I'm through with looking up. It rings and rings in front of me and I think that it is strange why those sitting next to me are taking so long to stand up and dance. Suddenly I feel a slight tap on my shoulder and am a bit startled – well by golly if it isn't the sunrise girls dancing in front of Pailzote and me! I'm ready to jump up but Pailzote suddenly nudges me, clearly indicating that one shouldn't be too quick here. We sit there a good while on the stump and let the girls dance. Then we slowly stand and with an air of indifference we join arms and begin dancing around the fire as if we had danced with the sunrise girls the entire evening.

Such is life. Once on the inside, luck often changes. Suddenly, we became very popular and women of all ages come rushing up to us at every dance. We even once dance with three charming nine-year-old kids who trip around in their long, wide skirts while they giggle and bashfully cock their heads against their dark hair.

Everything is wonderful – up until the "three witches" start in with their tricks. They are something right out of an old fairy tale: ancient, with scraggly gray tufts of hair, shriveled faces, and teeth missing here and there. When they catch sight of us, we're doomed. The seasoned, daring old women audaciously chase away the young girls and again and again latch onto us. The first time they even demand that we younger ones dance backward and they dance forward. We are senseless enough to agree to it, but bitterly regret it later. The bumpy ground is so full of holes that it's by the hair of our teeth that we don't fall head over heals a few times, all this of course to the sheer delight of the onlookers. Later we muster up the courage to ask that we dance like men, and begin dancing forward, one dance after another. But the three old women have the time of their lives, flirtatiously tossing their gray tufts of hair and smiling seductively with their gums – and us, oh we try to take it like men.

For a long time I grin and bear it because being the only white man I don't want to offend anyone. But then suddenly Pailzote disappears.

He's had enough. At the first opportunity, I do the same. I sneak into the woods and don't stop until I'm on safe ground.

The Apaches carry on with their sunrise dance for four days, and in the evenings the group dances are held. The strange devil dance (spirit dance) comes at the end as a concluding part of the ceremony. Seven near-naked men perform in the most horrid masks. It is a wild and eerie dance that is meant to drive away the evil spirits of illness. Afterward the Indians in the woods break camp and everyone goes their own way. The absolutely exhausted sunrise girls will now be able to sleep a long time.

Not long after this, I pay a visit to the master of ceremony of the festivities, my friend and one of the Indians I like the best, Medicine Man Tenijieth. His funny "Buddha" face always seems to humorously light up and there is also something so benevolently good about him. When I arrive at his tent he shakes my hand and says, "Indians happy that you not feel too big to join us in our festivities." It takes so little. He continues explaining some things about the dances and tells me that they are very, very old. For many generations, his forefathers danced the same way in the woods, the time when they wandered freely.

I tell him that soon I will be traveling off on my horse into the mountains and it would be a long time before we would see each other again. Then I mention that earlier he had talked about some "intense" stories and prayers that he previously didn't want to tell me more about because they were only intended for the Indians. But perhaps he would be willing to tell me now?

Tenijieth quietly sits there staring off into the distance. Then he turns his head and dramatically and intensely begins to tell the story of Nayenaezghani, the dragon slayer. Both this mythical figure and his mother, who was impregnated by the sun, are central figures in Apache beliefs and continually play a role in dances and rituals.

The story, which takes several hours to tell, begins like this: He who gave us life created everything and then gave it all to the sun. A woman stood naked on a cliff. The sun shone over her and the sun's spirit penetrated her and she conceived a boy, the sun's child. Then the time came for sun's son to be born. She stood on a mountain and to the east of her lay a black lake, in the south lay a blue one, in the west a yellow and the north a white lake. She stood directly in the middle of all these lakes. She stretched both hands high in the air with her palms facing up. She took the golden flower pollen in her hand and sprinkled it four times over her head, then made a stripe down her forehead. Afterward she made a stripe on her right side, one across her back, and another on her left side. She said, "This golden flower pollen will help me." Then she raised her hands with her palms up and fell on her knees. And this was how Nayenaeghani, the son of the sun, was born.

The mother of the sun's son, Isdzann-nadlae-hae, was alone.[1] After the sun's baby was born, she made a carrying basket for him. The bottom of the basket was woven with rays of lightning, the little covering over his head was made of a rainbow, and a blanket made from the black lake was the pillow to rest his head upon. Lightning bolts were tied in loops along the basket and rays of lightning were pulled through these loops. This was how he was held in place in the carrying basket.

The story continues by telling about how the sun boy, who had webbed fingers and toes, grew up with the other children. One day, a little insect sits by his ear and advises him to ask his mother who his father is. He follows the advice and she says that his father is the sun, but it is terribly difficult to get there.

The boy begins the journey anyway. He faces one obstacle after another, such as an impenetrable cactus forest and tremendous hailstorms, but wild animals help him, and often he rides over the obstacles on the back of a luminous snake.

Finally he reaches the sun's house, where the god himself lives with his wife and twelve sons. When the wife sees the stranger, she becomes very upset at the sun and says that this is a son he has had with another woman. The sun answers that he doesn't know anything about it but that he will try to sort it out. In the house of the sun there are four flaming ravines, a black, a blue, a yellow, and a white, and one by one the boy is thrown down into these. But every time, the little insect appears and whispers an important word in his ear so that he emerges unscathed from the flames. The sun now understands that this is his son and orders him to go into the steam bath together with his twelve half brothers. Inside they splash water onto the glowing hot stones to create an incredible heat. The webs between the boy's hands and feet loosen in the heat and then fall off so that he is now like other people. The entire time they sing a series of four songs and mystical things occur. There is no shade outside the steam bath, yet a tree grows high up into the sky and has very large leaves. It is also still, hot, and humid, but a fresh breeze begins to blow.

All of this is an initiation for the boy. For the first time, the sun now calls him his son and gives him the name Nayenaezghani, Dragon Slayer. He presents him with a yellow horse, a club made of turquoise, and other weapons that have the power to kill the dragon. The people in The Big Dipper give him a sword. He also receives a basket of food and a jug of water that never empties. Then he returns to earth and carries out remarkable acts.

When Tenijieth finally finishes with the long story, he quietly sits there lost in his own thoughts. Then he says, "Nayenaezghani was a great medicine man who taught the Indians everything. He taught us the way to the great powers. He taught us to reach the mightiest of all through prayer." I ask him how the Apaches pray and he replies, "We hold flower pollen in our right hand and blow it high into the air. We place our left hand on our chest and stretch our right hand with our palm up toward the sun." He does this, looks toward, the sun and says:

> Lord of life, our father,
> you have given us
> your own heart,
> your own thoughts,
> your own veins,
> your own fingers,
> your own limbs,
> your own body,
> we are of you.
>
> Father, lord of life,
> let good follow me wherever I may go,
> let everything happen for the best for me,
> let this prayer help me.

*I pray to you, my mother,*
*to you who were renewed by the sun.* [2]

*My mother, your path is made*
*from this wondrous golden pollen,*
*you have walked upon it,*
*you have walked upon it with delight.*
*Let me also walk upon it*
*and feel the song in my blood.*
*Your language is the language of the golden pollen,*
*a good language,*
*the language that leads to a long life.*
*This is the language you speak.*
*Help me to also speak it,*
*the same as you.*

*Lord of life,*
*to your house,*
*to the heart of your house I direct my prayer.*
*With this beautiful flower pollen I ask you:*
*Watch over me.*
*Watch over me with goodness.*
*You have created many types of people here on earth,*
*also watch over them with goodness.*
*You have created us,*
*look after us,*
*let us live long,*
*and rid the sorrow from our paths.*

Deeply moved, Tenijieth finishes the prayer, after which he turns to me and says, "All the things I have told you today are true. I feel them as an energy, they are a part of my life. This story and prayer will also be of good help in your life. I ask you to think of me when you use them."

He asks if my mother and father are still living and continues, "Tell them that I have told you this story and have given you this prayer. Tell them also that I'm not a very old man, only about seventy years old."

He then takes off his worn medicine hat with the feathers, lays his left hand over his chest, and stretches his right palm toward the sun. Afterward, he looks me straight in the eye, offers me his hand and says, ski-k'ii, "my friend."[3]

# 6
# Apache Cowboy Life on the White Mountain Reservation

I slowly ride up the slope toward mighty White Mountain, sacred peak of the Apaches. Far below, the Indian tents disappear and the valley river soon becomes nothing but a distant shimmering streak. My horse digs its hooves into the red sandy slopes and makes its way between ancient juniper pines with silvery-gray trunks and evergreen oaks. Soon we are surrounded by ponderosa pines. The high, tall trees grow dense around us and completely block off the view from all directions.

It is evening before I catch sight of the campfire that rises like a thin red pillar between the dark tree trunks. I hop down from my horse and walk toward the circle of light. About a dozen quiet, motionless Apaches are sitting around the fire staring into the flames; they hardly blink an eye as I approach. "Hello!" I heard someone say, and then Sid, the only white man in the group, stands and gives me a handshake. He is a husky fellow in his fifties, a real cowboy through and through, with a bold, rash demeanor typical of a southwestern pioneer.

Sid is in charge of the cattle drive here in the mountains, although the livestock itself belongs to the White Mountain Apaches, partly to the tribe and partly to individual Indians. Cattle ranching is still something that the Indians haven't quite managed on their own. The Apaches who are quietly sitting around the fire are the tribe's best cowboys and are working with Sid.

There are in all many thousand head of cattle roaming the expansive White Mountain forests and foothills, which rise about ten thousand feet high. The land is rugged and beautiful and its wilderness is peaceful. The Indians don't have any permanent dwellings this far up, and uninvited white people don't have access to the mountain, where deer and wild turkeys and bears and cougars and mountain lions roam.

Sid and his Indians have a lot to handle to ensure that the cattle business thrives. The half-wild cattle need to be found and rounded up from incredibly vast areas, calves need to be branded, those that are to be slaughtered need to be separated from the herd, the rest of the drove need to be herded to better pastures, and so on. Carefully weeding out the best of the herd is equally important to ensure that the beautiful Hereford breed continues to grow pure, healthy, and strong. Cattle ranching, which is of course based on beef production, has its busiest periods during the big fall and spring roundups. The entire mountain is then combed for cattle, and those that are to be sold are herded down to the lowlands. But even now at the end of July, the cowboys have their hands full, using a reserve of about a hundred horses to help carry out their daily work.

I throw my sleeping bag into Sid's tent. I'll be staying with Sid and his Apache cowboys for a while. Then I go around and greet the Indians, and then the dogs, four wonderful animals who are invaluable in helping out with the work. After a chat with Sid about cattle, cowboys, Indians, and pioneer times, I crawl into my bed.

In the middle of the night, I wake with a start. Sid is sitting straight up firing his gun off one shot after another and swearing to beat the band. Outside I can hear the fierce trampling of hooves. The entire herd of horses has been stomping all over our tent. One of them nearly trampled on Sid's head, and another had chomped hold and dragged off a sack of oats that had been lying right by the entrance.

At daybreak, we're up and ready to move our camp to higher ground, about seventy-five hundred feet. It's a wonderful morning with clear, blue skies across the forest and dew still on the grass and heather. Herbert, the horse-tender who smiles at everything a person says, including dreary news, has already been busy rounding up the horses. They're now stomping around in an enclosure, an area fenced off with a single rope stretched between tree trunks.

The quiet Indian cook, Sotta, who looks like a thin Chinese and who never opens his mouth but to eat or for a rare grin, bangs on a pan lid to signal that it's time to eat. Then we all chow down on breakfast. I notice that the cowboys aren't taking any pleasure in eating, they're just shoveling it in as if they are carrying out a tedious task. But after tasting the food, I understand. Sotta's incredibly bad cuisine, which for the time being will overshadow my existence, is quite unique. It breaks new culinary ground in creative cooking. The bacon is completely charred, the tea boiled for an undetermined amount of time, and the meat systematically cooked to pieces. The soup contains handfuls of salt and the biscuits, oh boy! But nobody dares complain, even Sid swallows up the biscuit crusts and inconspicuously slips the lead-heavy dough to the dogs. The problem is that a new cook is hard to find. Making food is about one of the worst chores an Apache man can think of, and at even the slightest hint of criticism, Sotta would jump on his horse and be gone.

After breakfast, we go over to the enclosure and every man has to lasso his own horse. It takes several tries for even the best because the animals are stomping around, bobbing their heads and manes up and down, and they're so crowded together it's difficult to find a target to throw at. Every cowboy has his own horse and alternates it with a fresh animal every other day, sometimes daily if possible. Chasing the half-wild, fleet-footed cattle can be hard on the horses.

After the morning chores are finished we tie on our chaps, jump into our saddles, and ride off.[1] The horse-tender, along with all the other horses and pack animals, makes his own way to our new campsite. The rest of us move on out toward a valley where there are supposedly several cattle.

We ride in a long line through the forest, fourteen men in all with Sid in the lead. The Apaches ride half-slung in their saddles, seemingly uninterested in it all but at the same time alert and ready to act in a second. They handle their restless horses with brilliant confidence but treat them harshly. Usually, they jerk so hard on the reins that the animals develop a nervous habit of throwing their heads back. To stop them from doing this most of the riders use what is called a distemper, a strap tied from the bridle down to the horse's chest harness.

The first rays of sun fade in over the forest and in through the branches, creating patches and streaks of yellow all over the soft green ground. Tall ferns swish along the sides of the horses. There is a kind of strange, cool, stillness in the big forest. Only a few blue magpies are out twitching their tails, and an occasional silver-gray squirrel peaks out from behind the trees. We are riding way down in the foothills, and the riders in front of me appear so small against the huge pine trees, whose tall tops sway in the blue sky.

We're now at the valley where the cattle supposedly are so we spread out. Our long row of riders make a slow approach. I'm riding on the outer flanks together with the Apaches "Chipmunk" and Ethelboh, one of the hardest-working of the cowboys and who incidentally isn't a full-blooded Indian. His mother was an Apache but his father was Mexican. As a boy he was captured by the Apaches during one of their fights and was later raised by them. Ethelboh's face shows finer features than his companions, a trace of Spanish.

We find a trail and the Indians lean down over their horses and determine that a herd of cattle has gone by only half an hour ago. We are quietly riding along when suddenly the Indians whirl their horses around, spur them to a gallop, and take off through the branches and underbrush sitting flat in their saddles. I follow but it still takes me a while before I see what the Apaches' sharp eyesight detected from an incredible distance: a small, brown patch far off between some bushes.

A herd of cattle break through the scrub. They are beautiful with their brown and white markings, alert and light-footed as any wild animals. Startled, they take off running but the Indians cut ahead and soon have them surrounded. Everything has to happen so fast because these cattle are something quite different than the gentle, sluggish dairy cattle back home in Norway. Year round these livestock roam freely up here in the mountains and become so quick and supple that if one doesn't get a jump start on them, they're gone.

As our row of men sweeps the area, more and more animals are rounded up, and soon we have quite a collection of cows, calves, and bulls. Some are still missing, so while a few of us hold watch over the herd, the other Apaches and dogs go off to find the remaining ones. We hear the dogs bark in the distance, and not long after, some furious rustling is heard in the bushes. All of a sudden, half a dozen cattle come crashing through. The Indians follow behind at a slow trot.

We now herd the livestock toward the beaver pond, always riding close on their heels. Some ride behind, some alongside, and some in front. We don't ride very fast as some of the cattle are less than willing to join us and every so often some old rascal attempts to break through and run off. Then we have to act fast, kick our horses, and chase after it. If it is an especially wild one, we throw out a lasso and catch the hind legs or head of the animal, which then tumbles to the ground.

Light begins to break through between the trees and we see a lovely meadow, an oasis in the heart of this great forest. This lush, grassy clearing unfolds amid all these tall pine trees, completely overgrown with yellow black-eyed daisies. They grow so dense that the grass nearly disappears. The small groves of white-trunked aspens and blue spruce rise like islands in a black-yellow sea. Behind, the river winds between reeds, rat grass, large ferns, and angelica with its white bulbs held high. The beaver dam lies over the river; opposite it stretches a quiet pond that reflects the narrow trunks of the aspens.

We ride on and the flowers crunch beneath our horses' hooves, almost a pity to watch. Then the Indians hop off their horses and begin decorating their hair and hats with the yellow daisies. They chatter, laugh, and act just like kids. These tough people love flowers.

Out in this meadow with the yellow daisies, branding starts on the calves, heifers, and cattle that hadn't been caught in previous years. If they no longer follow their mother, they are considered owner-less property and are called mavericks. They are then divided equally among the cowboys, who each has a small herd of cattle from before.

A fire is quickly lit and the branding irons are thrown in while some of the Indians keep watch over the stock. Ethelboh rides out and lassos one unbranded animal after the other and hauls it back to the fire. He is a master with that lasso and can throw it around the cows' necks just as easily as their hind legs. His horse is a perfect cow horse: it works with him and continually keeps the rope taunt when the calf is lassoed.

The branding and other jobs that they simultaneously carry out are not a very pleasant sight. The tribe's brand, a broken arrow, as well as the owner's brand are burned into the cow's hide with glowing irons. These brands and irons aren't exactly the small, modest brands used by the Anglo ranchers, but large, fancy brands that turn the entire side of the calf into a work of art.

While the branding continues, I take a little ride up toward Diamond Creek, and Buckskin splashes over the soggy marshes in the riverbed. It's amazing that the mountain should have such an abundance of water when the foothills and lowlands yearn for moisture. But as it happens, humid winds blow in from the Mexican and California Gulfs, are warmed over the desert and rise. When these winds reach the mountains, they release their condensation.

I halt Buckskin by the beaver pond in such a tangle of ferns that his head barely reaches over the top. Just in front of me is a beaver den, which seems to be lower and more haphazardly made than those that I have seen in the Arctic. Not far away lies an aspen trunk, about two feet thick, which the beavers have recently gnawed down for their dam. Suddenly, I see something dark making its way soundlessly across the pond leaving two long, thin streaks behind on the mirror-like surface. I hear a splash and catch the glimpse of a broad beaver tail.

The last time I saw one of these ambitious engineers was at the timberline in the northernmost regions of Canada. It looks as if they manage just as well down here in the Southwest heat. In the north, as in the south, it is incredible to think what these little animals have meant for the exploration of new land. It was hunting for them that first made adventurers brave the unknown wilderness and the hostile Indian tribes. Millions of beavers were butchered while civilization spread, and now these animals are only found in a few remote areas.

Farther up the river there are mink tracks, and at another place there are even traces of a bear trudging across the marsh. It must have been a black or brown bear roaming around because grizzly bears, which also can be found up here, leave behind very different, larger paw prints.

Up on the hillside I stop my horse underneath a huge pine tree and look back over the immense forest. It's soon evening; the sun is hanging low over the treetops and the air is crisp and cool. Below me I can see the river winding between white-trunked aspens, and there's the yellow-blossomed clearing where the Indians are still at work. Off in the distance are bluish silhouettes of faraway mountains.

Just to my right lies an exposed ridge and I suddenly see something moving up there. It's a small herd of wild horses. They are nervously stomping around, most likely because they have gotten wind of me. The leader, a shiny black animal with white markings across his chest, keeps flinging his muzzle up into the wind. They are wild and free and stand there twitching restlessly while the evening sun sheds a warm glow over their taunt, shiny bodies and flowing manes. All of a sudden they run off across the steep slopes and disappear into the forest.

At sunset we all leave for the new camp that the cook and the horsetender have set up while we've been out working. We haven't ridden far before some of the Indians all at once stop at an aspen grove, lean over, and glance down at the ground. There isn't much to see, just an intricate shape on a piece of moss and some bent blades of grass. But it was enough for the Indians to determine that these were fresh tracks of a deer. We carefully round a small hill. There on the grassy slope is the animal standing gracefully with its antlers tilted back and eyes full of surprise, looking straight at us. In a flash, everyone takes off in a gallop, Sid with his gun in his hands and the others with their lassos ready. The deer, however, slips away into a dense, craggy part of the forest making it hopeless to continue the chase.

Dusk falls and the silhouetted procession of riders continues through the forest. Now and then a cigarette is lit that momentarily illuminates the face of an Indian. A few words of Apache are exchanged every so often, but mostly we all just sit there riding along, absorbed in our own thoughts. Then moonlight begins to stream in through the forest, and its light casts long shadows between the trees.

A young Apache by the name of Frank rides beside me. He is a pleasant fellow and one of the few who can speak a tolerable level of English. He is also the grandson of the mighty and wealthy medicine man Baha, who owns eight hundred head of cattle here on the mountain. We begin talking about this and that, and very nonchalantly and unperturbed he tells me about his father, called "Chicken," who killed his mother. Then a little bit later he suddenly says, "I will soon be getting married." I congratulate him and say how nice that is. Quite fervently and solemnly, he replies, "A miserable thing."

This was quite a remarkable comment coming from a prospective bridegroom. I make a weak attempt to try to encourage him and say that perhaps it wouldn't be so bad with a woman to cook and keep house, and that his grandfather would surely give him a herd of cattle as dowry. Then he turns toward me and bitterly says, "I don't want a woman, I don't want cattle, I want to be like I am now, a single man." It sounds like a cry for help from someone who has a gun pointed at his head. I silently ride on.

We finally reach a beautiful clearing that is flooded in moonlight. A campfire with flames flickering high into the air is burning over by the edge of the forest. Sotta, our cook and evil spirit, scornfully stands there with all his pots and pans while the smell of bad cooking drifts our way.

Our new camp lies amid the forest in a long, beautiful, grassy meadow called Smith's Park. This will be our base camp for the time being. According to Sid, the place got its name from four Smith brothers who around the 1900s ran a kind of shady business in the Southwest. Their specialty was horse and cattle rustling. They stole horses in Arizona and New Mexico and kept them up here in this meadow on White Mountain until the herd was big enough. Then they drove the animals south to Mexico and sold them there. In Mexico, they would steal cattle that they would then herd back to Arizona and sell to the Americans. It was, in other words, a practical and profitable business. Unfortunately though, it also led to the killing of a sheriff and some other people. It didn't help either that one of the brothers took up a side job and began holding up banks. Everything grew too wild for the boys and in time three of them got shot. The fourth, George, was also in deep trouble but somehow managed to save himself. Later, he became a respectable citizen and was appointed sheriff. He must have been quite a clever sheriff, especially in catching horse thieves.

The weeks passed and we were continually on the move through the forest working the livestock. One minute we would be branding and the next culling chosen cattle to slaughter and herding them to better pastures. One morning we took off after a herd of cattle that supposedly hadn't had contact with people for quite some time and were considered especially wild. We struggled for half a day in rounding them up, and had it not been for the dogs it would have surely taken twice the amount of time. The most difficult job, though, was driving these wild beasts along without losing too many. There were two magnificent bulls in the herd that must have each weighed about fifteen hundred pounds. They seemed to consider all the commotion with the horses and lassos a personal insult and would charge at us furiously. When our horses just darted out of the way and the bulls didn't hit anything, they resolved their anger by fighting between themselves. And boy, could they fight. One eventually had to be lassoed and tied with a bell around his neck. It was a priceless picture, watching that bull and his bewilderment at having to carry such a clanging noise he couldn't get rid of.

But the worst of these animals was an old moody cow. She was like a fury when she first let loose. Time and again she broke away from the herd, attacked the horses, and made for the forest, with us following in hot pursuit. Once I was riding Buckskin right behind the runaway through the dense forest covered with the scraggly underbrush of fallen trees and such when Ethelboh rode up alongside me. He lay flat against the neck of his galloping horse with branches whipping all around him. In the tiniest opening in the forest he managed to aim and throw his lasso and in an instant, the cow dived head over heels caught by one of its hind legs. It was a swift and excellent toss.

There was never lack of work; we could spend ten or more hours a day in the saddle. The Apaches liked this type of life, and in the mountains there was a feeling of freedom. They would pleasantly go about their work, laughing, singing, and pulling the craziest pranks. Nobody was ordered about because that doesn't work with these people. Sid had his own quiet way with them and everything seemed to turn out fine.

The Apaches are skillful cowboys and are masters when it comes to tracking or finding cattle, so much so that they are probably better than the average Anglo cowboy. They are good at working with horses and with a lasso. But when it comes to the routine, more detailed points of cattle ranching, the restless Indians have much to learn. However, ranching is better suited for these people than any other business. The unfortunate thing is that it wasn't consistently carried out from the beginning. Currently, some Apaches own herds of up to a thousand head of cattle and are very prosperous, while others barely have more than fifty cows, and still others who don't own any because of too few grazing areas.[2]

During our jaunts through the forest, there was always something new to see. If nothing else, we would always go after rattlesnakes. They were everywhere and we could kill five or six a day. Sometimes we also came across a flock of grouse, which the Indians would begin throwing stones at with amazing skill, actually striking the birds. Stone throwing is an old Indian skill. Captain Bourke wrote about how during the period of fighting a small Indian boy was such an asset to the hungry American troops because he was so clever in throwing stones that he continually supplied them with fresh fowl.

As I was riding through the forest one day along with one of the Indians, something jumped out from under the brush in front of us, making a terrible racket. It turned out to be three wild pigs, one of them just a piglet, and we couldn't get them out of our way. Instead, the two grown pigs were so adamant about attacking our horses that we had no choice but to flee.

Later, Sid told me that these were the offspring of a group of domesticated pigs that had been released on the mountain in 1919. There is often talk of how animals adapt to domestication but here was an interesting example of a species that had to adapt back to nature. In only a short time it had undergone radical changes. The offspring of the fat pigs that were let loose on the mountain eighteen years ago are now slender, quick, and dangerous wild animals. Their snouts are more pointed and their tusks, which measured about one and a half inches before, can now measure nearly four inches.

At times, it wasn't very pleasant riding around in the woods. It was the rainy season, and we often ended up sitting for hours on the backs of our horses soaking wet. Every once in a while a storm would break that was like the wrath of the heavens pouring down. In a fifteen-minute period, lightning could flash across the skies, thunder rumble over the forests, and rain gush down. Forest fires here in the Southwest are often started by lightning, and just around our camp I saw about thirty trees that had been split or struck down.

But the bad days were soon forgotten. Even during the rainy season the sun would often shine over the forest and the air would be as fresh and clear as in the mountains back home in Norway. When we would ride out in the morning, dew covered the grassy meadow and red, yellow, and blue would shimmer on the hillside from flowers stretching their petals toward the first rays of sun. Now and then a red-speckled butterfly fluttered around or a glittering hummingbird would dart up into the air. When we rode deep into the forest it was like entering a silent world where it was wonderful to just move along on a swaying horse. In the evening the moon would sometimes rise and cast pale shadows over the camp, where flames from the fire rose into the air. Days like this, nobody had it better then these cowboys way up on White Mountain.

One such evening we were in an especially good mood because one of the heifers had just been butchered and we were being treated to fresh meat. Our enjoyment would have been cut short if the cook had been in charge of the feast, but fortunately the other Indians took over and did both the butchering and preparation according to old Apache practice. Like the Indians in Northern Canada, they discarded the meat and went after the liver, kidneys, stomach, and intestines. It was all grilled over coals and without any salt. When the meal was finished, we sat around the fire, lit our pipes and cigarettes, and relaxed and enjoyed life. The dogs, those large and chubby creatures, lay around us, and every once in a while my beautiful horse Buckskin would wander up to the ring of light for a snack.

It is quite a mixed bunch of people who are sitting here close to the campfire in the middle of this dark mountain forest. Sid, the Anglo cowboy, looms above all the others. He is lean and weather-beaten, a typical descendant of the bold pioneers who journeyed into the Southwest, conquered the Indians, and took the land as their own. Around him sit fourteen young Apaches, sons of those who only a generation ago freely wandered the land they ruled. To my side sits a huge fellow, William Alchesay, whose father was a well-known chief among the White Mountain Apaches. A bit farther away sits Baha, son of the great medicine man. Then I see the sharp profile of Ethelboh, the boy who had been adopted into the Apache tribe as a child after his family had been raided by the Indians. Over there sits

Chipmunk, Frank, and the rest, whatever their names are, and, of course, our horse-tender, Herbert. He's resting one of his bare feet up on a log, and I notice a swollen big toe, which is quite yellow and purple. A horse trampled on it, which must mean it is surely painful, but he sits there smiling as usual. The flames flicker up and illuminate those dark faces with the taut skin and high cheekbones. In the background away from the firelight, our cook, Sotta, stands quietly and alone, leaning against a tree.

We begin talking and a special feeling fills the camp. Even if we are worlds apart in our thinking, we all have something in common here in the forest. Only a couple of the Indians can speak a bit of English. They belong to the new generation but the old ways are still a part of them. It is a common rule that when one of them starts to talk, even the youngest one, the others are silent and focus their attention on the one who is speaking, interjecting encouraging sounds every now and again. Everybody gets to have their say, and their words are respected. When the Indians speak to us white people, it is with men whom they consider themselves to be equal to or better. Just as Norwegians, Eskimos, Americans, Japanese, English, Eastern Indians, Germans, Jews, Italians, and Ethiopians, the Apache are also convinced that they are superior to any other ethnic group.

Ethelboh starts to tell us about an event that took place long ago not far from where our campsite is right now and something that caused a bitter conflict between two close tribes. A group of Navaho Indians had come to White Mountain and kidnapped an Apache boy. His people took after them and retaliated horribly. Close to the place that is now called Gallup, the Apaches killed about three hundred of the Navahos.

Then we begin talking about hunting mountain lions and bears. One of the Indians tells of how he once lassoed a bear cub and killed it, which was no easy task because, he says, the lasso had to be thrown around the animal's legs. Throwing it around its neck was completely hopeless because the bear would just slide the lasso off with its front paws.

Sid confirms this and then tells how he and a friend lassoed a grown bear. They managed to get it flat on the ground while the horses held the lasso taut from every direction. But then they realized that they didn't have any rifles with them. There was nothing else to do but to go up and stab the bear with a knife. This was possible only because one of the lassos was around the bear's neck and forearm, which held its head down. Then our conversation turns to talking about horses and more horses: fast horses, wise horses, crazy horses, and wild horses. Sid says that a couple of years ago he took part in rounding up three hundred wild horses right here in the area where we have been traveling around.

By the time I crawl into my sleeping bag, the moon has shifted far across the forest. The Indians stay sitting and talking around the fire long into the night. Now and then, they start singing their strange songs, which I hear as muffled sounds in the distance as I'm half asleep, struggling to lasso a huge beast of a bear by its head.

Just as we feared, one evening we were riding back to camp hungry and tired and didn't see any campfire nor catch a whiff of any burned meat. Our cook, Sotta, had disappeared. Without warning, he quite simply hopped onto his horse and left. He was obviously sick and tired of the whole cooking job and didn't give a damn. But it didn't bother us too much because we only had a couple days' work left up there anyway. We organized some cooking arrangements to get us by.

By now, the toughest work with the livestock was done, so Sid suggested that we all take a trip up to the top of White Mountain for a few days. Everyone agreed, as we had all heard about "Baldy," which rose ten thousand feet, but few of us had been there.

Early the next morning we rode off, taking along three pack animals. We had a steady, gradual climb at first but then it got even steeper and denser. Huge pines barely let any light through and the moss and heather oozed a clammy dampness. At one place we frightened a bunch of wild turkeys that swooped up into the air with a heavy beat of their wings. Another time we came across a bald eagle that sat and scouted the area from on top of a dry spruce. It flew off and for a long time we could see it circling high in the blue sky. The forest began thinning only right below the summit. We came to an exposed, sandy hill and suddenly we were there. What a view! A realm of forest, mountains, and vast plains stretch beneath us. We can see all the way over to Colorado, New Mexico, and even get a glimpse of the blue mountains of Mexico. What a country the Apaches ruled over in their day.

In the very large forests to the west we can see fires burning in three various places. The smoke lies like a cloud over the green carpet. Lightning has struck again. Fires like these usually make only a small dent in this immense belt of pine forest, which is considered to be the largest in the world and of which the governments of Arizona and New Mexico own only nineteen million acres. Despite its lack of rivers, people will still probably tread deep into these forests to exploit the riches here. Hopefully, past mistakes will make them wary so that they will approach carefully and cautiously. If the forests in these regions are chopped down it would be like ripping out the plug of the land's water reserves because the trees help retain the mountain's moisture and regulate the water supply to the dry lowlands.

This might be what the future holds, but signs of past centuries are everywhere we look. The area bears witness to those who lived in these parts, and their sorrows and joys, at a time when white people didn't even know that this great American domain existed. Not far from the mountain's highest point is a cave in the cliffs. In its entrance lay pieces of a broken clay pot that shimmer in the sunlight, and nearby stand the ruins of stone dwellings. All of this was left behind by Indians who hundreds of years ago would often climb to the top of this holy mountain to pray and make offerings to the rain gods when drought ravaged the lowlands. What was more natural than to believe that the god who ruled the rain dwelled where a pinnacle of the earth pierced the clouds? Because this god could offer help for sun-scorched cornfields and hunger, the tribe's old medicine man would ascend these highest peaks. Way up here under the heavens these bronzed men would stand naked, raise their arms up to the drifting clouds, pray and chant, and offer their most precious treasures to the god.

At the old Indian offering sites, we discovered various artifacts such as flint arrowheads, turquoise, and nearly a thousand tiny, flat, bored bone rings that had been part of a necklace. The cowboy Apaches were so in awe of these finds that they forgot about their horses and everything else and began digging in the ground. By now we should have been making our way down the mountain to set up camp, but nobody wanted to leave. They just kept digging and digging. For them objects found at old offering sites contained certain powers.

We wanted to make camp in a small pine grove not far under the summit, as we were planning to head down again the following morning. It was a steep descent from the mountaintop until we came to a small clearing by a rippling river where we pitched our tents. Some of us went off to try some fishing. Ever since I first came to the Southwest I had often heard about the great fishing in the high country. I was given the impression that it took very strong men to haul in the tremendous trout that swam in the moss-strewn pools up here in the mountains. After four hours of heavy toil, I had twelve fish as big as grown anchovies, while the thirteenth was perhaps a bit too large to fit into an anchovy tin. When I brought these miserable little things into camp I was told what a fine catch I had and that the thirteenth was something quite special and considered a wallop of a trout.

The next day we continued down to the mountain plateau where the Apache tribal base was located. Along the way, we saw a bluff that could have well been about 120 feet high and which dropped off steeply. One of the Apaches pointed it out and told us that in the old days when the Indians tried to press a prisoner for information but weren't sure if what he said was true, they would throw him from this cliff. If he survived, he spoke the truth but if he didn't he had lied. I looked up at this steep rock and had to admit that it certainly must have been a simple and straightforward method.

Toward the end of our journey, I separated from my companions to swing across a beautiful part of the mountain that I previously hadn't seen. Just on the outskirts of the reservation boundaries, I finally got to see the poverty-stricken Mormon settlement called Show Low. Long ago, two fellows let the draw of the cards determine who would end up with the place. Whoever turned over the lowest card won, hence the name of the place.

One of the old-timers living here took me around and told me one story after the other about the Apache wars and local Indian raids. The Mormons had a difficult time back then. He also showed me how the settlement in Show Low was practically built right on top of some old Pueblo Indian ruins, a huge adobe complex. The Mormons found all sorts of beautiful pots and containers here.

I was just about to leave when I spotted something white tucked behind the houses. It was a real, old-fashioned covered wagon with a huge canvas cover and heavy, iron-laden wheels, a carriage of the desert. A small tent was pitched beside the wagon, and when I flung open the flap I found an old man sitting on a crate. He was holding his hands around his knees, starring off into the distance, and doing absolutely nothing. He just sat there.

I said hello and he walked out into the sun. He was a small, worn fellow who showed the signs of age. It looked as if he didn't have long to go. But his gaze was strong, and when the old fellow spoke there was definitely a spark of life in him. His name was Mac Sieber, and he was ninety years old and one of the first pioneers of the Southwest. He had been a roaming cowboy his whole life and had been through everything in this world from buffalo hunts in Kansas to battles with bandits and Apache Indians in Arizona. Even in his last years he was still living a carefree life, a true vagabond of the world. There stood his old covered wagon that had taken him so many places when there were no other means of transportation and the West was the great unknown. His four mules stood grazing over by the edge of the forest, and when he felt like it he could just hitch them up and take off. He had the sky above and God's green earth beneath him to wander as he pleased, and he was happy to do so.

During the course of our conversation, I discovered that his father was a Norwegian sailor. When I told him that I myself was Norwegian he looked at me in amazement, smiled, and said, "When it all boils down to it, maybe you and I are relatives."

In a typical rough and calloused cowboy style, Mac began telling me about some of the most extraordinary episodes of his life. He had an incredible memory and clearly described events without missing a single detail, including the white spots on the horse he rode in the autumn of 1875. Listening to him was like suddenly being back in the pioneer days when men trod through the great unknown West, where thousands of buffalo grazed on the prairie, and where the place was crawling with hostile Indian tribes. Many times I had heard my Apache warrior friends tell their version of that period and of the white men who intruded in their wilderness. Now I was hearing about it from the other side.

Three events seemed to especially stand out in Mac's memory: In Kansas he had once seen a herd of wild buffalo that he estimated to be several hundred thousand animals. The land was covered with them, he said. Then there was the great swarms of grasshoppers that in the 1880s plagued the West. "Doggone if I haven't ever seen the like," said Mac, "I'll be darned if we weren't wading in grasshoppers." But the most vivacious and fondest memory was the time he shot "the big, fat Indian." He told me:

> We happened to be riding up the canyon to the west of the place where the mail wagon had been attacked the year before. There were three of us fellows, Jimmy, Charley, not the one who was hung in Tombstone but Prescott Charley, the one who was part of the Gold Rush, and then me, of course. All of a sudden, bullets started flying out from some of the bushes up there on the hill and then Jimmy's arm drooped and was good for nothing after that 'cause the bullet had smashed his elbow to smithereens. It was an Apache who had fired a shot, a whole bunch of them and completely naked. It didn't take us long to jump off our horses and take cover on the ground. We then began firing away and made a few holes in a two or three of those red-skinned devils. But their chief, a real big fellow, let his people keep firing and it got pretty bad for us. Then they shot my horse, that beautiful dapple-gray animal with the black patches on its neck. It was a mighty good horse and had such a smooth and steady trot, and it could go from morning to night without ever getting tired. I'll tell you, that was one horse who could hold the steer when you lassoed it. It knew just how to do that; and smart, boy, I remember . . . Oh well, there I saw my horse tumble over and I tell you did I ever get mad. I didn't give a damn about anything else. I ran out and caught sight of that big, fat chief of theirs who stood there split naked next to a mesquite tree. I raised my shotgun and gave him a stomach full of lead. He collapsed with a grunt like a fat pig when it gets speared. The other Indians got scared and ran off.

Old Mac dwells a while on this memory, not because he thinks it was anything special to be attacked by Indians and kill a few of them but because he had gotten the better of that big, naked chief who was so fat.

As I jump on my horse and ride off, I see Mac standing there in front of his covered wagon. He seems to be so frail and old that if he makes it to the end of the year it'll be his last. But he speaks encouragingly and has a bold look in his eyes like someone who has lived a strong and free life and who accepts this last, long ride as part of the game.

# 7
# An Expedition Is Planned

I had returned to the Apache camps on the mountain plateau of the White Mountain Reservation when one evening I found myself once again sitting in front of the tent of my friend Tenijieth, the medicine man. We talked about Apache wars and how the Indian scouts contributed to helping the American soldiers. Then we began talking about the Chiricahua Apaches' fierce leader, Geronimo, and his desperate fight for freedom in 1885–86. He and a handful of warriors were pursued by several thousand soldiers and chased into the Sierra Madre in Mexico until they finally surrendered and were taken East to spend years in prison. It went quiet between us for a while and then Tenijieth said, "Geronimo and some of the Chiricahua Apaches surrendered and were taken prisoner, but not all of them." I bewilderedly asked what he meant by that and the medicine man replied, "Some of the Chiricahua Apaches hid in the mountains and the Americans didn't know. Today they are still living in the Sierra Madre. They are free people but have a difficult time. The Mexicans are always after them and there are many fights. The Mexicans have captured one of their women and several of their children. But Chiricahua Apaches are clever. Nobody finds them."

This sounded incredible. Had the American troops in 1886 given up finding any of the last remaining renegade Apaches or did a band really exist that they didn't know about? Could it really be possible that in 1937 a group of Geronimo's warriors still existed deep within the Sierra Madre and continued to fiercely fight with the Mexicans? I ask the medicine man one question after the other, but he could not, or would not, say any more. Nor was it possible to find out how he had heard about these things, he just said, "It is just so."

Now, it was a known fact that in earlier times the renegade Apaches had occasional contact with the Indians on the reservation and it's not impossible that some type of connection had been maintained. Whatever the case, I felt sure that Tenijieth wasn't just jabbering but had facts to support what he was saying. Time spent with the Apaches had taught me one thing: their observations and reported accounts were generally well supported and accurate. I just couldn't ignore Tenijieth's fantastic story about the mountain Apaches.

As I sat there pondering this, it seemed as if the Sierra Madres were suddenly closer and I could see scenes from the Apache wars and that wonderful mountain life south of here: A range of mountains so rugged and unmanageable that the American troops' mules just tumbled off the cliffs one right after the other; cliffs that rose like natural fortresses where the Indians could keep the enemy at bay just by throwing rocks down onto them; a summer heat so intense that the soldiers burned their fingers on the iron fittings of their guns and a rainy season so miserable that any attempts to make an advance were hopeless; country where the Apaches could wander like mountain goats but where the white men floundered; a rugged mountainous tangle of peaks and valleys with beautiful small oases deep in the heart of the forest-clad ranges where game was plenty and berries and edible plants abounded.

This all indicated that it was a most suitable area for a band of Indians who wanted to hide away and continue their native lifestyle. The more I thought about the whole thing and the history of it, the more I was sure that the old medicine man was right. Might it be possible to find the last of these roaming Apaches? It was an encouraging thought, and it took hold in me. When it was time to leave Tenijieth I told him that I was thinking of traveling down to the Sierra Madre to search for Geronimo's tribal relations. The medicine man looked at me, shook his head and replied, "You are a young man and many times the sun can rise for you. But if you follow the trail of the Chiricahua Apaches, I have much to fear. They are like sly animals. You don't hear them, you don't see them. Then suddenly an arrow comes whizzing by." He pretends to draw back a bow and send an arrow flying. I ignore this but remark that I would think about it. Then I say a final farewell to the noble old man.

So far, I had only scarce information about the mountain Apaches, but at least it was something to work with. I thought that if I could now add to and verify what Tenijieth told me, promising possibilities might open up for taking an expedition to the Sierra Madre. If one could make contact with the Apache band up there and have the opportunity to study their culture over a period of time, it would be of great ethnological importance. I didn't underestimate the difficulties and had to consider the possibility that these skittish people might not want any company. However, it would be interesting in itself to determine their existence, gather some of their cultural artifacts, and perhaps learn more about their hidden history from the time the band separated from the other Apaches fifty years ago. I also thought an expedition could discover some archeological finds. The only significant expedition in these areas, except for a few military raids while chasing Geronimo in the 1880s, was Carl Lumholtz's classic excursion in 1890.

The possibilities of reaching these Apaches were pretty slim. It was obvious that if there were any people in this world who didn't want contact with white people it would be these remaining Apaches. For years they watched as their people were trampled upon. They had paid a high price for their freedom and were still being mercilessly chased by the Mexicans. One thing was for sure, an expedition of only white men wouldn't have the slightest chance of coming in contact with the Indians. The only possibility of finding these mountain Apaches would be with the help of their tribal relations who lived on the reservations in the United States. These men living there were still adept in traveling through difficult mountain terrain, following tracks and interpreting signs. They could speak the Apache language and had their own means of coming in contact with their tribal kinsmen. It would be best to use the Chiricahua Indians, the people of Geronimo's tribe to whom that small band in the Sierra Madre supposedly belonged. Nothing would be better than taking along some of the old warriors who fought down there fifty years ago. How many Apaches I could bring along, however, would be a financial issue. But it was clear that I myself should be the only white member of the expedition.

This was the overall plan. However, the little information that I had received from the old man wasn't enough to base an expedition upon.

A few important historical facts put me on the right track: When Geronimo and his handful of warriors surrendered in 1886 and were being taken north toward Arizona, six Indians managed to escape, half of which were women. Nobody was quite sure what happened to them but it is possible that they made their way back to the Sierra Madre. Furthermore, Apache war veteran Captain Bourke writes in his book *On the Border with Crook,* "Not all the band Geronimo and his warriors in 1886 surrendered; there are several still in the Sierra Madre who, as late as the past month of January (1891), have been killing in both Sonora and Arizona."[1]

Carl Lumholtz also had this to say from his excursion over the northern part of the mountains in 1899:

> It was still very risky for a small division to try to cross this mountain range. Small bands of Apaches still remained . . . Therefore, no Mexicans could venture out alone in these mighty, mysterious forests and mountain regions that were so feared and held so many unpleasant memories of bloodshed. Years after my expedition traveled through these parts, the Apaches had on various occasions attacked remote Mormon farms and killed many people.

Now this was important information. It confirmed that self-reliant, roaming Apaches existed about the turn of the century. But where were they today? Which areas should be searched? To head into the mighty Sierra Madre without any clues would be like going to sea without a compass. There was nothing else to do but set off on an exploratory trip before the actual expedition.

I first visited the old Indians at the White Mountain Reservation, but they wouldn't talk. They kindly suggested that a person could choose a better end to his life than chasing the Apache Broncos. Then I looked up Sergeant Henry, who in his earlier days had participated in chasing Geronimo. That old veteran lived all alone in a cabin far off in the woods along with his cats and some wild turkeys that wandered in from the mountain by the dozens and strutted around his house like tame geese. Henry had many amazing things to tell from the Indian wars, but he couldn't answer my questions. At the time, it surprised me that he couldn't even give me some kind of geographical directions within the Sierra Madre and the routes that the soldiers must have followed. Later, when I myself was in the middle of this tangle of canyons and mountain ranges, I understood him all too well.

I would have to go elsewhere for information. For months I roamed Arizona, New Mexico, and parts of northern Mexico, approaching anyone who I thought might have some understanding of the Sierra Madre. I began with the old pioneers and continued with experts. Not even at the University of Arizona could anyone provide me with information, even if they had wanted to. However, the university's most renowned archeologist, Dr. Emil W. Haury, did contribute other invaluable assistance.

Finally, I ended up way down along the Mexican border at the American fort called Huachuca, which had been an important cavalry post during the Apache wars. There was a quaint old settlement here with long, low houses scattered about on an open plain and rolling hills in the background. Except for a few Apache scouts the rest of the soldiers were black Americans, and they were all having drill training when I arrived. They marched around in the scorching heat strutting to the chipper "dam-ta-dam" of the military music. I was hoping that the few Apache scouts here at the post who were often out riding along the Mexican border had had some possible contact with their tribal kinsmen. This, however, was not the case.

The trip to this beautiful fort was worth it anyway, mainly because the officers let me look through the old military records. From the brief yet detailed telegrams that I found here I could really envision the colorful history of the Southwest. Between the years 1885 and 1886, when Geronimo and his little band were being intensely pursued, one message after the other was dispatched: Apache tracks have been found; they are chased; the Apaches attack and kill Mexicans; they are chased; the Apaches attack new settlers in Arizona; they are chased; the Apaches steal the soldiers' horses; they are chased; pursuit abandoned in hopeless rugged mountains; Apaches raid and kill hundreds of miles away; they are chased; and so on. But just when these dusty old records nearly heave an exasperated sigh over this Geronimo who played cat and mouse with thousands of soldiers, the message of his surrender suddenly comes through like a burst of joy.

But in among all these reports, there was also this dreary telegram thrown in: "Bisbee (a mining town) raided by bandits last night." Such news was also a part of pioneer life in the Southwest.

The most interesting thing I found, however, was a report about eleven Apaches who in June 1887 (that is, *after* the Apache Wars had ended) were heading south toward Mexico. Cavalry troops quickly chased after these Indians, who zigzagged their way across the country, at times even backtracked to their old trail, and who masterfully escaped from Captain Lawton and his soldiers, struggling to keep after them. In the last telegram it was reported that the Indians had disappeared into the Mexican mountains. At last, here was some relevant information that directly related to my quest: these eleven Indians had undoubtedly journeyed to the Sierra Madre and probably assumed that they would meet their tribal kinsmen there. Indubitably, the collective force of the mountain Apaches could have been quite significant.

Word had it that in the Mexican town of Naco there was a remarkable old schoolteacher who knew more about the Indians in northern Mexico than most others. So I took off looking for him. Late in the evening I reached Naco, a strange little place with small adobe huts, donkeys in the streets, dirty kids, and friendly people. The man's name was San Domingo, an older fellow with a wise twinkle in his eyes and a high forehead. He looked to be quite a thinker. It was interesting to listen to his stories about the Indians of Mexico, who he knew inside and out. He also told me that he had written about the history of the State of Sonora, but added with a sad smile that he never got enough money to publish the book. He confirmed that great archeological discoveries could very well be found in the Sierra Madre, but whether Apaches were still living there he wasn't so sure. However, he did have faith in my venture, and for once here was someone who wasn't so quick to tell me that the Indians would do me in as soon as I set foot in the mountains. After my many disappointments, this meeting greatly encouraged me.

Unfortunately though, I knew just as little about the band of Apaches as I did earlier. Days passed and it began to look pretty hopeless to carry on with my expedition. Then as I was in the border town of Bisbee, I heard about a former cowboy by the name of Jim who now ran some kind of business in northern Mexico. He supposedly knew about the Sierra Madre and the conditions there. I was able to locate him out on a small ranch, where he was breaking in a new young horse. When I posed my questions, he replied that from time to time he had heard talk of some wild Apaches and of a few recent skirmishes. "But the person who can tell you the most about this," he added, "is the Mexican Martinez who just rode through here only a few hours ago. He said he was headed south toward Sonora, but when he left this side of the border he was so sloshed after a drunken spree that who knows where he'll end up."

Here was my chance but I had to be quick. I persuaded Jim to join me and quickly we got hold of some horses, jumped in the saddles, and rode off to the border and farther south into Mexico. It was incredibly hot but we pushed on, and soon the United States faded behind us into the distance. We followed a path that ran across rolling hills that were overgrown with junipers and evergreen oak and had small rippling creeks flowing in the coulees. Would I finally be lucky or was I about to be disappointed once again? Every time we reached the top of a hill, I anxiously looked out across the area but couldn't see any sign of life, only forest-covered ridges and blue, blue mountains. We had been riding for quite some time when we stopped at a place that had a pretty good view out across the land. That one, lonesome rider was still nowhere to be seen despite our quick chase after him. Now we were afraid that he had possibly taken another route. Then Jim pointed to something dark under a mesquite tree down at the bottom of the valley and said, "Doggone it if that isn't a horse tied to that tree." He dug his spurs into his horse and went tearing down the hill, hooves kicking up dirt and stones every which way.

Under the mesquite tree stood a skinny, gloomy-looking horse. A little farther away lay a Mexican snoring with his face under a straw hat and a gun at his side. When we shook him, he leaned up on his elbow, squinted his eyes and said, "Very much booze yesterday, heavy head today." He was a wiry, copper-brown fellow who almost looked like an Indian and was among the many carefree souls who lived down here in Mexico, men who didn't own anything, seldom worked, and had no place to live. They just wandered around on their horses beneath the bright shining sun and blue sky, untroubled about tomorrow and content with today.

When I asked him if he knew anything about the Apaches living in the Sierra Madre he casually replied, "A couple of years ago I and some others chased several of these bastards and did away with a few of them," and then continued to sluggishly ramble on. One thing, however, became very apparent. The Mexicans had often fought with some of these last remaining Apaches, most recently as 1932. But the drunken stranger most obviously thought there was a limit to asking such stupid questions to a man who was trying to sleep off a serious hangover. Trying to get rid of me he finally said, "The Mexicans in Douglas have talked about the Apaches, ask them." Then he turned over on his stomach, buried his head under his arms, and went back to sleep.

Onward to Douglas. This was a small town north of the border where in the 1880s American troops frequently passed through when they were chasing the Apaches in Mexico. It was a pretty and friendly town situated in the foothills of the famous Chiricahua Mountains, Chief Cochise's old hiding place. I inquired around and was told that the local newspaper, the *Douglas Daily Dispatch*, was to have had some articles about the Mexicans' last encounters with the mountain Apaches. And right they were. I was able to confirm what the inebriated Mexican had told me, as well as find some interesting new facts.

In an issue dated January 4, 1929, front-page headlines read, "Military Campaign Organized to Rescue Child Captured by Wild Apaches." In the article it said that in October 1927, the Apaches had attacked a Mexican man by the name of Francisco Fimbres and his wife near the small village of Nacori Chico in the foothills of the Sierra Madres. They killed Fimbres' wife and took their six-year-old son, Heraldo, into the mountains with them. This was all an act of revenge on the Apaches' part. A few years earlier, Fimbres had captured an Apache girl named Lupe, who was later adopted by the Mexicans and supposedly still living among them.

A thorough report followed in the newspaper article about the large force that took off to find the Apaches and rescue the boy. It said:

*This group of Indians, who are very much like their tribal relations who earlier roamed in Arizona, are sly and wild as animals, almost impossible to approach . . . As far as anybody knows, this small band of warriors does not have any contact with civilization . . . The old-timers in Agua Prieta and along Sonora's eastern border tell us that these Apaches have been roaming around as long as one can remember. They are believed to be the descendants of the warriors who guarded the strongholds of Geronimo and other raiding leaders when these chiefs were out stealing cattle, burning farms in Arizona and fleeing to Mexico while being chased by both American and Mexican military forces, settlers, Indian border patrols and riflemen.*

There was no further news in later issues of the *Douglas Daily Dispatch* that disclosed any results in rescuing the captured child. However, I did come across a short article dated January 29, 1931, with the following heading: "Fimbres Returns with Three Prized Scalps After Fighting Apaches Along with Rifles and Other Loot." It mentions that he had just arrived at Agua Prieta, and that these items were being held at the city hall.

A number of quotes from well-known American old-timers and Mexicans who had firsthand knowledge of the situation and conditions were also included in the articles. It appeared that the Apaches had been raiding and killing for a number of years. They had become such a terror that the Mexicans never dared to go into the Sierra Madre unless accompanied by a large group. Even though several of the Apaches had been killed, many still remained. Some people calculated their number to be about forty while others said approximately seventy.

Some of the old-timers were quite good at vividly and precisely describing the Apaches and the Sierra Madre. In one article dated January 6, 1929, Charles Ross stated, "There is probably no other place as rugged and naturally secluded on the entire North American continent than where these Apache live and from where they have challenged the world this last half century."

A well-known rugged fellow and tracker by the name of Hayhurst, one of the famous Texas Rangers who had also been involved in fighting the Apaches, was quoted in the *Douglas Daily Dispatch* on

January 12, 1929, as having said, "These mountains (Sierra Madre) encompass hundreds of square miles and are so rugged that a wildcat can hardly get around there. They're straight up and down, full of deer and bear, contain small rivers, huge trees, big rock slides, caves and prehistoric dwellings. No people live in these parts, unless you call those bloody band of wild Apaches people."

This said a lot. Based on what that drunken Mexican had told me as well as what I was able to clarify in Douglas and other places, I could now quite confidently determine that the Apaches still existed. Locating exactly where they lived was quite impossible, but I did have certain clues and could at least confine my search to a specific area where there was the greatest chance in finding them. My area of exploration would be the most northern ranges of the Sierra Madre, which by air stretch about 125 miles north to south and about 62 miles east to west. I could finally begin organizing my expedition.

The Mexican government and the governor of Sonora, General Román Yocupicio, were very accommodating and quickly gave me permission to take the expedition. At the same time, I was made aware that the areas I was planning to enter lay outside the government's jurisdiction and that I myself had to take responsibility if anything happened during the expedition.

Then began my search for suitable participants. As I previously mentioned, the plan was to get hold of some Chiricahua Apaches, preferably those who had fought together with Geronimo in the Sierra Madre.

Everything now depended on the American authorities' consideration of the matter. I anticipated that there might be some concern about letting a few of the old warriors travel down to the country of their archenemy, the Mexicans. On the other hand, this venture would also offer something of great interest: finding the last remaining Apaches who were a part of the United States. The background was the entire history of the Southwest. Fortunately, the director of Indian Affairs, Mr. John Collier, was interested and open-minded. I received all possible assistance as well as the opportunity to choose the Indians from the Apache reservations in New Mexico and Arizona I wanted.

1. The century, or mescal, plant.

2. Old Indian drawings on a cave wall in the western Sierra Madre.

3. Old Aztec Indian.

4. Sunrise Dance (puberty ceremony) in Day Canyon.

5. Mountains and more mountains.

6. Part of the cave dwellings near the Chico River. The picture is taken from inside the cave and shows the cone-shaped storage chambers.

7. After crossing the northern Sierra Madre, one winter's day we reach the Mexican mountain farms of Nortenia. A tame deer roams between the buildings.

8. The glistening Aros River at the bottom of the gorge.

9. In through the Sierra Madre. The old Apache Yahnozah points to the places where as a youth he roamed with Chief Geronimo.

10. In Nacori Chico, mules drive the grain mill.

11. Ruins of the old Spanish church in Nacori Chico.

12. A few items from the Spanish church treasure in Nacori Chico: gold crowns, silver chalices, and so on.

13. In Sierra Nacori, approximately three thousand meters above sea-level. From left, the old Apache Yahnozah, Yaqui Indian Mora, and Helge Ingstad.

14. Facing page, top: The old Spanish church bells outside the church ruins in Nacori Chico.

15. Facing page, left: The Apache girl, Bui, shortly after being taken.

16. Facing page, right: The Apache girl, Bui, after adoption by an American family.

17. The Sierra Madre area is a world of rugged mountains and deep gorges.

18. High in the mountains we came upon beautiful, luscious clearings surrounded by pine and oak forests.

19. Cave dwellings along the Chico River.

20. The old cave dwellers' storage chambers. They were made of grass and clay and could be up to three and one-half meters high.

21. Ruins of a stone home from a time when the Indians lived along the Aros River. The structure sat like a fortress high on a cliff with a view clear across the valley.

22. Old cave dwellings near the Aros River. The structures extend far back into the cliff and consist of several levels and various rooms.

23. Crossing the Aros River.

24. The Sierra Madre, home
of the free Apaches.

I then traveled to the Mescalero Reservation in New Mexico, where most of the Chiricahua Apaches have been living since 1913 after having served many years in prison back East. I met Mr. E. R. McCray, the director there, who actively supported my plans in every way. He took me around at once so that I could personally speak to the various Apaches who might be interested in the expedition. My trip around the beautiful and fertile Mescalero Reservation was a surprise. I had expected to find these Indians, commonly considered to be some of the most unmanageable, to be more opposed than others in taking up the everyday routines of modern society. Instead, I see resourceful people who are enthusiastically involved in farming and cattle ranching and who all live in small, tidy houses. Conditions here were so vastly different from those of the San Carlos and White Mountain Apaches that it was almost hard to believe. No doubt their wonderful progress is mainly due to McCray who seems to have a special influence on the Indians.

Choosing my first participant was easy. As soon as I met the reservation administrator, he mentioned an old Apache by the name of Edwin Yahnozah, a man who fought together with Geronimo in the Sierra Madre and who would probably enjoy a trip back to his old stomping grounds. The Indian would be delighted to take a trip down to Mexico because he supposedly knew where a Spanish treasure was hidden there. He ran across this treasure when he roamed the area with the other renegade Apaches.

At the time, gold or silver meant little to the Apaches, but now it was quite a different story. I couldn't deny that this old Spanish treasure sounded enticing. But I also knew that it would be all too easy to get sidetracked by this sort of thing. Therefore, when I went to talk to the old man I was determined that no Spanish treasure would disrupt my plans.

Yahnozah was a small, sturdy, broad-chested fellow with a deeply lined face and high cheekbones, Apache through and through. He was about seventy-six years old but still hearty and just as fit as any young man. When I asked him if he wanted to come along on the expedition, he agreed at once and then started talking about the treasure. It truly sounded like he knew exactly where it was and that all we had to do was go straight down to a cave and carry out the silver and gold bars. But I was firm and clearly explained the mission of the expedition and was insistent that there wouldn't be any treasure hunt. If we happened to be close to the place during our travels in the Sierra Madre we could then consider a short stop to investigate, but I couldn't honestly promise that either.

Yahnozah accepted this and was clearly enticed to come along for more than just the treasure. His gaze grew distant when I spoke of the mountains down there. Despite his unruffled Apache face, I could sense that the old warrior became anxious and eager at the thought of seeing that beautiful mountainous region where in his younger days he had wandered freely and fought many a bloody battle.

I asked him if he knew the Sierra Madre well enough that he could show us the way. Then he smiled and said that he could find his way around there blindfolded. He also mentioned that if any of those old Indians down there were still alive, especially those six who escaped when Geronimo was taken prisoner, they would be his friends and he could easily recognize them again.

I had now acquired one of Geronimo's men, one of those desperate warriors who fought to the very end and who in the 1880s spread panic over the entire Southwest and northern Mexico. It wasn't just an expedition member I had acquired, it was living history.

The next man was not as easy to find. There was a question of Geronimo's son, but just the mention of his name would cause the Mexicans anxiety, so I relinquished the idea of including him. There was one man I was especially keen on taking along, and that was the son of the great chief Victorio. He was an energetic fellow in his forties who looked alert and wise. But no, he didn't want to take off down to the Mexicans. It was quite enough that they had killed his father. Still, it was remarkable to see this son of one of the fiercest Apache chiefs standing there in his overalls digging a shovel into the ground.

Then we went to see Juh, son of another great chief. His father was the original leader of the Chiricahua Apaches until he got drunk and drowned, after which Geronimo gained leadership. Juh the son had an incredible temper but otherwise looked like an ambitious fellow with considerable leadership qualities. He agreed to take part in the expedition and added that there was one mountain down there in the

Sierra Madre that he especially wanted to see again. Once when his Indian camp had been ambushed, he jumped right off a very steep cliff.

I had now gained two fantastic men and was quite satisfied. Unfortunately though, Juh afterward had to be replaced with another man, which I will explain later. I originally had wanted to take along about six Apaches so that some of them could ride off on longer scouting excursions. This would have increased the chances considerably for finding the mountain tribe. But every expedition has its financial limitations, and so I had to make do with two.

I left for the border town of Douglas to organize some equipment and other things. The place was full of friendly and helpful people, and even the chief of police went so far as to let me borrow one of the station's rifles. During this time, I went back and forth between Douglas and the neighboring village south of the border called Agua Prieta, where I had to continually deal with the Mexican authorities. To go from the busy and orderly town of Douglas to Agua Prieta was like entering another world. On the Mexican side of the border, people took life easy and enjoyed the sunshine. Men sat happily in front of the houses in their wide-brimmed sombreros, even in the middle of the day. Everybody had a daily siesta and nothing but a revolution could stop them from doing so. In the evening, they'd go over to the cafe, where enticing banjo and guitar music poured out the door.

Just on the outskirts of Agua Prieta there was a short row of brothels where young, dark-haired girls would sit on the doorways, smiling and laughing in the sun, looking as if they didn't feel the slightest bit ashamed. In one of the streets in town, traffic had to maneuver around various bends and curves. Monuments had been erected to honor the brave men who were killed during the last revolution. They were placed right where the dead had fallen, which often happened to be in the middle of the street. This was a great honor for the dead but a bit cumbersome for the living. Agua Prieta was also usually one of the first cities to come under siege during a revolution, since it was such a lucrative port of entry. The revolutionary leader Poncho Villa made a bloody visit here during his time.

Unfortunately, it turned out that Juh, one of the Apaches I had chosen for the expedition, eventually declined. Instead, a younger fellow by the name of Andrew Little would come along. His mother was an Apache but his father was a Mexican who as a boy had been captured by the Indians in the Sierra Madre and adopted into the tribe. So in a way, Andrew also came from those mountains in the south. A great advantage was that he was not only fluent in the Apache language but also in English and Spanish. Whether he was equally competent in other areas was yet to be seen.

All our equipment was finally ready, and early one morning I met up with the Indians. We discussed the plans for our journey and then wandered around town to do some last-minute shopping. I dare say that we caused quite a stir when we walked through the town streets, not least because of the way we were walking. Getting the Indians to walk alongside me on the sidewalk was quite impossible. Their forest habits must have run deep because they would only follow me in single file as if they were on the warpath. I walked first, Andrew followed right on my heels, and old Yahnozah came lurking behind.

At last we were ready to leave.

# 8
## South into Mexico

Almost as a continuation between the Rocky Mountains and the Andes, the westerly Sierra Madre Occidental cuts through the Mexican interior like a huge reef. In the northern region, where the Apaches usually dwelled, the mountain range establishes the border between the neighboring states of Chihuahua and Sonora. Lowlands with rolling hills and wide, flat plains stretch on both sides of this mountain range.

I wanted to enter the Sierra Madre from Sonora, so our first destination was planned for the village of Bacerac, which lies about a hundred miles south of Douglas. There is a road, albeit a rugged one, that leads there, and a truck travels the stretch once a week. Strangers wanting to go to Bacerac are rare because the place is nothing more than a poor, small outpost in the middle of the wilderness.

On November 4, 1937, we loaded our twenty-three pieces of baggage onto the vehicle to Bacerac and headed south into Mexico. As we drove along we were for quite some time surrounded by nothing but flat, barren land overgrown with drab green creosote bushes, salt grass, and scattered yucca plants and mesquite trees. Then rolling green hills appeared and stands of oak stood out against the bluish-black juniper. Little by little, the most northern peaks of the Sierra Madre appeared on the horizon. Yahnozah suddenly got excited at one place and pointed out some hills to the northwest, explaining that that was where he and Geronimo surrendered to General Miles, only later to be taken to prison.

We passed a small settlement by the name of Colonia Morellas that had been established by American Mormons who sought refuge down here after the banning of polygamy in the States. These ambitious people exerted great efforts to clear the land, only to be driven out when the revolution came. Mexicans had now taken over the place.

The road gradually grew worse, that is, if you could call the ruts we were traveling on a road. It must have been first created when a cow came plodding along nipping at the grass here and there, later followed by other cattle using the same trail, as cattle do. Then perhaps a Mexican came riding along on his horse and chose the cow trail, as it was easiest. Other Mexicans followed and in time it became some sort of a thoroughfare that meandered here and there, sometimes even backtracking, depending on the grazing route of that first cow.

Our driver, a middle-aged Mexican donning a tilted hat and with a cigarette always hanging out of his mouth, was a funny, philosophical chap. Once when we were bouncing along sideways down a steep incline, I mentioned how this could really take its toll on his brand new car. "It'll hang together," he replied. Then I asked him how long he thought it would last in such terrain.

"Oh, in about a year it'll roll and die."

When I heard that he only received forty-five pesos for a return trip, I made a simple calculation and realized that his chauffeur service created a direct loss for him.

"That could be," he said, not too concerned, "but it's a living."

We arrive at a beautiful small and lush valley called Valle de las Caverneas (Valley of the Caves). On both sides we could see dark caves in the rock walls and cliffs where centuries ago people lived, and some still do. I got out to take a look at one of the caves nearest us, and inside it was as big as an apartment. A campfire was burning in the middle and a very young Mexican girl sat beside it, frying corn tortillas while a small child tottered around her. It was all such an idyllic Mexican scene.

I was completely astounded when suddenly from deep within this cave I heard in clear English, "Hello! Step inside and have a look around." A young American stepped into the light and, smiling, he reached out his hand and gave me a handshake. How he ever landed down here in a cave in the middle of the wilderness was his business and nobody else's. Whatever the reason, he now ruled over a small domain that anyone would have envied. A beautiful, fertile valley with a rippling stream, wild vineyards along the hillsides, as well as a spacious cave with a young, dark-eyed girl. What more could anyone want?

I give the American a newspaper that I had with me and he voraciously engulfs himself in it. After he reads a while I hear a sudden gasp. He sits down on a rock and stares straight ahead with a pained expression on his face. Poor fellow, I think to myself, he's probably come across some bad news about one of his loved ones. He suddenly stands and throws the paper down and then begins to restlessly pace back and forth in the cave. "It's all through," I hear him mumble.

I feel sorry for the guy and think that that's what happens when sorrow strikes a person way out here in the wilderness: it must feel twice as bad. Finally, he stops in front of me and with a sad smile he says, "It's almost hard to believe." Then, he clenches his fists and bitterly says, "But they'll get theirs, they'll be beat, just wait."

I feel terrible for him, but I don't say anything. There's nothing that can be said. Then the fellow says, "And to lose to such a lousy team!" I must have looked completely amazed because he repeated himself even louder, "Yeah, a rotten team compared to California, the greatest football team on the entire West Coast." Even out here in the middle of nowhere it's hard to escape football-crazy Americans.

A deep darkness descends upon the forest and mountains and the car bounces along over the rough, bumpy road that emerges bit by bit in front of the headlights.

After a while, we stop at a grove, where I could see a few dim lights and the contours of tents in between the trees. This was a camp for some soldiers who for a long time had been working on improving the road. However, along our entire route I had hardly noticed any results of their hard labor other than some nice guard stones that had been placed where the road ran across a perfectly flat field.

One man after another appeared out of the dark bringing a letter or asking for mail. During this exchange, the driver studied each letter, scrutinized them front and back, and gave his expert opinion. He wasn't one of these perfunctory mail carriers who was content with just delivering the mail. Instead, he thought it was his duty to keep informed as to who wrote whom and get a hint of why they wrote to each other.

Hour after hour we bounced along. Suddenly some small, beady-green lights shone in front of us. Three coyotes were standing on the road, staring at the headlights. The driver grabbed his gun and fired a few shots into the dark and the green lights disappeared.

We continued down a steep slope over a road like no other. The worst of it was that we tilted so much to the side that at any moment I expected the car to roll. "This ridge drops hundreds of feet here," the driver said casually, "and only a week ago a car went right over the edge." Then he added, "Ramon and his wife were in the car. They had just gotten married and were coming down from the north with some things they had bought for their cabin. And there was a mirror, a big, beautiful mirror. It had gold all around the edges and you'd never seen the like. Yeah, and then the car rolled off."

"What happened then?" I asked.

"What happened! Well, there was nothing left but smithereens, as you might guess. Not a bit left."

"I mean with the people, the newlyweds," I continued.

"Oh them. Well, the same happened to them too. But, boy, that was too bad about that mirror. Nothing that magnificent has ever been seen down here before."

We passed another village but couldn't see much of it because of the dark. The car bounced by a short row of adobe huts where dim lights glowed from the open doors and women and children stood clustered together starring at us. We finally reached Bacerac late at night, ate some dried meat and cornbread, and got a floor to sleep on. I anxiously awaited morning. What did this country look like when darkness lifted and the sun came out?

We weren't disappointed. Glimmering sunshine flooded the little village, which consisted of short rows of adobe huts built in a square around an open plaza. The town lay high up on a vantage point from where there was an extensive view, and right below rippled the Bavispe River over shiny stones. Along its banks grew leafy trees. Farther away, there were rolling hills covered with forests and behind these the mountain kingdom of the Sierra Madre rose like a mighty, endless mass.

This was a place where people could live and not have a hurry in the world. Men loafed around the plaza square or sat along the shady walls of the houses and smoked. Burros wandered through the streets and children played in the sun. Nothing was planned, but everything turned out fine. A meal of corn and a little dried meat could always be found. There were also berries, mesquite beans, sweet cactus fruits, and other good things around in the wild. It was also easy to bring home a pail of honey. The sun shone above, so why struggle?

Bacerac consisted of about four hundred people, all of whom were a racial mixture but with a strong strain of Indian. This was true for most people living in the foothills of these mountains. They were not strong, as they had been weakened by intermarriages and disease. This makes it easier to understand that for centuries these people have been an easy target for the Apaches. They lack the Apaches' stamina, wise ingenuity, and irrepressible drive and are almost like children the way they loaf around in the sun. They do a little ranching and grow just enough corn, sugarcane, tobacco, and such to survive. They are incredibly poor, but happy in their way.

Our little expedition created quite a stir here where new faces are seldom seen. With mixed feelings of fear and awe, the people kept staring at the Indians accompanying me. They had heard that they belonged to the fierce people the Mexicans had learned to fear like the devil himself. Younger children and women kept a safe distance while Yahnozah and Andrew confidently sauntered around the town square as if they belonged there.

First on my agenda was to pay a visit to the local authorities. I had received careful instructions that I was supposed to register my arrival here before I continued into the mountains. In front of a very nice old house I met the mayor and his council committee, who sat on the steps having a quiet smoke. My request to be registered, the first of its kind in the history of the town, rose quite a new problem. The authorities were in serious doubt as how to handle the situation. The mayor, however, rose to the occasion and ordered my papers to be copied word for word. This took hours because there were many documents and they were long. But at least it turned out to be an absolutely certain registration that filled half a book.

Later, I photographed the county officials who, like all county officials, appreciated that. Afterward we became good friends. I realized later with some surprise that nearly the entire male population of the town belonged to the mayor's council or held one or another important position in the county. After thinking about this more, I concluded that this was not such a bad arrangement and well worth following in other societies where disregarded politicians poison the place with their professional jealousy.

The mayor came over to me and said quite seriously, "We have a murderer in jail and would appreciate it if señor would take a picture of him and later send it to us." There was a certain amount of pride in this statement because keep in mind Bacerac didn't lag behind in anything. They even had a jail with a murderer in it. I replied just as seriously that I would be honored to immortalize the criminal. So we all headed toward the jail, the mayor and I in front and all the other county officials trailing behind.

We came to a small, square plaza surrounded by low houses. In one of the cement walls there was a cell that had no windows, just a dirt floor and a door made of thick iron bars that scarcely let the sun shine through. I peeked through the bars and the murderer lay there stretched out on the dirt floor with a clay jar by his side. He could envy a lion in a zoo. While some of them went about opening the door of the cell, I organized my film and camera. I was finally ready and I looked around for the murderer, who had already been let out. I scanned the thirty or forty men who stood around me but I couldn't see anyone who looked especially like a murderer. The only one I was sure about was the mayor, other than that I was in real danger of picking out the wrong man from all those other county officials. Most of them had gruff faces and dark stubble, and all of them were standing packed together. Who the hell was the murderer?

They watched me intensely as I fidgeted with my equipment. I knew that I had to do something. Then to my great relief, I spotted a big fellow with black stubble and a low forehead who seemed to be the likely fellow. There wasn't any doubt. Just as I stepped forward to position the man for the picture, the mayor quickly shoved another fellow forward, the right one. I later discovered it was the town's vice-mayor whom I nearly so wrongly seized.

The murderer, by the way, was a great disappointment. I had hoped for a mean and hardened criminal whose picture would make people shudder when I showed it in other countries. But instead, I had here a young fellow smiling from ear to ear, so clean-cut and handsome in every way that it was incredible. Nobody would have believed that he could have chopped off the head of a chicken.

When my picture-taking was finished and the criminal had been taken back into his cell, I asked why he had committed the murder. One of the men standing there replied, "No particular reason, he just wanted to see what it was like to kill a person." The Mexicans and Indians who live along the eastern boundaries of the Sierra Madre are said to be the kindest and most cordial one could meet. But of course there are a few gangsters and desperados here like anywhere else.

I was now most interested in clarifying as much as possible my information about the Sierra Madre and the Apaches there. But even though these Mexicans live at the foot of the mountains, hardly any of them have any knowledge about those higher areas. They are so afraid of the Apaches that they don't dare venture into them except when they occasionally have to travel there in groups to punish the Apaches.

They then told me about a few skirmishes between the Mexicans and the Apaches that had occurred within the last few years. Some of the stories sounded so astounding that at the time I must say I was a bit skeptical. Later these accounts were most accurately confirmed, as I discuss farther on in the book. For now, I'll only mention that a fur trapper by the name of Bill Bye, supposedly a Norwegian, one day in 1934 found a twelve-year-old Apache girl in a dry riverbed not far from Bacerac. She was naked except for a short buckskin skirt and was ill, starving, and shaking with fear. Bye took her to the village of Casas Grande, but she died there a couple of weeks later. The girl had either been lost and unable to find her way back to her people or she was the sole survivor of a group that had been slaughtered in one of the later fights. Exhausted and alone she had wandered around in the mountains, surviving on roots and berries.

It turned out that the Mexicans had killed quite a few Apaches during the last several years. The Indians were usually shot when every once in a while they came down from the mountains to steal cattle. The Apaches were clearly regarded as outlaws, and the Mexicans ruthlessly shot them down at any opportunity. It was also considered good sport to scalp the dead and mishandle their bodies in other ways.

These are horrible things, but remember that the historical background of today's situation explains a lot. For centuries, the Apaches were like a bloody scourge across Sonora, where the people constantly feared for their lives. The tables are turned now, and today the Apaches are the minority and the Mexicans have the power. It's time for revenge.

I needed mules and horses and was inquiring into this when two Mexicans approached me and offered their assistance. It was Jesus Valencia and another man, both influential and important fellows in these parts. When they heard more about my plans, they were a bit hesitant but then felt that I had a good chance at finding the Apaches if my Indian companions could interpret the obscure signs and traces that they occasionally leave behind. Valencia himself had chased some of these mountain people so he knew what he was talking about.

They thought the best approach would be to first make my way south to the Sienequita Ranch, which lay at the foot of the mountains. From there I could begin my ascent and also rent mules and hire the people we needed.

This sounded good, and so we got hold of some riding and pack animals as well as two Mexican helpers who could take us as far as the ranch. It didn't take long before our trail of riders and pack animals were headed south through the forest. When it comes to loading packs on the animals, not many are as quick and assured as the Mexicans. The pack saddle, *aparegjos*, consists of two wide, flat bags stuffed with hay. Three hundred pounds is about an average load on a mule and two hundred for a donkey. Mexicans have little sensitivity for their animals and treat them hard. Many of the mules have large, raw patches on their backs that never heal and are continually pestered by flies.

We traveled across a rolling landscape with semitropical vegetation. On the hillsides, acacia were in full bloom, and in small forest clearings patches of yellow and red flowers glimmered in the sun. Now and then we wandered by the crystal-clear Bavispe River, which flowed under the shade of poplar, walnut, and sycamore trees. Small bright birds flew around, and at one place a funny green parrot sat peering at us with his head cocked. It was quite hot, about 95 degrees Fahrenheit in the shade, but nothing compared to the heat of mid-summer in these parts when the temperature can rise to 120. This season was by far the best for us.

We made camp along the Bavispe River and had a pleasant evening around the fire, eating dried meat and cornbread our Mexican helpers fried over heated stones. When we crawled into bed, I noticed that the Mexicans carefully took their guns and laid them on the ground beside them. Later I realized that this wasn't unusual, but customary out here. During the first night I understood all too well the reason for doing this. We had barely fallen asleep when a bunch of drunken Mexicans came riding over the river. They really raised a ruckus over in the forest, and judging from their yelling they must have had quite a fight going. In the end, we heard two shots followed by the sound of horses splashing across the river again. Afterward, it all quieted down until the coyotes started up. There must be huge packs of them in these parts because I had never before heard such a howling racket. At dawn, I also saw a pack of about fifteen of these animals run off and disappear into the forest on the other side of the river.

We carried on our way and soon we neared the village of Huachin-era. What a sight! Small, attached adobe huts, built in a square, perched like a crown atop a high crest, where the blue Sierra Madre rose behind. There were also single huts strewn about on the hill-side, surrounded by fences of planted cacti, with golden-red peppers hanging on the walls that could be seen from far away.

Huachinera is considerably smaller and poorer than Bacerac. In this isolated little community at the foot of the mountains, everything was incredibly rudimentary and utterly picturesque. Young girls ap-proached from the river walking tall and gracefully with clay jugs balanced on their heads. Now and again we would see women with flowing dark hair heading toward the village with burros carrying firewood. Other women were sitting under leafy awnings holding a stone and grinding corn in *metates*, curved stone bowls. Their tools and lifestyles were not much different from the time when Cortez conquered Mexico. Civilization had nearly passed this part of the world by.

We now headed farther into the Sierra Madre and the amazing pine forests that covered the mountains as far as one could see. Now and then a fascinating peak rose toward the blue like a majestic spire. Yahnozah called one of them Nabow-dah-hitsons, "the mountain on the edge of a range." He called another Isa-dahsia, "the mountain with a bucket on top." He said that he had often been there with Geronimo, who had preferred to keep to higher elevations in order to better scout the land and be able to see the enemy from far away.

We were riding through an open wood of large oaks thinking we were far from any people when suddenly two Mexicans appear. They were carrying a pole between them on their shoulders from which hung two great wooden buckets filled to the brim with wild, fragrant honey. There must have been at least seven gallons in all. They offered us some and I didn't hesitate in taking some of these wonderful honeycombs, which I sucked on as I continued riding. Much of this delicious honey dripped onto my saddle.

We turned into Sienequita, the ranch of Gildardo Moreni, who welcomed us and said to make ourselves at home. There was something very Spanish about Moreni, more refined and courteous than one would expect from a man who is enticed by a lonely existence in the wilderness. This wasn't for show either. He really did his best to make us feel comfortable in every way.

His ranch lay in a small oak hollow at the foot of the Sierra Madre. The houses were made of clay and had slanted roofs covered with chips of wood. His farmyard was a real zoo: cattle, horses, and mules trudged around, as well as seven dogs that were used to hunt birds and mountain lions. There must have also been half a dozen cats and a mass of ducks, chickens, pigs, and turkeys. In the middle of all this, a tame deer gracefully walked around, stretching his soft muzzle toward the naked children who played in the sand.

We stayed at the ranch for a few days, checking over our equipment one last time before setting off into the mountains. We lived like princes. Moreni's beautiful, quiet wife dished up the best the house had to offer. There was no lack of wild honey, brown sugar, tortillas, dried meat, and white Mexican cheese. It was astonishing to see how much of that dynamite-hot spicy food the Mexicans could put down, great portions of chili pepper that would have gagged me seemed to slide right down their throats.

The day after our arrival, we took a trip into the mountains to explore a cave Moreni had talked about. We rode through endless oak woods where the horses plowed through the belly-high grass that grew between the trees like golden fields and covered the slopes. Looking over this unbelievably fertile area where practically everything lay untouched, I couldn't help but think of my own country, where at places along the barren coastal regions farmers have to carry buckets of soil to make fields on the bare rocks.

We found the cave, and I crept inside on all fours while frightened bats flapped around in front of me. There wasn't much in there other than some pieces of broken pottery left behind by people who lived there in prehistoric times.

On our way back to the ranch we passed by a river, where we could see trout swimming around in the crystal-clear pools. At a place just beyond this river, the Mexicans explained, the "white-haired one" was shot a few years ago. He was one of the mountain Apaches, a very old man whom the Mexicans knew about for a long time but who was too sly for them to catch. They think that he might have been the Apaches' chief.

The moon appeared from behind drifting clouds, a kind of fairy-tale atmosphere in the dim forest and on the dark mountain. The Mexicans, children of nature as they are, had fun and lightheartedly sang and laughed. Then we kicked our horses to a run and galloped wildly off through the oak woods, branches whipping us as we tore by. We sped the entire way back and didn't stop until the horses stood panting at the ranch.

That evening we talked about the Apaches, and Moreni had much to tell us. It was extremely difficult to follow an Apache trail, he said, because they would sometimes tie branches under their moccasins and if they had horses, they would tie hide under the hooves. All those he had seen had been shot and were dressed in hides. Every once in a while they would find them with some type of old gun dated back to the Apache wars, but otherwise the Indians used bows and arrows. Nothing indicated that they had any contact with civilization. During the course of time, a good number of the men had been shot and killed, so he believed that now there was a majority of women. Then he startled us by saying that just recently he had spotted fresh signs of six Apaches. Indians were still out there, that was for sure, but finding them was the question!

# 9
# Through the Western Sierra Madre

Not far into the Sierra Madre and a day's ride from Sienequita, there was supposedly one last ranch at which the Yaqui Indian Ysidro Mora and his family lived. He was known to be a tracker and mountain man that few could match, and he was considered to be the only one in the area who knew so much about the Sierra Madre. He was also considered to be a rough type. With mixed feelings of fear and admiration the Mexicans said that once he shot down five Apaches.

On this first trip I wanted to look him up and then ride farther in through the Sierra Madre. Moreni let us have some pack animals and horses, and early one morning we took off for the mountains. We rode up and up the steep terrain where forests of oak grew in all directions. Every now and again we startled a herd of deer, which snorted and took off running with their white tails high in the air, leaving a wake of swaying yellow grass.

The slopes grew even worse and the pack animals worked hard. On the steepest inclines, the packs would sometimes tip them over and they would tumble down the hill. The first time I witnessed this I really thought that we had a tragedy on our hands and ran down thinking that I was going to find a lifeless mule. But I was mistaken. The animal just slowly got up, flapped its big ears a bit and was in good as shape as before. In time, I learned that mules simply don't die from accidents.

The acrobatic feats our pack animals did every once in a while caused us a lot of trouble. The ties on the packs often loosened, and we were in continual danger of losing some of our things. The next day I found out that I had been about as unlucky as possible, and so soon into our trip. The case holding the aneroid barometer, the temperature gauge, and so on had been lost during the night. Despite intense searching, I didn't find it again. This was especially aggravating because the height of some of the various summits in the Sierra Madre were fairly unknown and it would have been considerably interesting to collect some measurements.

On a small plateau at about six thousand feet we found the Santa Clara ranch, a humble cabin by a river. The rancher and hunter Mora lived here, the only one in these parts who dared to stand up against the Apaches in their own mountain domain. When I saw Mora, I quickly understood that he was a sly devil and rough fellow who didn't put up with much from the Apaches. He was completely different from the Mexicans I met earlier at the foot of the mountain. He very well might have had white blood in him, but he looked like an Indian through and through. He was a descendant of the Yaqui people, who dominate large parts of Sonora and are known to be the most ferocious and fearless natives anywhere in Mexico. He was a small, middle-aged man with intense, narrow, hawklike eyes. His face was deeply lined and thin and he had a bristly black mustache above a tightly clenched mouth. He was agile and limber and fit as a well-trained Finnish runner, fast as lightning.

On our trip up, I realized that it wasn't going to work out to continue with the unfit mules that we had gotten from Sienequita. They had been out in the pasture way too long. It was also unfortunate that our Mexican helper didn't have more knowledge of the mountains. It was different, however, with Mora. He had a herd of tough, conditioned mules that had been raised in the Sierra Madre and that could endure almost anything. I made an agreement with him then that he and his mules would join us on our expedition, and I sent the Mexican back.

It was true that Mora was a rough fellow, but he knew more about the mountains and the Apaches than anyone else. I just had to chance the rest. I also admit that I had a weak spot in my heart for such an adventurer and mountain man who practically blended right in with the wild nature in which he lived.

We stayed a couple of days at Santa Clara while Mora gathered together the mules. During this time, I became better acquainted with his wife and two daughters, who helped us out with various things. It must have been awfully lonely at times for the two seventeen-year-old girls to live alone up here in these mountains year after year. They seemed shy, but also appeared to crave contact with other people. Otherwise, they had plenty to do because Mora ran some kind of farm.

It was interesting to see how generous the earth was up there at six thousand feet and how it was used. The corn is planted in May and harvested in October. The wheat is sown in December and cut in June. In the same field, the beans are planted in July and reaped in October. Tobacco is planted in May and harvested in October. Fertilizer isn't used, and everything ripens to maturity. Only the sugar cane is slow to grow and is used for horse feed.

Our big task now was how to plan for our search for the Apaches in that great mountain area surrounding us. I wanted to have as organized a plan as possible for the search but that wasn't so easy. The existing maps of the Sierra Madre were so totally worthless that I had to get rid of them after Mora and I spent half a day puzzling over them. Instead I chose to use what he could provide me with about the country. We had a few clues and we also knew that the more recent encounters with the Apaches had mostly occurred in the western areas, where Mora had also discovered some of their camps. So I decided that we would begin by traversing the mountain southward all the way to the lowlands around the village of Nacori Chico. From there we could carry on toward the mountaintops traversing farther east, and in that way gradually move deeper through the mountains.

We started off, first going eastward, then southward. Leading our small procession was Mora riding his wild mule. Andrew followed leading the black mare, and then came the four pack mules. Yahnozah and I rode behind and around the animals, keeping an eye on everything.

Without the mare in front to lure the others on, it wouldn't have been possible to get those stubborn pack animals moving along at a steady pace. The mules loved her and just turned their noses up at the females of their own kind. That mare was quite a female! The mules couldn't even get close to that black beauty, whose flowing mane fell softly over her shiny, sweet-smelling fur.

It didn't take long before we were in a land that was more wild than any other: we were riding through the notorious Sierra Nacori.[1] I compassionately thought about the American soldiers who half a century ago struggled along somewhere up here in pursuit of Geronimo. They certainly had quite a challenge, and it was no wonder so many of them collapsed. Deep gorges cut through the mountains in all directions. No actual valley exists, you either travel straight up to the top or straight down to the bottom. The oak forests were gone now, and instead we were in the huge pine forests that begin at about six thousand feet. Like slender pillars, the pine trees rose about ninety feet into the air.

Like a true Mexican, Mora sets our course pretty much straight up and down the steep slopes. At first I thought this would put too much strain on the mules in the long run. But I was wrong. They climbed like goats and showed an endurance equal only to what I have seen with polar dogs. In such difficult terrain as this, they are much more practical than horses, not the least due to the surefootedness of their small hooves.

I must admit that during the first days, I found it a bit scary when my mule would now and again balance right on the edge of a cliff. Later I was able to calm myself with the thought that the mule was just as interested in going on living as I was.

The seventy-six-year-old Apache, Yahnozah, sat as straight as a Russian Cossack in the saddle on his white mule as he scouted out across the country where earlier he had roamed free. Occasionally he would stop on a ridge and point out peaks and valleys saying that he had once been over there with Geronimo, fought over that way with the Mexicans, and made a camp over yonder. Among other things, he also explained that each of the great Apache chiefs from the old days ruled over their own sections of the country down there. Cochise ruled in the mountain range west of the actual Sierra Madre, and Juh, and later Geronimo, reigned in the western and central parts, while Victorio considered the area closer to Chihuahua to be his hunting grounds.

The days passed. We searched for signs and tracks everywhere we went. We continually ran across herds of deer, and when we needed meat we would shoot one of them and tie it on the backs of our saddles. Sometimes we also startled large flocks of wild turkeys and even discovered wolf and bear tracks. Besides brown and black bears, there are also grizzly bears in those parts.

There was no doubt that we worked hard during the days, but we were justly rewarded with our evenings around the campfire. At one particular spot, we make camp by a small river protected by some leafy trees. The wine-red autumn leaves hang and flutter in the evening breeze. We have a good view of the mountains to the east, where the sun is shedding its last golden rays across a hill. The grass is so thick and tall we can barely make out the antlers of three deer standing quietly a little distance away. A chill is in the air and the fire feels good.

We chow down on some deer meat, have a smoke, and then discuss our plans for tomorrow. Darkness drapes over the Sierra Madre's forests, and the fire becomes a sole spark in the night. Yahnozah begins singing his tribe's strange and wild songs, and Andrew sings along. The melodic sounds drift far into the quiet forest, just like the time when that old Apache sat up here with his people defying the rest of the world.

We eventually crawl into our sleeping bags, but not without first making sure that our rifles are loaded and laying beside us on the ground. Mora even takes his pistol with him under his blankets. He is familiar with the mountains, and one never knows.

Morning is a busy time. Besides preparing breakfast, we also have to continually track down the mules, which have inevitably wandered up to the highest surrounding hills. They love to enjoy the quiet morning hours wherever the sun first appears. Later, the packs have to be tied on. Every day we have a couple hours of hard work to do before we can leave.

After a while, my accompanying Apaches made it a routine to sing every evening. Yahnozah was quite a singer and had a vast array of songs, some of which he made up himself or substituted with his own lyrics. Like other artists who specialized in ballads or opera, he too had his own niche – morning songs. He was one of the few who knew the Chiricahua Apaches' long series of morning songs, which he incidentally always sang at night. I was pleased that the Indians continued with their concerts because if we were to come into contact with the Natives, our chances wouldn't depend on sneaking up on them undetected. On the contrary, it was important for them to know that there were tribal kinsmen close by. Perhaps the sounds of these familiar songs might reach them and lead to closer contact.

We soon came upon the first of the old campsites of the free-roaming Apaches. It lay on top of a mountain below some large pine trees and had an extensive view across the area. One or two families had lived here in a small, low grass hut. Stakes that had been used to hang and dry meat were still leaning against a large rock, and down the hill were signs of a hole in the ground for cooking mescal. By the remains of bone and other things, it looked as if the Indians had stayed here for quite some time. But we did not find a single trace of clothing, utensils, tools, or such. This showed how badly equipped these people were. They owned practically nothing.

One evening, Mora told us that we were now fairly close to the place where he had fought a band of the Apaches in 1932. In the same area, he knew of a strange, old cave where the Apaches used to live and where there might be a chance of coming across them. We headed westward and reached a lower-lying mountainous area with deep ravines and steep slopes. In the background rose a mighty mountain Mora called Gaotivos.

The farther we descended, the slower our progress, and in the end it was impossible to continue with the mules. We tied them to some trees, climbed on down, and came to a very different place than what we were used to up where the cool pine forests grew. Cactus, yucca plants, grapevines, and other semitropical vegetation covered the hills. Deep in the gorges, bamboo brush grew along the riverbanks and tall palm trees rose from sun-filled hollows.

We eventually found the cave that Mora had talked about, but we didn't see any of the Natives. But I was satisfied with taking our strenuous side-trip because the cave was one of the most beautiful and incredible that I have ever seen. A bunch of palm trees grew in front of the cave and the leaves draped down, framing the entrance. Remarkable drawings and fantastic figures of people, wolves, deer, eagles in flight, and so on decorated the sooty walls. The depictions were made with some sort of gray clay that had been brushed on the rock and later hardened like cement. Long before the Apaches occupied the cave, a prehistoric people must have lived here.

In danger of losing life and limb, we climbed up the mountain and onto a small ledge we found another cave that had also been inhabited. Other people had also found this to be a nice, safe place to stay in the steep mountains. As I crawled along the rock shelf, I came upon the warm lair of a jaguar or mountain lion. Most likely we had scared it off.

We sat a while on the sunny ledge in front of the cave to catch our breaths. I just started to say that a bite of food would taste good when Mora took a few steps sideways and picked a few pear-shaped fruits from a small tree that had attached itself to a crack in the rock. He called it a *pochote* and explained that it had such long watery roots that in a pinch you could quench your thirst from it. The fruit contained lots of tasty white seeds that were delicately encased in silky-soft fuzz.

As we sat there enjoying the view, Mora pointed to one of the highest plateaus on the great mountain Gaotivos and proudly said, "It was over there that I shot a band of Apaches in 1932."

In the following, I repeat what happened based on what Mora himself has said and what I have heard from half a dozen Mexicans who were partly involved in chasing the Natives and who helped tend to the wounded who were brought to the village of Nacori Chico:

It is early in the morning on Mora's mountain farm, Santa Clara. At daybreak, he walks down to the corral just below the house where the day before he had put his mules. But what's this? The corral gate is wide open and not a single animal is to be seen. Like a bloodhound, he searches the ground until he finally discovers some faint moccasin tracks. The Apaches have stolen his mules. Mora's eyes flash with anger, for the mules are his pride and most valuable possession. He would never part with them without a fight. But to take off alone after an entire band of Apaches would be futile. He quickly gets hold of one of the horses grazing up in the hills, jumps in the saddle, and chases on down the mountain so fast that he sends dirt and rocks flying.

Down in the lowlands, he gathers a dozen robust fellows and together they head back toward to Sierra Madre, where they find the Apaches' tracks and quickly pursue. It's the rainy season and it's pouring. The rivers gush with dirty yellow water in the canyons, making it treacherous to cross in many places. But with stubborn determination, Mora leads his group farther along. Sometimes they lose the trail, and then they find it again, and the Apaches don't get a moment's rest. But the Natives are used to fleeing for their lives, and they know every nook and cranny of the country. They zigzag their way across a maze of ravines and cliffs, circle back to their old tracks, head way east to the heart of the Sierra Madre, then turn back toward the most rugged part of the western mountains. How they ever find time to sleep or eat is a mystery, and they never light a fire.

For twenty-five days they are chased like wild animals by a pack of hounds. They know it is a matter of life or death. They know the Mexicans will slaughter them to the very last man if given the chance. They themselves don't have proper weapons to attempt a fight with the well-equipped opponents. Finally, after they have let all the mules go, they are able to shake off the pursuers.

Dead tired and drained by the futile chase, all of the Mexicans are ready to give in – all but Mora. He is a Yaqui Indian, a born warrior and relentless avenger. Every time he thinks of his beautiful mules, his anger flares up and drives him farther on. He now parts from the others and circles around, trying to cross the trail again. In the end, his search leads him up the western side of the mountain called Gaotivos. He stops his horse under some oak trees near the summit and scans the area to the east. He sees something down on the plateau below. Coming through the sparse forest is a single rider, and around him is a small group of people. The Apaches!

Mora spurs his mule to a run and speeds down the hill. Before the Apaches know what's happened he is right on top of them. The Indians are gripped with wild panic, and screaming they flee for their lives. But Mora takes aim with his rifle and very slowly shoots them down one by one. A woman with a child on her back on the verge of collapse scrambles up the mountain. Mora puts a bullet right through both of them. He sees another woman and once again his bullet hits its mark. A third, who is also carrying a child, runs for her life up toward a cliff. She lets go of the child and just barely escapes. A man runs right behind her and just about makes it around the cliff when Mora fires a shot and hits him in the side. The man falls but makes it up again and disappears. Mora follows the trail for a while and spots blood, although it is difficult to see. The tough, level-headed Apache gathers his blood in his hands as he runs and scatters it into the bushes so that he can't be tracked. Finally, the pursuer gives up his chase. The man would die from his wounds anyway.

Mora rides back to the mountain plateau where the shooting started. Stillness now lingers in the Sierra Madre. Sprawled all over the ground is a small group of people who, for fear of their lives, had tried to grapple their way into the mountains with the hound on their heels. They have all been finished off except for a little boy and some small wounded children who are crying and clinging to their dead mothers' bodies. The prey has been caught.

Mora picks a bit of corn husk out of his pocket, rolls a cigarillo, and feels generally satisfied. His desire for revenge has been fulfilled. That's what they deserve, anyone who tries to steal from a man like him. The thought of what other Mexicans will say also gives him a tinge of delight. He realizes that from now on he will be looked upon with respect and admiration; they will call him *valiente*, a brave man.

But all those who were killed were women, and not one of them fired a shot because none of them owned a single weapon. One of the dead women is older but the other two are middle-aged. Beside them lie a three-year-old boy and girl who are clearly twins. One of them was hit by a bullet right through the foot and the other's right hand has practically been torn off. The third child, the one that the fleeing woman threw aside, is a chubby, dark-haired boy about two years old.

The other Mexicans who had heard the firing off in the distance from the top of a mountain now appear. The twin children, the wounded boy and girl, were taken to Nacori Chico, and the other boy was taken to Cumpus. There he was adopted by Cheno Medina. (Later I discuss my meeting with this Apache boy.) The Mexicans also took the clothes from the dead Indians and the little that they owned. The Apaches were all dressed in hides. The women wore short, wide skirts, small shirts, and knee-high moccasins. Basically, their cloth- ing was very much like the Apaches of earlier times. Among the bits and pieces that they had were a knife made from scrap iron, small leather purses, a doll carved of wood, a drill, and a few rough iron needles.

Later I was able to get hold of one of these.

The women in Nacori Chico took care of the wounded children and nursed them as best they could. The girl lost her hand and the boy lost some toes and they both had a tough time. The girl was a mild and sweet little thing, while the three-year-old boy was a hotheaded warrior. It was clear that he was intended to be a chief because his clothes were ornately decorated with a number of glittering things and he also carried himself with high respect. They wanted to give him other clothes but he stubbornly refused to wear anything but his chieftain apparel. He couldn't stand having women tend to him, he only wanted to deal with men. His foot that had been shot must have surely caused him great pain, not to mention the agony when they had to amputate his big toe. That little warrior clenched his teeth and took it like a man. But he was nothing more than a small child, and sometimes he would confusedly lift his foot up to understand why he suddenly couldn't run around on it.

About three months before these murders, another small Apache girl by the name of Bui, Owl Eye, was captured in the Sierra Madre and brought to Nacori Chico. When she met her two wounded companions from the mountains, they spoke to each other in their native language. It was quite an unusual encounter. At that time, an Apache woman called Lupe also lived near by. She too had once been taken captive by the Mexicans. So this small group of nomadic, mountain Apaches were all brought together in their archenemy's community, where they mourned their bitter fate.

After the amputations, it appeared that the two wounded children would pull through. Their physical condition was actually quite strong and they had a remarkable ability to heal. But a change in their diet caused them terrible stomach problems and they both suffered from severe diarrhea. This is what did them in. Soon they were nothing but skin and bones and they faded away. Thus ended the short lives of these nature children who had never known anything but forests and blue mountains.

We proceeded back into the high mountains to continue our search. As we moved along the edge of the steep gorge that ran just north of Gaotivos, Mora pointed to a small ledge in a cliff and said that some of the Apaches had once spent the night there during his pursuit. There had been seven of them, one only a child, who had separated earlier from the Indians whom Mora had come across. They managed to escape and are still roaming the mountains, where both Mora and the other Mexicans have quite recently seen signs of them.

We now rode straight up toward one of the highest mountaintops in that part of the Sierra Madre, which is called Sierra Nacori. It was hard work getting there and so steep that we couldn't manage to bring the mules. But we were rewarded for our toil because at the very top the view was tremendous. At an elevation of eight to nine thousand feet there is a mountain range that extends south-southeast like a threatening barricade to the Sierra Madre's western border. The mountain slope down to the lowlands was so steep that it looked as if it had been sliced with a knife. I looked out over staggering high peaks, faint distant gorges, and an endless number of dark-red and green rock heaps. Way down below to the west, the rolling hills of the lowlands stretched out to the southeast, where they formed a shallow bowl. There is where the village of Nacori Chico was located.

Just below the summit from this panoramic view, we found an abandoned Apache camp among the pine trees. It was the most pitiful human habitation I have ever seen, yet it looked like the natives had lived there for quite some time. On the steep slope they had placed some poles, supported these with a root and some rocks, and then filled in with dirt to create a shelf about six feet wide and nine feet long. Behind the shelf was a small cliff against which they had propped a low slanted grass roof, their home. It all appeared so cramped and dangerous that I would have thought twice about spending the night there in fear of rolling down the hill and off the cliff.

This is the way that the Sierra Madre Apaches are compelled to live, since they are constantly being pursued. No other group of people anywhere in the world is so mercilessly chased to death as these last, free Indians of the proud and previously powerful Apache nation. They don't lack courage, only weapons. The only thing they can do against their mighty enemy is to hide and flee. So they set up their humble grass huts in places where they believe no pursuer would imagine that anyone would live. On a steep mountain ledge at nine thousand feet they have built a home – an eagle's nest.

But even here they wouldn't have managed to escape. In May, 1932, a few months before Mora massacred that group I previously discussed, a Mexican cowboy by the name of Aristeo Garcia came riding over the mountain top looking for some cattle that had gone astray. He spotted the grass hut and threw some rocks at it, which made an old woman and a young girl of about five leap out and run down the hill. Aristeo, *valiente*, raised his rifle and killed the woman with one shot in the head at close range. The girl hid in some bushes, but the Mexican's two dogs caught scent of her and found her. Aristeo threw her over his saddle and rode to Nacori Chico. He left in a hurry fearing that several other Apaches lived at that camp, something that was later confirmed.

The girl's name, previously mentioned, was Bui, or Owl Eye. She too became inflicted with serious stomach problems, but recovered. By coincidence, she was later taken north, where an American family adopted her. She is now living in the United States. Later, I will discuss my meeting with this girl who was raised in the eagle's nest on one of Sierra Madre's highest mountains.

Besides a primitive knife made from a pot, the Mexican had taken a lot of other small items he had found in the camp: the dead woman's clothes, which consisted only of a short buckskin skirt, an animal stomach used as a water container, a crudely hammered knife, some primitive needles, a leather purse, two large and carefully carved wooden dolls dressed in hides and decorated with black hair, and two toy horses cut from thick rawhide and supplied with a mane and tail and saddles made of an iron plate from a wolf trap stolen from the Mexicans.

I was later able to get hold of one of these horses. It was remarkable to see this simple toy for a nature child. It could have been their only joy up there in the eagle's nest. They weren't allowed to play and run around like other children because they might have exposed the hiding place. Perhaps they weren't even allowed to go outside that cramped camp for fear of them rolling down the hill and over the cliff.

Some carved wooden dolls were also found. It is quite probable that these were not intended as toys but instead as fetishes. This is much more likely because such humanlike idols have been used not only by Apaches of olden times but also by the White Mountain Apaches of today.

Food for these free Apaches consisted of berries, roots, mescal, sprouts, small game, and occasionally dried beef. They stole the cattle from the Mexicans, but the bone remains found at the various camps showed that this type of theft wasn't as common as assumed. These people were primarily nourished by products of the wilderness, and they mostly eat their food raw because they only seldom, and preferably only at dawn, dare light a fire, even in the wintertime.

Down the hill lay the skull of the old Apache woman the Mexican had killed. There was a hole in the back of the head. Without thinking, I asked Yahnozah to hold the skull while I took some photographs of the camp with the dazzling view in the background. He shook his head in horror, but Mora stepped forward and was thrilled to be immortalized holding the trophy in his hand. Afterward, Yahnozah was very quiet and kept to himself while he looked over this camp where his tribal kinsmen had been slaughtered.

We later climbed down to a lower-lying plateau and made camp by a clearing in the pine forest. It was an unusually still evening with a full moon that drifted over the mountains, casting its dim light in between the trees. The fire consumed the resinous pinewood, and a glowing red column rose high toward the stars. But there was no singing that evening, and closest to the fire sat that old Apache quietly staring into the flames.

After searching the western regions of the Sierra Madre, we headed as planned toward the southwest, in the direction of the little village of Nacori Chico. However, the mountains seemed so steep everywhere that any descent seemed hopeless. Fortunately, though, Mora knew the area and led us down some staggering slopes southward where the Santa Clara River cuts through the mountains. And we made it, though not without trouble on my part. In the middle of the steepest part of the hill my mule, Bago, happened to step right into a wasps' nest. If there is anything that makes a mule shudder it's wasps, and Bago was no exception. He flattened his ears, bucked, and took off down the hill. I was thrown off head over heels and went rolling down until I landed in a bush with a bang. As I crawled up and out while the Indians roared with laughter, there were parts of my body that were hurting more than my neck, and I discovered I also had been stung by four wasps.

The lower-lying knolls we now had reached form a continuation of the Sierra de Bacadehuachi. They are built up of agglomerations so rugged that we had to continually climb up and down. We were now outside of the Sierra Madre Occidental, whose steep ridges rose above us to the east. In the middle of the wilderness by the Agua Clara River, we came upon a single cabin. It was covered with bear grass and lay in a clearing in a deciduous forest of flaming red autumn leaves. A bin full of corncobs sat in front of the house. Only women were at home, two older ones and one beautiful eighteen-year-old who appeared to be full-blooded Indian. There is something very pleasant and quiet about the Mexican women, who often seem to stand above their men. "Que dios te guarde!" (May God protect you) shouted the oldest woman as we left. There was a beautiful ring to it out here in the forest.

Eventually the mountains turned into rolling hills. The warmth of the sun was like that in midsummer at home in Norway, and instead of that endless pine forest we were now surrounded by mesquite trees and all kinds of cacti, from the giant cactus and cholla to the prickly pear, which often had fewer needles here in comparison to similar plants in Arizona. Tall, sweet-smelling clusters of blue flowers bloomed in a canyon cleft. Along the river grew a dense thicket of willows, and their wooly seeds covered the branches like snow.

About three miles from Nacori Chico, we set up camp by the river. As we sat around the fire, two half-blood Indians emerged from the forest with a tame deer trotting along after them. They looked incredibly alike, with long skinny faces and a small tuft of beard on their chins and big childlike eyes. We traded for a pumpkin and roasted it in the ground under the fire. Later, we followed our guests to their home, which was a mountain cave. There we met two young boys who had just come down from the forest carrying between them a huge coyote on a pole.

We crawled into the cave and sat around a small fire that cast its light all over the sooty black walls. Corncobs lay ready for roasting in front of the fire. At the entrance, the tame deer had laid on the ground, and in the furthest corner of the cave lay a pile of kids under some hides. Every so often, a little tot would stick his head out from under the hide and stare at these peculiar strangers who had suddenly appeared in his home.

As it grew darker and darker outside, we sat talking long about this and that, but mostly about the many ruins, hieroglyphs, and cave dwellings that were thought to exist in this strange, sunny country where people still chose to live in caves.

The next day, we carry on to Nacori Chico but stop along the way to investigate a small round mountain the cave dweller had talked about. On the top, I found two round holes in the rock. They were about a foot deep and half a foot in diameter. The Mexicans claim that in prehistoric times these were used for crushing corn, but possibly there was a religious significance to them.

Close to Nacori Chico we came upon a cluster of leaf-covered huts that we were able to see from quite a distance because of the pepper plants with shiny red fruit that hung from the walls. The friendly Mexicans who lived there showed us a round, green rock about twice the size of a soccer ball and told us that it came from a prehistoric settlement. But what I remember most about these people who lived in the light, leaf-covered huts was a young demented girl who was pushed around by everybody and had such a beautiful smile and pretty brown eyes.

# 10
# Nacori Chico

Slung in a hollow amidst endless mountains lies the village of Nacori Chico. No road leads there, just steep trails over the mountains where riders have to travel for days to reach any kind of civilization. In this little corner of the world there are few modern conveniences, but there isn't much lacking, either. The people here are able to supply their own corn, dried meat, tobacco, pepper, and sugar, and other than this they don't have much need for anything else. These four to five hundred inhabitants live in blissful ignorance, sauntering about under the dazzling sun. What would they want with knowledge? They have what they need and everything else is nonessential and far, far away. This is a world of its own, existing deep within the mountains.

The location of Nacori Chico is indescribably beautiful. I have seldom seen anything as stunning as when the evening sun sets and the contours of the village's low rows of adobe houses stand out against the intense blue of the Sierra Madre. The settlement was built around a square plaza at the eastern end of which lay the ruins of an old Spanish church. In front of the building stood four church bells hanging from a crossbar. One bell even had the year 1718 engraved on it, but the church itself is older than that.

The Spaniards were led to this faraway place in search of gold and silver, here where the mountains are unusually abundant in precious metals. Close to Nacori Chico, there was a thriving gold mine that supposedly had fantastic yields. It went by the name Toyopa and is one of the many "lost" mines from the Spanish rule. It isn't so strange to think that these mines sunk into oblivion: for hundreds of years the Apaches ruled the mountains and rampaged the area so horribly that almost any mining over a period of time came to an end.

We settled down into a small farmyard of sorts that bordered the old church ruins. It was pleasant there with the pigs, a pair of donkeys, a tame deer, and some lemon trees that hung heavy with golden fruit. A primitive grain mill stood close by, which consisted of two large millstones being driven around by an old donkey. The animal was blindfolded and tied to a long, extended pole and went around and around, hour after hour.

I noticed that Yahnozah had a peculiar, searching look on his face when he rode into the village, and I asked him whether he had been here before. He told me that in his wild youth he had many times lain outside the rows of houses here fighting against the Mexicans. This, however, was one of the few towns in this region that the Apaches didn't manage to conquer. In fact, not only Geronimo but also the great chief Cochise had to give up after four attempts to storm the town. And now, fifty years later, this old warrior peacefully rode in.

When I asked Yahnozah how it felt to come inside these walls, he replied, "I not feel it is my place to be here. Long time these people my bitter enemies. Now I only see the ordinary and good people." The village people themselves were no less astonished to suddenly have a real live Apache of the older generation among them.

It was a clear, starry night, and as we lay there in our sleeping bags sheltered by the old church ruins, Yahnozah, as usual, began singing his native morning songs. Half the town came and gathered around. Behind shrubs and rocks and by the open portal hordes of people carefully stood poking their heads out and staring at us. Most of these people had relatives who in the course of time had been killed by Apaches, and Geronimo was considered the devil himself. They still feared the remaining Apaches who continued to roam the mountains, and very few of them dared to travel in through the Sierra Madre. Occasionally, the mountain Apaches would steal horses and mules from them. I saw an animal that had been stolen but later retrieved by the Mexicans. It bore the Apaches' brand: two opposite-facing arrows.

I was told many stories and accounts about the Indians and their activity since the turn of the century. It seemed they were responsible for a number of attacks and killings, both in Chihuahua and Sonora. There were stories about Mexicans who drove their pack animals through the mountains and whose mutilated corpses were later found. Other reports claimed that at far-off cattle ranches entire families had been massacred. It was said that the Indians tied an American by the name of Jack Fisher naked to an anthill. The Mexicans later took revenge and didn't give in to the Apaches.

Once again I heard about the old white-haired Indian who for ages had been chief of one of the bands until he was shot. Another warrior was found wounded in a cave and died a short time after, and many others over time "bit the dust," including those I have already mentioned. An old Apache woman, Salome as the Mexicans called her, was captured around 1908 and imprisoned in the village of Opoto. She killed herself by throwing herself head first against a rock.

Finally in Nacori Chico, I was able to confirm what I had heard elsewhere, namely that a single white man had for years lived together with the mountain Apaches. Mora also knew about this, and among other things he said that a hairbrush made of mescal leaves had been found in an Apache camp with tufts of red hair. For the past few years, the Mexicans had not seen a sign of this white man, who was supposedly rather old the last time anyone heard of him. This was quite a far-fetched story, but it was confirmed by so many independent sources that it wasn't easy to ignore. My later research shows that it might be connected to a well-known tragedy that took place in the United States about fifty years ago.

I had hoped to find the captured Apache woman, Lupe, who lived with her foster parents in a cabin near Nacori Chico. But it turned out that she had moved to Chihuahua, where I met her later. This meeting with Lupe and her foster parents will be discussed elsewhere.

The owner of our campsite by the church ruins was Ramon Hutardo, who once had led a retaliating search for the Apaches and had himself been involved in killing four of them. He could be happy that he had an unusually resourceful and friendly wife. I got off on a good start with her and she helped us in many ways. One day, she called me into a hallway, where an old trunk lay without a lock. She lifted out some objects and removed the rags that covered them. I couldn't believe my own eyes: old Spanish church treasures made out of the most beautiful gold and silver. There were three large crowns in hammered gold studded with turquoise and blue stones, as well as pots, silver vases, trays, and dishes, everything made out the solid precious metals and very decorative.

The woman let me take photographs and film the objects, but to sell them was out of the question. They were such an inextricable part of the people's religion. Besides being used in other ceremonies, they were used during Easter festivities, when young girls dressed in white wore the gold crowns and walked barefoot leading the procession across the plaza square to the old church ruins. It was customary for each family to keep the church treasures a certain number of months, but no one other than the head of the church knew where they were located at any one time. In all likelihood, the treasures came from the church that now lay in ruins. The Spaniards probably didn't manage to take the items with them when they fled.

Besides these valuables, there were more treasures of one kind or another in this small village. I came upon a young fellow who was wandering around quite intoxicated. I heard that he had been on a drunken binge for fourteen days. Not so unexpected, for the boy had discovered a treasure of old Spanish money near Satachi. Something like this could go to anybody's head. I was able to trade for some unusual copper coins, but I never got to see the silver and gold.

This isn't the first Spanish treasure to be found in this region, and there certainly are others, although one can't believe all the incredible stories one hears. Wars and other turmoil throughout history forced the Spanish to quickly hide their valuables. They were especially concerned about the silver and gold bars from isolated mines. Later, however, one thing or another happened to the owners of these things. They were either driven away or killed.

Word quickly spread that I was interested in buying or trading for items that had belonged to the mountain Apaches, and people came rushing to me. I was able to get hold of a few interesting things, such as the aforementioned toy horse, tools, and so forth. But these were not the least of what they brought forth. They came with all sorts of rarities, from Spanish stirrups, stone axes, flint tips, and strange coins down to uninteresting trash and junk. The most difficult was when the young girls would come with their embroidery and such things. There were a couple of things I liked, but I quickly ruined the trading because I proved myself to be a hopeless businessman. Right at the beginning, an absolutely beautiful half-Indian girl came with some of her embroidery. It was a rather shabby piece of work as far as I could tell but as she was such a beauty to behold, well, I said I would take it. Then I took out the brooches and rings I used for trading with the fairer sex. Right away she started contemplating whether to choose the rings with blue or red stones or pick a brooch instead. I said that she could try on some of the items and so she put on a bundle of rings and a bunch of brooches. They all went so incredibly well with her hair and supple fingers that it was a shame that she had to take any of them off. So I generously said that she could keep them all. Her mouth broke out into wide smile revealing rows of white teeth, a sight in itself, then she turned and disappeared out of my life. Later, other women with truly beautiful work came and demanded exactly the same pay and so my whole embroidery business went to pot.

It is a cool evening and the stars shine above the plaza and rows of adobe houses. Over by the dark walls of the houses, some half-naked children squat around a fire they have started from cornstalks and twigs. They hold the palms of their hands against the warmth of the fire. Close to the church ruins, a door to a shabby room is open; it appears to be a small chapel with a white altar cloth and two lit candles inside.

Next to the four bells hanging on the pole in front of the church ruins and closest to the plaza stands a young donkey with long, somber ears atop a funny, little body. It contentedly rubs against one of the bells, which suddenly makes a soft, clanging sound that reverberates into the evening and then dies down. An even deeper stillness follows. Then an old man potters over to the church bells and begins ringing them. The silence is broken and the tingling resonates through the clear evening air and far off across the dim Sierra Madre.

A barefoot girl gracefully and quickly comes walking across the plaza. She is wrapped in a black, fringed shawl that covers her head and drapes down over her shoulders. She walks into the chapel, tosses the shawl from her hair, and kneels down in front of the white altar cloth with the burning candles. It is almost like a painting framed by the dark night.

The baby donkey is asleep where it stands. Close to the walls of the house the fire smolders with small, flickering flames, yet the half-naked youngsters still sit there with their hands stretched toward the heat.

I was very interested in finding out whether any archeological discoveries could be found around Nacori Chico, and I received what was thought to have been valuable information. Among other things, I was told that on the other side of the Aros River, about a three-day trip south, there was supposedly a mountain that was almost like a shell that covered a world of caves in which prehistoric people had once lived on several levels. The rocks there were said to have countless number of plate-sized holes that had served as ventilation or as windows, and at the top stood two large clay ovens. The Mexicans called the place Cureda and were quite excited about it. Regardless of the fact that most of them had seen plenty of old cave dwellings, they claimed that Cureda was the most remarkable of them all.

I then decided to sacrifice a few days to investigate the place, and we got ourselves ready to travel south on this side trip. Along the way we would also pass the old village of Satachi, which the Apaches had conquered many times and which now supposedly lay in complete ruins. Gold had recently been discovered around there in a sandy hill, and several old gold miners were now busy "dry washing" for the precious metal, using small billows to blow the sand away from the gold pan to leave the heavy gold behind. This is a very common method in northern Mexico, where access to water is often difficult.

Just when we are about to leave, Mora showed up dead drunk. "I'm holl reit," he said as he staggered around his mules, making a sad attempt to pack our things on one of the pack animals. The whole lot came tumbling off, knocking Mora to the ground, where he sat giggling his head off. I carried him over to the shade of the church ruins, where he immediately fell asleep.

Mora hadn't been down from the mountains in over half a year, so I didn't need to take his short bout of drinking too seriously, especially since no other useful guide could be found on the spot. But at the same time, I felt this was a warning that I should try to get Mora away from people and into the Sierra Madre as quickly as possible. On that planned side trip to the south, we would have run into gold miners near Satachi, and possibly other people. If I knew Mora right, he would try to snatch a bottle of booze every chance he got. I decided to forgo the trip to investigate the strange caves south of the Aros River. We would instead head east toward the Sierra Madre and continue the search for the mountain Apaches.

In the morning when we were about to leave for the Sierra Madre, I first swung down to the blacksmith to pick up thirty muleshoes I had ordered the day before. I found the gray-bearded old giant of a man in the blacksmith shop along with two young Indians. They stood there half-naked pounding the sledgehammers in even rhythm on the pliable, red-hot iron causing sparks to fly from the anvil. Every once in a while embers flew up, and the flickering flames reflected over their sweaty, shiny brown bodies.

A huge heap of muleshoes was piling up on the floor and I thought that these village blacksmiths sure had a lot of orders to fill. Then I asked for my shoes. The blacksmith pointed at the big pile and answered, "You can take those for now but there aren't more than a hundred and three, so you'll have to come back in a couple of hours and get the rest." This sounded a bit strange and I explained that I had ordered thirty shoes, no more, no less. The blacksmith took a deep breath and puffed out his chest. Under shaggy eyebrows, there was a threatening look in his eyes when he replied, "You ordered shoes for thirty mules and that's that." A deep silence fell over the blacksmith shop and trouble was brewing. There I stood. I thought quickly and realized that I held the weakest cards. It wasn't rare that my strange use and twists of the Spanish language caused difficulties. In this case I probably had given my order in such a way that it could have been misunderstood. The expressions "thirty mule shoes" and "shoes for thirty mules" touched on grammatical nuances that were not my strong suit of the Spanish language. Whatever the reason, here stood the blacksmith and his two apprentices holding sledge-hammers in their fists, and quite honestly I didn't like the looks on their faces. All in all, I concluded that it would be wisest to settle with an unaggressive agreement. I paid for the one hundred and three shoes and was able to escape paying for the rest of the order.

We rode straight east and soon Nacori Chico disappeared from sight.

We rode through extremely dry, rolling land and then over two mountain ranges that extended below the actual Sierra Madre. On a steep slope we saw a single wooden cross planted in the ground. A tragedy had occurred here that caused quite a commotion, something I briefly mentioned earlier. It was back in 1927, when a Mexican by the name of Francisco Fimbres and his family came riding down from the mountain after visiting a ranch higher up. His wife rode in front with their six-year-old boy, Heraldo, sitting in front of her on the saddle. Francisco followed behind with their little girl. His wife, who came from the highly respected family of Grajedaenes, was beautiful and fair-haired, just as the children were.

It was a lovely, sunny day in the mountains, just the right day for a journey home to the village. The little family felt happy and safe; down here in the foothills of the Sierra Madre there was nothing to fear. But right where the path winds down the mountain, there is a sudden turn that leads past a small boulder pile by the edge of a steep slope. Here lay a band of Apaches watching the family's every move.

The woman rode past the rock pile and continued down the hill. Then suddenly a gunshot rang out. She and the boy fell to the ground while her husband, a short ways behind, jerked his horse around and galloped off down the valley to get help from some cowboys who he knew lived down there. On the way, he quickly put the girl down in some bushes. He did have a loaded revolver with him, so something could be said about the predicament in which he left his family.

Francisco finally got hold of the cowboys and charged back. He found his wife's bloody body on the ground, which the Apaches had practically cut to pieces. Even worse, it turned out that the shot that had been fired hadn't even struck her. It was the knife wounds that had killed her. The little boy, Heraldo, was nowhere to be seen. The Apaches had kidnapped him. The Mexicans tried in vain to pursue the attackers but the crafty Indians seemed to have vanished into thin air.

As previously mentioned, this all had to do with taking revenge. Many years earlier the Mexicans had kidnapped the Apache girl Lupe, and now they were even.

In utter desperation, Francisco Fimbres immediately went about organizing a rescue trip into the Sierra Madre. This was an extremely sensitive situation, however, because if they did not first succeed in taking the Apaches by surprise the Indians would surely and quickly kill the boy. The captured Apache woman, Lupe, explained this clearly and advised them to bear with it until the natives had had the boy long enough to develop affection for him.

The years went by and little Heraldo lived up there in the mountains with the Apaches. In 1929 various expeditions were organized to the Sierra Madre in search of the boy. They were experienced people who used the utmost caution. They often trekked in on foot, covered their faces and straw hats in black, and seldom lit a fire. For months they pushed on through the most rugged regions of the mountain ranges, but all in vain.

Then in 1931, a small expedition under the leadership of Ramon Hutardo, my host in Nacori Chico, by sheer chance came upon four Apaches, a man and three women. They were riding mules and were not aware of the Mexicans until they were close in on them. The Apache warrior was not one to leave his women in a bind but immediately began fighting against the more powerful forces. He sought cover behind trees and fired away with a rifle dating back to the 1880s. All the Apaches were shot down on the spot except for one woman who managed to escape despite her fatal wounds. Afterward, the Mexicans scalped the Indians and sent these to the Governor of Sonora. The belongings of the deceased included some hides, a little ammunition, and four carved wooden dolls, one for each of them.

Obviously, this kind of slaughter was the most foolish thing the Mexicans could have done if they wanted to get hold of the captive boy. What followed was to be expected. When a few Mexicans sometime later passed the place where the Apaches had been killed, it turned out that the mountain Apaches had been there. The bodies were covered with hides and stones. Nearby lay the white boy with his throat slashed. The Mexicans buried them all and placed a cross over each of the graves. There in the heart of the Sierra Madre now rests the little fair-haired Heraldo, side by side with the Natives.

We made camp by a river right below the Sierra Madre's steep mountain slopes. It was beautiful there, with shady trees hanging over dark, deep pools and rippling water. As we sit around the fire, a Mexican comes riding into our camp and hands me a letter, explaining that it arrived in Nacori Chico a short time after we had left. A rider on his way south through the mountains had brought it with him and given it to the Mexican, who then had ridden as fast as he could to catch up with us again. The letter was from my brother in Norway. Among other things he writes that Spot is dead, my wonderful lead dog from many polar sled trips.

I sit a long time by the fire that evening. My thoughts wander far away to the snow country and to all that Spot meant to me since he came into the world in a snowdrift up in Greenland, a scruffy little puppy with only a stump of a tail. For many years we shared good and bad together. There were musk ox and bear hunts, endless sled trips in the sun, darkness, and snowstorms. Spot's bushy tail was always waving ahead of all the other dogs as he cut his way through with his head tilted to the side, alert and ready for the slightest command. There was also the time of the raging snowstorm when everything seemed so hopeless. I dug myself into a snowdrift and used Spot as a warming pillow – Oh well.

The moon has risen and sheds its light through the dark forests of the Sierra Madre. The fire has died down into a glowing heap. My three Indian companions lie there in their sleeping bags like strange mummies, each with their rifles beside them. Even I have settled down for the night. Then suddenly something moves down by my legs. I jump up and there's a dog, a little raggedy rascal of a brown dog that had lain down by my bag and fallen asleep. It had probably followed after that Mexican rider, and when he left it decided that it might as well stay with us.

This was how we acquired our newest expedition partner, who followed us throughout our entire journey. Mora dubbed it Chikapu, which was a distorted name the Mexicans used for a certain Indian tribe. He found it so incredibly hilarious that a dog should have such a name that during our whole trip he unfailingly burst into laughter whenever I called the animal.

There wasn't much to say for Chikapu; he was no good for hunting or as a watchdog. In fact, if the mountain Apaches were to come at us intending harm Chikapu would come wagging his tail to meet them. This was just a very hungry and lonely dog that had an infinite trust in people.

# 11
# Through the Heart of the Sierra Madre

We seemed to climb forever up the steep slopes. If they had been any steeper, people and mules wouldn't have been able to cling to them. Finally, we were back up to the wooded areas just below the Sierra Madre peaks at about nine thousand feet. Below us to the west lay the precipitous cliffs with their vertical drops and large screes where patches of autumn-colored trees flared up like dazzling flames. An endless sea of rugged, dark-green mountains stretched to the north, east, and south. Somewhere within those towering pine forests lived the mountain Apaches, and now it was only a matter of finding them.

We didn't get off to a very good start because as soon as we reached the territory right below the summits, all the Indians succumbed to altitude sickness. They curled up in their sleeping bags, laid with their heads covered, and didn't make a sound the entire day.

I flung my gun over my shoulder and took off alone to look around in the woods. I was soon in the middle of some strange, jagged terrain jumbled with canyons where there were hordes of deer. Small herds of the animals grazed in the knee-high grass that covered the slopes, and they were very easy to approach.

During this entire journey through the Sierra Madre, I found many signs of a prehistoric people who had lived in those mountain regions. Obvious evidence was what the Mexicans called the *trincheras* structures, which Carl Lumholtz also talked about. Stone walls were built across the steep hills and then filled in with soil so that small, level areas could be used for growing crops. There could be up to seven of these terraces on one hill. Nearby lay some stone houses in ruins, and in them I found a variety of artifacts such as arrowheads, axes, rock clubs, pieces of pottery, and stone mortars for grinding corn.

I ran across tracks of wolves and bears, but not of Indians. On the top of a ridge, however, I found a rock cairn that looked as if it had been some kind of Apache offering site.

When I returned to camp, the ill Indians were considerably better. Yahnozah had dragged himself to his feet and was busy making *izae*, a medicine. Every evening he and Mora, individually and routinely, would collect plants and roots and brew up medicines. Yahnozah made his according to Apache traditions, and Mora did as the Mexicans. It was obvious that each of them considered his own recipes to be the best. Both of them knew the names of the every plant and tree that grew in the mountains and knew exactly which one to use as a cure for certain illnesses. Judging from the medley of medicinal concoctions they now and again gulped down, one would have thought that they were in complete agony with stomach pains, liver diseases, backaches, headaches, and lung and heart disease, plus a fair amount of other ailments.

This evening Yahnozah was clearly brewing a very exquisite medicine because he was more secretive and zealous than usual as he mixed his herbs and cooked the brew over the hot embers. When I asked him what the new medicine would help for, he replied, "This medicine works against everything." Later, he began to rely more and more on this universal remedy.

The medicinal and healing know-how of the Apaches, not to mention the Mexicans', deserves a closer understanding. A variety of medicines are used based on ancient Indian traditions. A thorough study of these different plants and roots would surely be interesting and possibly applicable in modern medical science.

As soon as the Indians were feeling better, we headed northward, first along the Sierra Madre's western crest and later more toward the northeast. We generally spent several nights at each campsite and took short day trips in through the country. Mora and I would head out in one direction and the two Apaches would go in another. We were all anxious to be the first to find fresh signs of the mountain Natives, and the others were even more eager when I offered a reward to the first one who caught a glimpse of the Indians.

It was becoming more and more clear that if we were to succeed in finding such a group of reluctant, shy people in such rough terrain, we were going to need a lot of luck. We were now drawing closer to the heart of the Sierra Madre, which was just as rugged a wilderness as the western parts. Every which way there were deep, tree-lined gorges that made progress as difficult as possible, and farthest to the east ran a blue mountain range from north to south. Each canyon provided perfect hiding places where great numbers of people could be living without anybody knowing. There were also several deep caves that were well concealed by surrounding shrubs. In short, this place was a haven for anyone who wanted to hide away.

Now and then we came across old trails that, most likely, were from the time when several Apaches populated this area. It was here that we found almost invisible signs of the mountain Apaches, such as a rock turned over or a minute slash on a tree. Mora brought these things to my attention that I otherwise would have probably overlooked. Another sign the Apaches used that Mora was familiar with was some straw or grass braided in the shape of a clover. Usually, two of these were laid side by side on the ground and held in place by some small rocks. The clover in front would then point one way or another, indicating the direction.

It was now the beginning of December, and the nights were getting chilly. During the day, though, it was pleasantly warm and the sun shone high in the blue sky. Flowers still bloomed, and between the pine trees we could see small colorful patches whose fragrances filled the air.

As we rode through the forest, something flaming red would suddenly stick out amongst all that green – the strawberry tree, madroña, which was now full of cascading red berries. We would occasionally stop the mules and break off some branches so we could have a tasty treat as we rode along. The branches of the strawberry trees were often dotted with silky bags about eight inches long in the bottom of which were black larvae.

The birds didn't take the coming of winter too seriously. We constantly spotted blue jays around, and every once in a while we saw a flock of doves. One time we even saw a mighty eagle soaring over the deep canyons. A few of the world's largest woodpeckers, indigenous birds of the Sierra Madre, even appeared. It was a beautiful bird about eighteen inches long with tremendous black and white plumage.

When it hammered away on a dead tree it sounded like a machine gun firing through the woods.

The days passed and we continued wandering and searching. We first went up some very high knolls and next down into deep canyons where small creeks trickled between steep, rocky slopes. Bears often used these creekbeds to make their way around, and we once surprised one of these creatures as it was feasting on a deer. Another time, we caught a glimpse of a forest wolf as big as a grown polar wolf. Mountain lions, jaguars, lynx, wildcats, raccoons, mountain goats, and even elk live up in these parts, and once in a while we would catch glimpses of them or run across their tracks.

Once on one of our side trips we reached the steep precipices of the westernmost Sierra Madre. We climbed out onto a crag from where we had a panoramic view in all directions and then searched the place with our binoculars. Straight to the north, the cliff formed a sort of cove in the mountain chain, and we had a perfect view over this to a tree-lined ridge. As I scanned the knoll with my binoculars I became aware of something alive moving upright at the edge of the forest, hurrying between the trees. It must have been a human being!

We immediately took off to investigate, but the path was long and arduous and before we got there it started to rain heavily, destroying any tracks. We looked around but didn't find any sign of people. My Indian companions, who were skeptical about my sighting, suggested that it might have been a deer I had seen. But I felt certain about what I saw.

It could have been one of the Apaches' scouts I had caught a glimpse of. They would have kept themselves informed about our travels in the mountains, so this probably wasn't the first time they had been close to us.

Torrential rains continued now for days and it became increasingly difficult to travel onward. The clay soil became a slippery mess, and the mules had a hard time finding a foothold on the steep inclines and declines. Our dog Chikapu also wasn't very happy about the conditions and seemed droopier and gloomier than ever.

However, the sun returned and it was once again pleasant to wander around so high under the blue sky, regardless of the tough going at times. Mora had to swing up north to look in on his family. We agreed that in the meantime we would wait for him here within these mountains where we would also let the pack animals have a break. After we had made camp, we found out that the place where Yah-nozah's old Spanish treasure was supposedly hidden wasn't far from where we were. As it turned out, we would be able to take a look for it. Yahnozah then told us about the treasure.

About fifty years ago, when Yahnozah roamed the Sierra Madre as one of Geronimo's faithful followers, the chief's son-in-law Djae-ilkinnae happened to find a strange map in the pocket of a Spaniard he had killed. He later had a white friend translate the text, and it turned out that the map showed three different places where the Spaniards had hidden their treasures. He succeeded in finding one of these, a great pile of gold and silver bullion hidden away in a cave. However, neither he nor the four Indians who were with him touched any of it. Precious metals did not mean much to the Apaches at that time, and they couldn't possibly take anything like that with them, continually chased by the enemy as they were.

Yahnozah first heard about this treasure from his hunting buddy Chili-yae-innae, a Mexican who at a young age had been captured and adopted by the Apaches and who later was killed in a dramatic fight near Nacori Chico. During a hunting trip, Yahnozah's friend had pointed to a cliff wall in a deep canyon and explained clearly how he had run across a cave there that contained an incredible amount of gold and silver bullion. The cave was partly covered by a rock. Yahnozah took note of the place but he wasn't interested enough at the time to investigate it more carefully.

During this same time, Geronimo and his people had their perma-nent camp on a ridge across the canyon. When their enemy continued to chase them through the mountains, the Apaches were forced to move farther south. But before they left this old camp, Geronimo gathered his people around him, pointed toward the canyon's rocky wall, and said, "If something should happen to any of us, the others must remember that down there in the cliff wall, there is a cave full of gold and silver." Yahnozah, who at the time was standing right by the chief, again noted the spot where the treasure was supposedly located.

Geronimo and his old guards were later taken as prisoners to the United States, and nobody had had a chance to search for the treasure – not until fifty years later when Yahnozah returned.

Yahnozah's story, which included all the details, seemed to be entirely true. He was determined to find the treasure, which had haunted his thoughts since the time he was in American prisons and learned the value of gold. What he said also corresponded with old Mexican traditions. As previously mentioned, there was nothing strange about precious metals being hidden far away in the mountains. It is a fact that back then the Apaches rampaged across large parts of Sonora so much that several mines had to be abandoned and the owners had to quickly hide their gold and silver as best they could.

On the day of our search for the treasure, we started with a turkey hunt. Early in the morning, Andrew and I were awakened by a peeping sound that seemed to rise from the hillside. We were out of our sleeping bags in a flash, grabbed out guns, and sneaked up toward a forest higher up on the hill. We soon saw scores of turkeys holding their morning concert in a small sunlit patch between the trees. We shot a huge bird and afterward quickly prepared it for breakfast. It was a delicious and nourishing meal, something that we could surely use, since emptying a cave full of heavy silver and gold could be quite a strenuous job.

It was a ways to ride but after a while we reached the place where we could see over toward the treasure canyon. It was deep and rugged. Yahnozah pointed to a ridge and explained that there was where the Apaches had their camp when Geronimo explained about the treasure.

We tied up the horses and climbed down. Yahnozah was all fired up, in fact he was so excited that he slid long stretches on his rear end. When we reached the steep cliffs that led down into the depths, he climbed along a ledge and stopped at a spot with jagged rocks. There were layers of huge boulders with deep, dark caves behind them. We searched them all carefully but with no luck. I asked Yahnozah if he was quite sure he had remembered the place and he answered that he thought he did but there were some things that had changed from when he was young. I insisted then that just to be sure we should systematically search one of the cliffs. However, getting him to collaborate with a specific plan proved to be quite hopeless. But we climbed around in the rocks and searched the different caves with suppressed anticipation, thinking that at any moment we might grab onto a gold bar.

We continued like this for days. It was strenuous. There were plenty of caves but to get to them wasn't easy. Sometimes I would balance on the edge of the cliffs, other times I clawed my way along the steep rock by jamming my fingers into the small cracks. It was worse still when I dangled in the lasso over the abyss. This reminded me of stories by courageous authors who described how fun and exciting it is to hang like this with your feet suspended in empty space. As for me, I didn't like any of these aerial acrobatics and instead felt incredibly uneasy. This was especially true when I was once hanging down a rock trying to swing over to a particularly alluring cave. The thin tree to which the rope was tied began to give way and all of its roots started to loosen from the rocks. The tree swayed back and forth, keeping time with each of my swings. After that, I preferred solid ground under my feet, but this was actually not easy to find on those crumbling rocks. Once when I had climbed quite a ways up my foothold suddenly gave way and I tumbled back down the steep slope. The only reason I escaped unharmed was probably because there must be some other way that I was supposed to die.

We didn't find the treasure. I don't doubt that it was there in those rocks, but Mora was probably returning soon, and I didn't want to use any more time searching for treasure. Besides, it was evident that half a century of varying degrees of rain and erosion had changed the landscape. It would have surely demanded both time and hard work to give the many nooks and crannies of those cliffs a thorough search.

There were three worn out and disappointed treasure hunters who sat around the fire that night chewing on turkey meat. The most discontented person was Yahnozah, who for so many years had looked forward to the moment when he would crawl into the cave and retrieve that old Spanish treasure. He sat there heavy and quiet, until suddenly he burst out, "Hundred times I hunt in the canyon with my friend and walked past treasure. I could have said one word and he lead me to cave. Now everything too late." I then said that perhaps what had happened was best for all of us. Yahnozah pondered on this a while, brightened up a bit and seemed to find a kind of comfort in these words of wisdom.

But a treasure is a treasure, and I can still see the rock wall before me where just a little farther up a deep, enticing cave, huge piles of Spanish silver and gold lay hidden. But I never got to search that cave.

Mora returned and we headed south through the heart of the Sierra Madre. The map was still quite useless, but my Indian friends knew the way. The Bavispe River, flanked by brilliant red leafy trees, wound its way down a canyon at the bottom of the mighty mountain range in the west. After a while, we rode by the spot where the Apaches had been shot when the Mexicans had tried to retrieve the captured boy, Heraldo. I found a simple, worn-out old pot here that the Indians must have had with them. There were no fewer than eleven holes in it that had been roughly patched up. The pot had undoubtedly been considered a greatly valued item. On a nearby ridge, some human bones lay under a large oak tree. I was later told that they belonged to the Apache woman who had escaped during the fight. She had died from her wounds and later her body was found and hung from the tree.

Our progress was slow because the country was just as rough a tangle as before. The surrounding mountainside was made of volcanic rubble and heavily eroded. I never did see granite. The soil was quite fertile up here at higher altitudes, and the grass grew thick and tall. Every so often the forest would open up and peaceful meadows would emerge before us. There were hordes of deer, and we spotted anywhere from thirty to seventy of the animals a day. Mora said that it was getting close to the deer's mating season, which in the mountains began about the third week of December, a month later than in the lowlands. He also explained that in the spring the animals would have large clumps of larvae in their nostrils, something that could also be found on the wild reindeer in Arctic regions. There were also scores of wild turkeys, and sometimes we startled large flocks of them up into the air, sending them flapping in all directions. Now and then we also ran across snakes, regardless of how late in the year it was. Besides the usual rattlesnakes, we saw one that was blue and another that was almost completely white. The bees made their hives up underneath the rocky overhangs, and if we wanted a good taste of honey, we would shoot one of the nests down. This took a bit of talent because the hive had to be hit right at the base.

We continually ran across *trincheras*, rock terraces on the hills, and ruins of the stone homes left by prehistoric people. Every once in a while, we also found caves and buildings, which for the most part consisted of stone homes but were different from the meticulously made cave dwellings I would later discover farther south. In most of the caves and in other places along the cliffs, primitive drawings and signs were often drawn in yellow, green, and red.

We carried on down to the Bavispe River and crossed it many times, to the great despair of Chikapu, who did not like swimming in cold river water. Mora told us that there were large fat trout in the river, but I didn't catch any despite tempting them the entire evening with delicious grasshoppers. We were now in the portion of the Sierra Madre that lies within Chihuahua, and we continued our systematic search of the mountains here. Relations between the three Indians I was traveling with and myself continued to be very good, and they pleasantly and willingly went about their tasks. It was no use to be militant and issue orders because an Apache won't be ordered around. But if they are treated congenially and are made interested in the venture, everything works out just fine. In fact, I even got Yahnozah to wash himself in the mornings, and I consider that to have been quite an accomplishment.

On the other hand, it was a bit odd when we sat around our evening fires. Mora only spoke Spanish, Yahnozah only Apache, and I spoke English and just a little Spanish, but not enough to get a real conversation going. Andrew spoke fluent Spanish, Apache, and English, and it ended up that he often took control of the conversation as he could alternate between the three languages. Otherwise, he was the one that I liked the least, because I never knew where he stood. Mora was a killer and a rough fellow but in the mountains he had so far been all right. This, however, would later change. Yahnozah was the one I trusted the most. The seventy-six-year-old Apache seemed to become more fit every day. He sat like a grenadier on his white mule and never said a word if he sometimes had to carry out heavy chores. When we would take off, he could suddenly gallop ahead and disappear into the woods for hours before we saw him again. He might have been checking out one or another familiar spot from his younger days or perhaps he was scouting for his free-roaming tribesmen. He never explained his disappearances and we never asked. Moreover, he continued his songs at night and his prayers in the morning. The first thing he did after getting dressed was to walk a short distance into the woods and kneel facing the rising sun. He then took out a pinch of yellow pollen from a leather pouch he had with him, put it in the palm of his hand and blew it up into the air.

One dark morning, Andrew and I happened to be the first ones up and were building a fire while Yahnozah was still getting dressed under the canvas cover of his sleeping bag. Suddenly, I stopped and listened. Through the still morning air, I could hear the sound of some type of bird. I looked around puzzled, thinking that it was strange that birds had already started their morning singing while the forest was still very dark. I heard the sound again, this time closer. Andrew listened intently, then said, "I'll be damned, if that sound isn't coming from Yahnozah's sleeping bag." Sure enough he was right. I could now clearly hear a fine, trilling sound coming from that dark bundle over there. "He couldn't possibly have a bird in his sleeping bag, could he?" I cautiously suggested. "It almost sounds like it," Andrew replied.

Yahnozah was almost finished dressing and then he threw the canvas to the side. We eagerly looked for the bird but none flew out. He sat for a while tying his boots and suddenly I heard a new sound, beautiful and pure. This time though I caught the songbird; it turned out to be Yahnozah himself. The sounds were coming from his nose. Except for a few pauses in between, the concert continued throughout the day and picked up again later on in the trip despite Yahnozah's desperate attempts to ward it off. We pretended nothing was wrong as it was obviously a sensitive issue with the old warrior. We all have our burdens to bear and his was that in his old age he had to deal with a nose that occasionally whistled like a bird.

It was getting colder. Water puddles froze at night, and once in a while a light snow would fall but quickly melt again. The mornings were perhaps a little nippy, but then again there was nothing more beautiful. I shall never forget those quiet, crisp sunrises when the forest-covered ridges that reached so high into the blue sky glistened with layers of frost.

One day I learned from Yahnozah that Geronimo's well-known stronghold was not far away. This was the place where the Chiricahua Apaches had their main camp in the old days and which was supposedly located in such a rugged spot that they felt safe there against any attack. It was natural to assume that the Apaches who still existed in the mountains would seek shelter in their old hiding place, so we headed in that direction.

After a few days' journey south, we rode through a high pass that Mora called Puerta de los Apaches. Directly to the south, we came upon a large and rugged mountain. We crossed the headwater of the Bavispe River and climbed up its steep banks. Beneath the summit, Yahnozah stopped his mule and said, "Here we stayed."

A better place to make camp could hardly be found. It was a small, grassy field surrounded by large pine trees and with a rippling brook winding through the green flora. Mountains and gorges were easily seen through small openings in the forest.

It appeared that not only had the Apaches in their time found shelter here, but prehistoric Indians had as well. On a little hill there were remnants of some old stone homes, where I found various flint tools and a stone ax.

Yahnozah then told us a thing or two about the times when he lived at the camp with Geronimo. He pointed at two terraced clearings in the pine forest and said that Geronimo lived on the lowest one and Juh lived on the upper one, each with his own people. Juh was actually the Chiricahua Apaches' chief and Geronimo his good friend, and they ended up dividing the people between themselves. After Juh drowned in a drunken stupor, Geronimo became leader of all the Chiricahua Apaches.

We walk into the tall pine forest, nearly ninety feet high. Yahnozah points and says, "Many hundred tents stood here. They were made like tepees and covered with grass, leaves, or branches. There was much happening here." I ask what else they spent their time on when they were in the camp and Yahnozah replies, "We gambled, hunted, and ate. We always had lots of food." Then I ask, "What were the raids like?" He answers, "Often good battles. First we send scouts. They checked out every little thing before the attack. We held many talks and would decide what each man do. Then all carefully approached and on signal pounce upon them. We almost always defeat the Mexicans. One time we kill many people in little village in Chihuahua and take large booty."

When I ask if Geronimo had all the authority during the planning sessions, Yahnozah sneers and says "No leader can order over Apaches. All Indians have their say and make decisions together. He who is dissatisfied takes his gun and leaves. But Geronimo gave wise counsel, therefore we often listened to him."

I continue, "What was Geronimo like?"

Yahnozah is evasive but says, "We stayed with him because he was good at bringing our people into safety. Geronimo was a great medicine man who saw the enemy in a vision even when far away. He had a spirit in the mountain that helped him, and to this spirit we all prayed."

I then ask if the captured American boy, Charley McComas, had been in this camp.

Yahnozah answers, "I often saw him here. He played with Apache boys and enjoyed it here. Later he came to the camp that General Crook attacked. Then many Indians fled and he was gone. I don't think he was killed. I was in the Sierra Madre with Geronimo to the end and knew everything that happened in the mountains."[1]

In the end, I ask what the Apaches did with the white women whom they often took prisoner.

"We treated them well," he briefly replies. A bit agitated, he then adds, "This I don't like to talk about. That was a long time ago." It was almost as if he wanted to shake away some of his memories.

Just beyond the camp on the other side of the grass clearing stood the Apache's old dance area, a firmly stomped square on the forest floor. It was at least ninety feet long and sixty feet wide. I could almost see the warriors dancing there after a raid, the fire burning, the drums pounding, and tempers rising. But in among the people stood some trembling white women fearing for their lives.

We now head west and to our surprise happen upon a small ranch. The rich mountain pastures had tempted a Mexican family to try making a living in these dangerous parts. So far, the people had made it work, but they didn't wander far from the house without having their guns along. It was true that cattle and horses were stolen from them quite frequently but they realized that this was something that could happen.

I asked if they had seen any Apaches lately and was told that only a few weeks ago the Natives had stolen two horses from their corral, one which even had a bell tied around its neck. Furthermore, the Mexicans had also recently seen a campfire way up in the mountains to the northwest.

We rode a ways down the mountain and made camp for the night. It was a beautiful moonlit evening in the forest, and a small creek glowed in the light as it flowed over the edge of a nearby knoll. There was a wonderful view to the south, where dim mountains stretched for miles and stars shone above.

As we sat around the crackling fire, it occurred to me that there was something odd about the Indians that evening. They sat together a long time talking and something was clearly brewing. Even Chikapu lay there with his head on his paws, ear sticking straight up, staring into the fire.

Eventually, Andrew came over to me and said that they had concluded that the Apaches must be close by. We knew that they had recently stolen horses from the ranch we had visited and that a fire had been spotted up in the mountains to the west. But something else strange had happened, he continued. Early in the morning when we were nearing Geronimo's stronghold, all three of them had heard someone shout from the forest on the other side of the river. They had shouted back and were answered once. They later discussed this with the people on the ranch and were now sure that it had been Apaches who had shouted. He suggested then that he and Yahnozah should ride up the mountain where the campfire had been spotted and take a look around there a while. Every evening they would beat their drums and sing Apache songs. In the meantime, it would be best for Mora and I to stay farther back so that the mountain Apaches wouldn't be frightened off.

This was good news! Now that he mentioned it, I also remembered that Mora and Andrew had turned and shouted back that morning as we were riding up a steep hill. I had been trailing behind with the mules and assumed that they had shouted to me. So it was the Apaches that they had answered.

I quickly agreed with Andrew's suggestion and began to discuss it in more detail. There was a renewed feeling in our camp, excitement was in the air. After all our toil through the mountains it looked as if we finally might have a bit of luck. Afterward, Yahnozah and Andrew began singing some old Apache songs more fervently than ever before. Between songs, Yahnozah would shout loudly into the woods, "Kodih nogk'ii hikah!" (Friends are coming!). It felt as if the Natives were standing right behind those dark trees beyond the fire-light watching us.

Early the next morning we took off toward the steep mountain ridge to the west where the campfire had been spotted. After a distance, Mora and I stopped and settled down on a very old dancing field close to some stone ruins as the other two continued on. While waiting for them I used my time to investigate the ruins, which were quite ancient and now overgrown with moss. There were about ten houses in all, most of which were built as squares, about six by nine feet. Deer grazed in the surrounding hills, and at night the wolves howled so much that it sounded like they were holding congress out there in the woods.

But disappointment struck. After singing and scouting for several days, Yahnozah and Andrew turned back empty-handed. We now headed south toward the little mountain village of Chuichupa. We would replenish our supplies and then continue west toward the notorious mountain region Espinosa del Diablo, or the Devil's Back-bone. This also had been a popular place for the Apaches to stay in the old days. Someplace there in the west, Yahnozah had also hoped to find some booty that he had hidden in a cave when he roamed around fighting the Mexicans. A saddle and some Spanish shawls were supposedly a part of what was there. As we were riding along, we met two Mexicans on horseback who each had a deer tied to the back of his saddle. One of them was Jesus Ortega, a man with whom I would later have contact concerning other matters. It turned out that he was some kind of officer or police chief in these parts and was now searching the mountains for four bandits who had recently killed five soldiers in the little village of Granados. They had stolen the military safe containing four thousand pesos and then took off through the Sierra Madre. They had good weapons, plenty of ammunition, and were pretty desperate so we'd better keep an eye out for them, he said. "What should we do if we run into the bandits?" I asked. "Shoot 'em down," replied Ortega.

"I'd like to have that in writing please," I said and afterward received. Mora, who was used to shooting down people, considered the whole thing an everyday affair. Bandits quite often drifted around the mountains, he said. For me, however, this was quite a unique situation. I had been given many authorizations in my life, but up until now none of them had ever empowered me to shoot people.

Three days before Christmas, an intense snowstorm began to blow. A fury of white, heavy snowflakes whirled across the green forest. Something special about snow often triggers memories. Soon Christmas would be here again.

We had not ridden far before we hit milder drafts and the snow melted as soon as it touched us. Soon we were soaked to the skin. Water poured off the mules and big blobs of heavy snow and pine needles clogged up under their hooves, which caused them to keep stumbling down the steep hillsides. Then we rode over a mountain that was probably about nine thousand feet high and came up against bitter cold and knee-deep snow. We froze like Popsicles sitting there soaking wet on our horses.

We rode for eleven hours straight until we reached a forest clearing in the early morning hours where there were about a dozen cabins scattered about. This was the small ranch settlement of Nortenia, which lay about six miles north of Chuichupa. The first thing I saw was a large black pig that groveled and grunted around in the deep snow while two bouncy little puppies tried to grab onto its ears. A straggly, frozen rooster stood on the fence with its one leg, wholeheartedly detesting the snow.

Mora knew the people here and led us into one of the cabins, which was small inside but very cozy. Sitting around the crackling, thick pine logs in the fireplace were a woman and small children as well as a gray-bearded blind man with a little girl in his lap. There was something about the man that was pure and good, qualities of someone who has suffered much. The owner of the house was out hunting and was not expected back for a while. I learned that this person had been captured by the Apaches when he was young and had lived with them for about twenty years. I expect that he is quite old by now.

We were incredibly hungry, frozen, and tired so it felt wonderful to come inside and meet these humble, gracious people. We sat so close to the fireplace that steam rose from our wet clothes as we warmed ourselves. While we waited for the food that was being prepared, Andrew mentioned that they didn't need to go to all that trouble. Old Yahnozah, on the other hand, didn't make a sound. He was so tired that he kept nodding and dozing off right where he sat. That guy was made of iron, he was.

People in these regions did quite a bit of fur hunting, and I got hold of some beautiful wolf, mountain lion, and beaver skins. It was surprising to find beavers so far south. Yahnozah was very interested in the beaver skin and said that these were highly prized with the Apaches' old enemies, the Comanche Indians. The men would cut thin strips from the skins and tied them to their long braids, he said.

The next morning the sky was blue and sun glittered over the snow-covered fields and forests. When I walked out into the dazzling light I just about stumbled over a tame deer that lay by the door next to the farm dog. A herd of white goats stood in the sun next to a wall, and over in the field two bulls plodded off in front of a wagon loaded down with wood. The rooster had regained his strength after the bout of heavy weather and was happily facing the sun and crowing.

We continued south toward Chuichupa. The sun quickly grew warmer and the snow slid off the branches in heavy clumps and melted as soon as it touched the ground. Small creeks trickled with water, patches of grass and heather cropped up, and the blue jays carried on like crazy. It was Christmastime but the feeling was of spring in the woods.

The forest began to thin and soon we rode out onto a large open plain where several houses lay close together. The homes were larger and nicer than usual, compared to other Mexican villages. We rode up to one of the closest farms, where a husky fellow came out to greet us. He looked us up and down a bit and for good reason: we were shabby and bearded after our trip through the mountains. I stuttered away in my Spanish and asked if there was any possibility for us to put our mules on his farm for a short time. In clear English the stranger said, "That's fine, but step inside and have something to eat." These were full-blooded Americans we had run into way out here in the middle of the rugged Sierra Madre, a small community of Mormons.

# 12

# Dramatic Christmas

When polygamy was outlawed in the United States, small groups of Mormons immigrated to northern Mexico and began new lives for themselves there. About forty-five years ago, one small group journeyed into the Sierra Madre and settled at Chuichupa, a small mountain plateau about six thousand feet above sea level. They cleared the land for agricultural use, built houses, and began raising cattle. Then about twenty years ago the revolution broke out and many of the new settlers were killed and the others had to quickly flee back to the United States. After conditions settled again, the Mormons returned to Chuichupa. The farms lay in ashes and everything else that they had owned was destroyed, but they didn't give up. They cleared the land and built it up and today, once again, a small, tidy settlement stands here on the highlands.

Up here in the mountains surrounded by wilderness in every direction, the people live a pioneer life just as difficult and dangerous as the settlers of the Wild West in America. They have had to continually guard themselves against the Apaches, who not long ago massacred Mormon families in the vicinity. Mexicans who have also settled in the village have not been that easy to deal with, either. Some of them are certainly good people, but others are rough and temperamental fellows who have been involved with this and that and are quick to grab their guns. As time goes by, I learn of some of the nasty deeds that some of the Mexicans have had a hand in. The number of people that these fellows have killed would be enough to fill a good-sized cemetery. Human life meant uncomfortably little in these parts.

Despite the many difficulties, the Mormons managed well. They are industrious people who do not buckle under hardship, and their determination and honesty have won respect from the Mexicans.

New land is constantly being cultivated. Corn, potatoes, and oats grow favorably at this elevation, and the cattle fare well in the rich mountain pastures.

The Farnsworth family owned the place we happened upon, and more hospitable and friendly people are rarely found. They had a pack of grown sons on the farm and one beautiful blond girl. The wife was of Scandinavian heritage, as with many of the Mormons here, and she had the true courage of a real pioneer woman. Once when I was talking with her in the kitchen she said, "Our laundry situation is completely awful. The Indian woman who usually helps us hasn't been here for several days, so I guess she's probably been killed." She said it calmly and matter-of-factly as if there wasn't anything extraordinary about such an incident. When I asked how she might know this she replied that the woman lived in continual fear of her husband, who had many times threatened to kill her. Later, sure enough, it turned out that the woman had disappeared. Her shoes and some of her clothing had been found in the forest.

When we arrived in Chuichupa, old Farnsworth took us to an empty house at the edge of the village where he said we could stay as long as we wanted. It was a pleasant dwelling with a fireplace and a floor to sleep on and we enjoyed it after our toil in the mountains. One of the first things I did here was fire Mora. Toward the end of the trip I realized how little this fellow could be trusted. Worst of all, he had gained influence over Andrew, who absolutely idolized this unscrupulous Indian who smiled when he told about all the people he had killed. Mora was outraged by the firing but as long as he was sober he didn't venture to express his feelings.

Then came Christmas Eve. I was sitting in front of the fireplace at our place chatting with Jess, the eldest of the Farnsworth boys, when suddenly Mora and Andrew sail in very drunk. Mora is feeling braver now and immediately starts to argue about being fired. He proposes several ridiculous demands, waves his arms about and acts like quite a man. I tell him what I think and in the end he and Andrew take off in a rage.

After a while, Jess and I stroll across the fields toward the Farnsworth farm to feed the mules, which are in an adjoining corral. We finish our work and stand chatting by the small shed where all of our expedition gear has been stored. The evening is cool and dark. We can barely make out the dim shadows of the nearby mules as they stand chewing on corncob stalks. High above us is a world of twinkling stars.

Two men appear in the corral. It's Mora and Andrew, both quite inebriated. As they come closer, they turn sideways and start talking quietly together. In an instant, Mora darts into the shed and a moment later he's back with a rifle in his hand. He quickly loads the gun and at about forty-five feet away he aims it at me. He doesn't say a word, but just threateningly stands there in the dark swaying a bit because he's so drunk. Andrew is standing nearby with his hands in his pockets enjoying the predicament.

The satisfied smile on Mora's face every time he talked about the people he had killed is the first thing that passes through my mind. Then I think to myself it's important not to excite the guy. We have to pretend that nothing's wrong and continue our conversation. With all my might I pretend as best I can and light my pipe, look up at the stars, and say this or that about the weather. Jess mumbles something in reply but there's little flow in our conversation, which soon threatens to end altogether. I fumble for something else to talk about as I glance over at the gun pointing straight at my chest. I find it difficult to keep a light, trivial discussion going as long as a drunk Indian is aiming a loaded rifle at me. A long, silent pause ensues. The only sounds we hear are the mules chewing over by the dark walls of the house and the distant howl of a wolf in the mountains. Suddenly, Jess says calmly and slowly, "I guess this is about enough." Then we both turn and very slowly walk up toward the farm, uncomfortably slow. We get closer and closer to the house and with every step I think, "Now it's going to go off!" Finally, we reach a spot alongside a small shed and one step to the side, out of firing range.

I sat in front of the Farnsworth fireplace until nearly midnight. Then it was time to go to bed. I would rather have not spent the night with my bunch because the two drunk Indians couldn't be trusted. On the other hand, this would mean that I would "lose face," as the Chinese say, if I now showed any sign of fear. I wandered over the dark fields, stumbled in ditches and over rocks and fumbled my way to the house. Yahnozah lay there asleep but the others had not yet returned. I loaded my gun and took it to bed with me and then dozed off.

When it was almost morning, I awoke to a tremendous commotion. It was Mora and Andrew staggering into the house, both in a drunken stupor. They fumbled around in the dark, struck some matches and finally got a lamp lit while they boisterously chattered away. I kept an eye on them through a small opening in my sleeping bag and was ready for anything. But nothing happened. Mora checked his pistol and rifle, put them both in his sleeping bag with him, and soon I could hear the steady, even breathing of sleeping men.

It was Christmas morning but sorry to say there wasn't much Christmas spirit in the house. I was furious and didn't try to hide it. Mora and Andrew kept incredibly quiet, their courage from yesterday deflated now that they were sober. It was obvious that I no longer could use Andrew on this expedition either. I told him so and that he should go back to the reservation in the States within the next few days. He didn't like this at all and insinuated that he would find a way to get revenge. As for Yahnozah, he hadn't been involved with any of this and I never suspected any disloyalty from the old warrior.

The next day, Mora disappeared into the mountains. I heard later that he had been quite cocky as he left and even hinted something about being man enough to hold a gun in front of any white man and shoot him down if needed. I was annoyed that I hadn't given him a real fistfight before he left. He deserved a lesson to remember. Then by chance I heard that there was a Mexican who had some sort of legal authority in the town. This was a surprise. I hadn't thought of the possibility that anything like a lawman existed in these parts. On the contrary, I had the strong impression that a person only had a gun to depend on here.

I went straight away to the official's house, a small cabin on the outskirts of the town. When I got there I had to step over a pig to get into a low room where a flock of frightened chickens scurried about and flapped between my legs. There were two beds over by the fireplace where a woman sat nursing her child and a middle-aged fellow was smoking his cigarette: the judge. I explained to him that

Mora had threatened me with a loaded gun, and now I wanted to put the case into the hands of the law.

The judge grew very serious, scratched his nose and stressed that the law would prevail. Two men were called in and a while later they came out armed to the teeth and galloped off toward the mountains after Mora.

The next day as I was standing by the gate having a smoke, three riders came riding by. Riding in between the two armed men was Mora. They passed right by me, but Mora just stared straight ahead and didn't glance my way. His moustache, which was usually bristly and standing on end, now drooped like a pair of gloomy old brooms.

The hearing was to be held the next morning and together with a couple of white men here I went to the judge's cabin. The judge, Mora, and a few other Mexicans had already arrived and were seated on the edge of the bed. Ortega was one of them, the man I had met in the mountains searching for the bandits. As mentioned earlier, he was some sort of military commander and now turned out to also be some kind of associate judge. The judge's wife sat over in the corner grinding corn, and under a table in another corner stood two sleepy chickens that reminded me of a couple of court witnesses like we have in Norway.

The hearing started with everybody talking at once and everyone enraged. When it finally quieted down the judge asked what I actually wanted to achieve with the case. I replied that I came as a peaceful foreigner to this country, was threatened with my life by Mora, and demanded that he be punished. In my own mind, though, I had already decided that I wouldn't force the case to a final sentence as that could take time and trouble. My purpose was to give Mora a real scare and to rectify the relationship with Andrew. I proceeded, however, as if I intended to take the case to the supreme court in Mexico City if need be.

The judge and his self-commissioned advisors put their heads together and came to the joint conclusion that I should let the case drop. Mora pretended to be so nice and even called me "mi buen amigo," my good friend, and was scared to death as he sat there on the edge of the bed fiddling nervously with his mustache.

I answered that I was not used to having my friends try to kill me and insisted that this case should be continued. The judge said then that the case could not be conducted in his district and that I would have to take it to Madera, which was quite a long trip away.

I replied that I would go straight to Madera and added that it was a city that I had always wanted to see. The judge and his friends were completely perplexed now. It was obvious that they were all on Mora's side, but to get him out of this pinch wasn't as easy as they thought. I myself felt right at home because this was just like trying my cases in court when I was a lawyer.

I won the first round and insisted that witnesses be heard. The judge and my other opponents answered that no American could be brought as a witness in Mexico. Right away I insisted that I wanted this in writing. The judge was taken aback by this, but then went over to the table in the corner, found a piece of paper and bit of pencil, carefully flattened out the paper, spat energetically on the pencil and next stared straight ahead. Then he shuffled back and mumbled something about the law being uncertain and that perhaps American witnesses could be used. I began to suspect that perhaps this fellow couldn't write.

The Mexican's next objection was that no one could be a witness in a case when the crime had been committed on that person's property. I didn't attempt to question this interesting court rule any farther but instead just insisted to have it in writing. The judge once again walked over to the table, flattened out the paper, spat on the pencil and came back. It was now quite clear that he didn't know how to write. I was holding a trump in my hand and I used it ruthlessly every time a critical question came up.

Two of the Americans who had witnessed everything that had happened between Mora and myself were finally questioned. Andrew was examined afterward and defended his drinking buddy as best he could. In the end, old Yahnozah was called up and said, "Me not understand all this uproar. When we were in mountains all us Indians work like men. Now just talk."

The hearing continued for hours. Every time a new question came up, the Mexicans flared up in violent discussion. They waved their arms around and talked incessantly about everything except the case.

The only one who didn't make much of fuss was the judge. He stood in the middle of the floor with his hands behind his back staring blankly into the room with sad, round eyes while he fiddled nervously with his pencil stump.

There was one fellow among the Mexicans who especially irritated me with his nonstop chatter. I finally got mad and asked him what in the world he had to do with the case. He then stood up straight and answered, "I'm a soldier in the Mexican army."

Another time I criticized Mora for having a loaded revolver and rifle with him in his sleeping bag during our stay in Chuichupa. All the Mexicans had a good laugh at this and the judge explained that it was common in these parts to sleep with a gun under the covers. This was how I sometimes erred in following the court rules, but for the most part I had a strong plea and my opponents were beginning to back off.

The hearing was to continue the next morning but didn't take place because Mora was dead drunk and had to be carried off to his bed. We finally got going again on the third day, at which time one of the judge's advisors brought a huge wolf skin with him. He pulled it out during the hearing and said that I could have it if I dropped the charges. However, I didn't fall for this or any other sneaky trick but continued to force the issue. Mora seemed to grow smaller and smaller as he sat there. When I finally felt that he had had enough I agreed to drop the case on the condition that a written statement be completed concerning the things that had been proven and that it be signed by Mora, the judge, and the others. The associate judge, Ortega, who turned out to be more literate than his colleagues, helped carry this out. It was quite a remarkable court document. The meeting was then adjourned and everybody walked out the door feeling relieved. Even the two gray chickens who had consistently slumbered under the court bench happily fluttered out the door.

Then came New Year's Eve. That night Judge Ortega had been out drinking heavily and shot a man in the stomach. The wounded man died shortly thereafter and Ortega was taken south to Madera under heavy guard.

Meanwhile, Andrew had convinced Yahnozah to return with him to the reservation in the States. Jess, who from the very beginning had witnessed all that had happened during these dramatic Christmas days, also rode up there and reported everything that had happened to the Mescalero Reservation administrator, McCray. This was a bit unexpected for that clever Andrew.

My initial expedition had fallen to pieces. At the time it was a tough blow as I had just gotten a handle on the conditions and now had more information that opened up new possibilities for finding the mountain Apaches.

Later I took various trips through the Sierra Madre with a half-blood Apache who lived in Mexico, and in the mountains I caught glimpses of some reluctant people who seemed to be those we had been searching for. However, from information I received later this might not have been the case. My new helper was a good fellow, but he didn't come close to the full-blooded Apaches who knew the Sierra Madre so well. Without the old warrior Yahnozah, nothing was as before, and I missed his morning songs.

But every cloud has a silver lining. I now had time to investigate some interesting things that otherwise I wouldn't have had the opportunity to do. First I wanted to check out some strange cave dwellings that an old Indian had told me about that were supposed to be somewhere around the Aros River in the southwest of the Sierra Madre. Afterward, I would look up some of the Apaches whom the Mexicans had taken prisoner, most recently in 1932. I hoped to gain information from them that would supplement what I had heard and seen during my travels and try to get a more complete picture of the lives of the mountain Apaches since Geronimo's time.

# 13
# Cave Country

In the middle of the cave, a fire flickers and casts a strange glow onto the dark corners of the rock, where old Indian ruins vaguely appear. Outside the darkness of night hangs like a black wall. The only sound we can hear out there in the dark is the hushed rushing of water from the river flowing in the canyon far below.

Old Farnsworth pierces a piece of deer meat onto a skewer as he says, "Confound these mountain lions, they're everywhere, and they ravage the livestock something horribly. The wolves aren't much better. But nobody hunts them because there's nothing but a bunch of Indians and Mexicans wandering around out here in this Godforsaken wilderness. Nope, it sure isn't easy trying to raise cattle in these here parts of the world."

This was a befitting description of the area where I now found myself, about a day's travel southwest of Chuichupa in the Sierra Madre's southern region. A more rugged and jagged mountainous country would be difficult to find. Farnsworth kept his cattle down here and lived in the cave. After my Apache companions traveled back to the States, I had followed Farnsworth down here to investigate the fascinating cave dwellings I briefly mentioned earlier. Supposedly they were located farther into the mountains toward the southeast. I was planning to ride down there as soon as Farnsworth finished the heaviest workload with his herd.

Early the next morning we ride off from the cave to tend to some cattle up in the mountains. All around us grow oak forests and strange sorts of cacti, and up on the hillside the grass grows tall and thick in waving fields. Herds of deer leap here and there and disappear into the brushwood. We pass by a strange contorted rock that resembles a monolith. It rises a good 120 feet into the air, and at the top sits a large rock that doesn't seem to be resting on anything. Farther on we pass one of Farnsworth's mountain lion traps and find a hissing wildcat caught in it. Next, we arrive at the edge of a canyon, a sheer drop down about twenty-five hundred feet. Far below we can see the glistening Aros River.

We take care of the cattle and afterward stop on the top of a ridge to give the horses a rest, light a fire, and relax. The sun sheds its dazzling light across the mountains, which extend in all directions. Bare, sheer cliffs descending to the depths of the canyon are streaked with strata of steel blue and rusty red. Far below next to the Aros River I spy a small grove of palm trees.

The notorious mountain range Espinosa del Diablo rises to the west of us. Farnsworth points and says, "Over there was where the old outlaw Emanuel Lugo hid his loot." Then I heard the story about this strange Aztec Indian, a descendant of the highly cultivated people who ruled over parts of western Mexico until the Spanish came.

For quite some time, Lugo was an outlaw who spent his days attacking and rampaging and who made the mountains his home. Once he joined up with a couple of other bandits and together they attacked a caravan of mules loaded with silver and gold. They buried the loot somewhere in the mountains. Not long after, authorities caught Lugo, who then had to serve twenty years in prison.

When he was released, he was too old to continue a life as a bandit. He wandered from one place to the other and was a frequent visitor to Chuichupa as well. Farnsworth liked the wise old fellow, gave him food and shelter and became good friends with him. Lugo talked about many things, including the last crime he committed before being dragged off to prison. He even took Farnsworth and his two sons to the place where he had buried the booty. They didn't find any gold and silver; others had already been there and taken it. They did, however, come across the skeletons of two of Lugo's companions. He and the other bandits had killed them while burying the treasure.

In many ways, Lugo was a gifted man. He knew more about Mexico's extended history than almost anybody else. On quiet evenings by the fire his stories could awe everyone there. Lugo, however, was first and foremost an excellent blacksmith. The craft of forging had been handed down to him through generations of his family. He was, after all, a descendant of the incredibly adept Aztecs, whose ironworks astonished the conquistadors. As proof of his skills, word has it that once at a sawmill east of Chuichupa, Lugo had repaired a broken piston rod so well that the welded joint could hardly be seen. Farnsworth also said that many times Lugo had told him that he knew how to temper copper. The method, which supposedly wasn't so difficult, depended on a very different process than with steel and required an accurate tempering process. Several times the old Indian had offered to show Farnsworth and his sons how to do it. They didn't realize its importance, however, and never did accept of the opportunity. Once though, they were talking with Lugo right after he had finished tempering a copper pipe. When they ran a new file across it, not so much as a scratch was made in the metal. Farnsworth, like most settlers, knew enough blacksmithing for household needs and could judge the quality of such work. Later I also discovered from other sources that Lugo really was very good at tempering copper.[1]

It is evening before Farnsworth finishes telling about Lugo. We hop into our saddles and trot off toward our cave. The sun's last rays cast a crimson glow over the Espinosa del Diablo, and cool gray light eventually descends over the canyons. Over yonder I can see the valley with the white stone monolith, and over there is the narrow path that leads to the camp in the face of the cliff. Our little campfire is soon crackling in the cave, and its flames dance upward to the rock ceiling, which is black with soot from centuries of Indian fires.

Farnsworth finally finishes with the most pressing work with his cattle and a few days later we take off southeast toward the Chico River. This is where the Mayan Indian Luna Bonifacius lives, who will guide me farther south through the mountains to the place of the strange cave dwellings.

As we're riding along we suddenly hear singing, wistful Mexican melodies drifting through the wilderness. Up on a ridge we catch sight of a train of pack burros, and behind them rides the singer, a young Mexican fellow. The train heads down to a grove from where smoke rises. We discover a *destileria* where half a dozen Mexicans are busy distilling spirits. The alcohol is made from the sotol plant, which grows wild in these hills, and this is what the singer was bringing down. The plant's firm top is peeled, cooked for a few days on heated stones in the earth, chopped fine, set aside to ferment, and then distilled. It produces quite a strong drink, about 60 to 75 proof.

It's common for Mexicans to do such distilling way out here in the wilderness, where customers journey in from near and far. But it is also a bit of a precarious business because the officials in the nearest villages demand a certain payment, and if this isn't paid it could be the end of their business. At most distilleries, a cross, or sometimes several crosses, have been erected near the building. Perhaps it is in silent hope that the workers think that these will also protect against greedy officials.

We continue southeast toward the Chico River. Not far up this river we find a small, remote cabin where Luna Bonifacius lives. He approaches us and reaches out his hand to say hello. He is sturdy and solid as a bear but retains a certain calmness. He carries himself with a natural dignity common to those from an old race and has an honest gaze and a warm twinkle in his eye. Farnsworth described him as a good friend and a dangerous enemy. It occurs to me that Luna's ears are very strangely shaped in that they have no edges. I find out why later in the evening as we are sitting around the fire in front of his cabin. Bonifacius begins talking about various episodes from his dramatic life. In his time, he worked at mining silver from an old Spanish mine. Once when he was leading half a dozen mules loaded with silver bullion across the mountains, he was attacked by the renowned rebel General Pancho Villa and his people. They trimmed his ears like they used to do with prisoners in order to recognize them if they ever later escaped. Then they forced him to fight on their side. In time, Luna managed to escape but afterward took off on one illegal venture after another. He soon was a bandit who was always on the run from the law. He fought the Mexicans, the Tarahumara Indians, and the hostile Yaqui Indians. After a while, he made some kind of deal with the officials, built a cabin in Chico Valley, and started raising goats and things.

When he finished his story, he opened up his shirt and showed how his upper body was riddled with knife and bullet scars and said,

"It is a wonder I'm still alive, but there must be a reason." He was a hardened fatalist.

Farnsworth considered the Indian one of his best friends and said that his word was as good as gold. Without Luna's support it also wouldn't have been as possible for Farnsworth to run a cattle ranch way out here in the wilderness. Farnsworth would just send word to Luna, who would quickly go out and handle what ever needed to be done. Nobody dared to stand up against him. Once though, some Mexicans did defy him. They stole about twenty of his goats and took them east. Luna saddled his horse, caught up with the thieves, and coldly said, "Within four days those goats are to be taken back to my cabin along with just as many cattle."

Then he turned his horse around and rode home. Both goats and cattle were brought back within the allotted time. In another incident a Mexican ran off with his daughter. Luna followed the couple, shot the lover, brought the daughter home, and gave her a good whipping.

The following day, Farnsworth heads back, and Luna and I cross the Chico River and journey in through the mountains. We were probably at about seventy-five hundred feet when we reach a series of narrow valleys with steep, rocky slopes. As we are riding up one of them I notice something strange far up on the steep hill opposite us. There in the opening of a cave, measuring about a hundred and fifty feet wide, rises a large two-story structure with a number of big and small window-type holes. The building fills the entire entrance of the cave, except for one small flat area where three mighty dome-shaped containers stand. Everything is radiant yellow and glimmers in the sunshine between the leafy trees. As we approach, I see one settlement after the other on the hillside.

I find a place to settle in one of the largest caves and make myself at home there. After a quick meal, Luna hops on his horse and starts back down again to his place. I'll be staying here on my own.

It was remarkable to wander around these hills from one strange cave settlement to the next. I sometimes came upon huge spaces where large, narrow rows of two-tiered houses were built like terraces. They stood there shining in the sun under monumental dark archways. In other places, smaller clusters of houses clung to shallow dips in the mountain. Within a radius of about three miles, I discovered twenty-five different structures, where the largest might have had nearly thirty rooms. They often lay high up in the steep cliffs like small castles overlooking the fertile valley below, and they weren't always easy to reach. But I was able to find trees leaning against the steepest cliffs and sometimes steps that had been chiseled into the walls. Many of these steps were deeply worn into the rock, which made the climbing easier.

In general, the buildings were amazingly well preserved, including the objects I found within them, despite their antiquity. The extremely dry air created this condition. Everything seemed so freshly current that I almost expected people to show up by the houses or see an Indian girl come climbing up the rocks with a water jug on her head.

The principal building material of the houses was a mortar made from water and limestone powder, the dust from which covered the floors of the caves in thick layers. Some of the walls were merely plastered rock piles with layers of smoothed-out mortar on one side. The roofs were supported with solid pine or juniper logs, many of which carried dull tool marks because they were felled with a stone ax. Others had been burned off.

The doors of the buildings were U-shaped or had parallel sides at the top, which then ran together in a point at the bottom. They were narrow and so low that I really had to bend down to get through. In the outside walls were several windows, which were often square or round but mostly the same shape as the doors. The rooms were generally small, with a floor space of about forty-five square feet and a height of about six feet. There were also larger rooms but others were so low and narrow that I had to crawl around on all fours. Each room undoubtedly had its own purpose. Some were designed for living quarters or for storage, others for religious purposes. The floors were made of thick layers of compressed clay. There was a depression in one of them about three feet long with a bowl-shaped hole at one end. Painted signs, patterns, or primitive drawings of people and animals in black, green, and yellow often covered the walls.

The most peculiar item at these cave dwellings was what they call *ollas*, or jugs, which were huge dome-shaped containers. There could be as many as five in a cave and they were up to eleven feet tall. Usually they had three or four windows. They were constructed from the same mortar as the houses and sometimes had a roughcast of braided blades of grass. These containers were used as some sort of storage space, probably mostly for corn. Inside the caves, I found numerous corncobs, but they were only about a third of the size of those grown today.

Besides caves used for living, others seemed to have been used exclusively for religious purposes. I found a massive cave where round rocks were piled up in large and small cairns.

It wasn't easy finding any remaining cultural relics from the people who lived in these caves hundreds of years ago. Inside and outside the houses was a thick layer of limestone dust that billowed up into the air at the slightest touch. It was also very dark in the rooms, which made it necessary to use a flashlight. I did, however, find a few interesting things, such as a couple of stone axes, arrowheads, pottery pieces with black and white detail, braided mats, baskets and straw hats, spoons made from gourds, metates (bowl-shaped rocks), and other items. Luna had told me that the dead lay buried under the floors of these cave rooms, always in the northwest corner. I started to dig.

I dug and dug for days, toiling like a plowhorse in clouds of chalk dust, but I didn't find so much as a single bone. In the end, though, my efforts were rewarded. In a very small house about two feet under the floor I found a woman's body lying in a fetal position with her face pointed toward the west. It was incredible how well the body had been preserved. The flesh was dried out, but the face still retained its expression. Some of the hair was still intact but was so brittle that it disintegrated with the slightest touch. The same thing happened to a piece of clothing that was draped over the woman's shoulders. A humble piece of jewelry was buried with her: a necklace made from carved pieces of bone and two turquoise stones.

Similar cave dwellings can be found scattered over a large area in the rugged and difficult-to-reach areas by the Chico and Aros Rivers. The northern parts of the Sierra Madre, on the other hand, are quite different. The cliff dwelling I found there, which I have mentioned earlier, was more primitive and consisted only of stone houses loosely mortared together with clay. There were no dome-shaped containers. A cultural division seems to lie here.

Little is known about the people who lived in these caves or when they lived there. What became of them is also unknown, but it is not improbable that the Apaches chased them away. Whether there are any close connections between these cave dwellers in Mexico and those who lived in the southern parts of the United States is also still a mystery. Only when the central parts of the Sierra Madre and all the various cultural remnants that can be found there are better studied and understood will these mysteries be resolved. Many fascinating challenges lie here. Not since Lumholtz's expedition in the 1890s have archeologists ever really worked in these hard-to-reach regions.

I continued searching the mountains, looking for other caves and old dwellings. I always carried a gun because there were so many things I had to watch out for. Mountain lions, jaguars, and wild boars roamed these areas, and you could never be too sure whether an Apache or an outlaw might show up. Mountain lions loved these caves, and hardly a day passed without finding some of their fresh tracks. These animals would often lie on top of the buildings, which caused large portions of the upper levels to break off.

I take off one day to a rugged area to the south where the steep cliffs seem to contain further discoveries. I reach the bottom of a deep gorge, and high above me on the slanted rock I can make out some dark openings and then rows of houses. I start climbing the difficult inclines and declines, first up to one cave then down to the bottom, then up again, and so on. Finally I come to an unusually large cave that could well be ninety feet high. It's like a dark opening in the cliff wall. I reach a spot just below this opening and am faced with climbing up the difficult pitch. I leave my gun in a cleft in the rocks, jam my fingers into small cracks, and finally manage to scramble my way up.

Like a huge hall, the cave arches over a cluster of houses and a couple of dome-shaped containers about ten feet tall. One of them is barely visible in the dark, deep recesses of the cave. I look around in the houses a bit, light my pipe, and then shuffle deeper into the cave. I haven't gone far when I suddenly stop in my tracks. Right there in front of me in the dark I can just make out two gleaming green lights.

First I see them in front of me, then they disappear and two seconds later reappear farther to the side of me. I hear a scratching sound and then a rock comes loose and falls with a thud onto the floor. A huge animal suddenly bounds forward and runs along a narrow shelf on one of the walls, takes a mighty leap to the top of the large container, and from there leaps back to the rock. It all happens so fast that I only can catch a glimpse of the fleeting brownish-yellow body. After that it wasn't often that I parted from my gun in mountain lion country.

From the valley of caves, I eventually start back to the beautiful Chico River to check out some of the caves, which, according to Luna, were located somewhere around there. I pitch my tent on a riverbank close to a warm spring that rises and gurgles up out of the rocks. It is a beautiful place. Right by my camp the river ripples along between huge white-trunked sycamore and cottonwood trees. A deep pool with rising steam is only a few paces away from my tent, and I bathe here as often as I can, a rare luxury. The water is so warm that I feel pleasantly drowsy while I'm splashing around in it. I like to lie there facing the part of the spring that bubbles out just above the pool. The water tastes fresh and lures me to drink and drink.

When dusk slowly settles over the valley, a deer sometimes appears on the grassy hillside over on the other side of the river. It gracefully makes its way down the hill, carefully splashes across the river with its muzzle twitching, stops by the small creek that flows from the spring, and starts to drink. It is a young deer, barely a year old. At first it is reluctant and scares off when it sees me, but after a while it gets used to seeing me. Many evenings I sit there in front of my tent watching my gracious friend. But if I'm not careful to keep quiet the animal takes off and is gone in an instant.

It's remarkable that both the deer and the birds search out this spring to drink from when a crystal-clear, cool river flows nearby. The spring water most likely contains certain minerals the animals instinctively want.

Right by the spring is a mountain trail that leads from the distillery I mentioned before to the nearest village, a few days' journey to the southeast. Now and again a few Indians or Mexicans ride by leading small caravans of pack burros with kegs intended for liquor tied to the animals. They all stop at the spring and drink from it and then bathe in the pond below. This fountainhead in the middle of the wilderness is thought to be a sacred place with healing waters. Farnsworth told me later that an Indian who was so crippled with rheumatism that he couldn't even mount his horse by himself was completely cured after he spent only a short time bathing here.

After being alone in the mountains a while it is nice to see a fellow human every so often. My first guests are Luna's young and hopeful offspring, three barefoot boys aged three to twelve, with the rascal Bavian leading the way. All three of them come riding in one day on an old donkey. Like an army, they charge into camp and laughing and playing make a real mess of things. First, they tumble around in the leaves, then splash about in the river, then take all their clothes off and jump head first into the pool by the spring, making quite a commotion the entire time. Those little brown bodies splash around for hours. Then they insist that I join them and in I go. They jump and crawl all over me. Later they command me to bake bread and cook meat while in the meantime they go snooping around in all my things. They are tough tyrants and know what they want. In the end, they decide to stay for the night. It is the middle of winter and the nights can get pretty chilly. But barefoot and scantly clad, those little men just lie down in the grass side by side and peacefully fall asleep. The following morning they wake up completely rested and climb onto the patient old donkey. They ride off with the little three-year-old hanging onto his brother for dear life so he won't fall, and that's the last I see of them.

On another day, a dark-skinned Tarahumara Indian rides by wearing almost nothing except for sandals and a huge straw hat. He's an exceptionally agile and well-built fellow, a descendant from a people who are among the world's best distance runners. A Tarahumara Indian can cover ninety miles in a day without difficulty and will gladly race with a rider if the distance is long enough. A week later this man passes by on his return. He is then pretty inebriated and is well on his way to draining the small keg of hard liquor tied behind his saddle.

A few quiet days pass and then an Indian family comes wandering by. A man, his wife, a young girl, and three small kids are crammed together on three donkeys. Some are barefoot and others wear sandals, and their clothes are so tattered that patches of brown skin shine through. They are leading a pack animal behind them that is loaded with a little corn sack, a couple of small blankets, and a crate with two motion-sick chickens flapping around. This is the whole of their earthly belongings, and they are on the move to some place or another. As soon as they reach the spring, the whole family strips off their clothes, splashes into the pool, and enjoy themselves to their hearts' content. Afterward, they come over to my fire and sit there for quite some time, and I chat with the woman who can speak a little Spanish. During our conversation, she stops and looks at me with concern, and then tells me that it's not good for a man to live alone like this. She nods toward her daughter saying she's clever and gracious. The girl looks to be about thirteen, quite beautiful and almost a mature woman. She understands what we are talking about and, embarrassed, she glances down again. Occasionally, though, she can't help but look up. There is anxiety in her eyes.

I carefully and as gently as possible refuse the proposal and give the girl a large chunk of dry meat to soften the matter, but she takes the gift quietly and with cool resignation.

My last guest at the sacred springs is the jolly cousin Japaro. Even before I can see him in the brush he begins jabbering away and laughing. He appears out of the woods, a long, lanky half-blood Indian on a skinny, bony old nag of a horse. He is bubbling with life and is a true carefree boy of the woods. After a dip, he settles by the fire and spends the night by my tent.

I had previously met Japaro when he had shown me a cave where he had uncovered a mummy that obviously must have been a dwarf. I very much wanted to get hold of the mummy but was told that he had promised it to a big man in Chihuahua. He said, though, that he also knew of other dwarf mummies and he would be more than happy to show these to me when the opportunity arose. Japaro later disappeared into the mighty mountains only until now to reappear here at the springs.

I was extremely eager to get some more information about these dwarfs the Mexicans, Indians, and Mormons often talked about. Old Farnsworth had also found a mummy of a full-grown man that measured four feet, four inches and that lay in a braided basket beneath a cave floor. Although we're not talking about a tribe of pygmies here, this type of frequent abnormality was incredibly interesting.

I question Japaro for further information concerning these discoveries. He acts a bit curt, like someone who has all the answers, and says he knows of a cave several days' journey to the south where there are mummies of "three little men." They lie in braided baskets in a small chamber between two rooms of a cave dwelling and are, as he says, *muy chiquito*, very small.

It turns out that Japaro hasn't seen the mummies in three years, and the way he gabs I'm sure that others must have gotten word of this, too. It is possible that one or another smart Mexican or Indian understood the business opportunity of this discovery, took the mummies, and possibly sold them to collectors in Chihuahua. Whatever the case, I would still like to investigate the issue. If I find the "three little men" it would be great, but if not, I will still be satisfied with the trip through the fairly unexplored mountainous area in the south together with someone who knows the land.

We agree to set out as soon as possible. But first, Japaro has to help out at the distillery for a few days. Three days later, I ride off to the distillery to fetch him. The Mexicans have just finished making a big brew of about fifty gallons. To celebrate a job well done, they indulge in a real drinking spree, and when I get there Japaro is blissfully staggering around. When he sees me his face lights up, and slurring he begins to prattle away about the "three little men." He fervently reassures me that they are *muy muy chiquito* and shows how big they are by holding his hand over the ground. The "three little men" have shrunk considerably since last time and are now only three feet, four inches tall.

There is no way that Japaro will be able to ride on the back of a horse that day. I ride over to Farnsworth's cave and spend the night there. The following day I ride back to the distillery. The situation is even worse than before. Four men are crawling around a full keg like half-dead flies. Others are sprawled out sleeping in all sorts of awful contortions. Japaro crawls over to me, sits down in the grass and again begins to slur and tell me about the "three little men." Then he says he has to have five hundred thousand pesos to lead me to the cave where they lie because that is the price he could get if he were to sell the mummies to the Mexican president. When I suggest that that is an awfully high price he sweeps his hand out and solemnly declares that he will get hold of all the dwarfs *alive*. When I don't show any enthusiasm about this generous offer, he tells me again how small they are and shows me their size with his hands. Just within the last twenty-four hours they have shrunk even more and are now less than two feet tall. Jasparo in the end feebly mutters *muy, muy chiquito* and then falls over in the grass and falls asleep.

Two days later we took off together with Melvin, the youngest of the Farnsworth sons. At the time he was staying in his father's cave, and when he heard about my plans he was enticed to follow along. He was an unusually sincere and clever fellow who helped us out considerably. His father, also helpful as always, provided the necessary horses and pack animals. The Farnsworth boys had dubbed my mule Dolores del Río after the enchanting Spanish actress. The animal certainly had the whims of a prima donna.

We rode southwest, crossed the Chico River about six miles from the place where it joins the Aros River, and then swung up the steep hillsides. There in the first deep gorge we toiled along and finally found the cave dwellings where old Farnsworth a few years back had seen the mummy of a dwarf. I vaguely hoped that it might still be there but it turned out that large parts of the two-storied structure had collapsed and slid partway down the rock-strewn slope. I found a few bones and the remains of a basket but that was all. A large dwelling constructed of mortared rocks had been built just above the cave. It lay like a fort far up on the knoll with an extensive view out across the rugged valley. This was the only time I ever found a stone house out in the open.

We carried on and continued crossing one gorge after the other, each steeper than the last. The rocky slopes consisted of beautiful red sandstone conglomerates that erosion had formed into various fantastic shapes. Caves were everywhere and they were often built up the same as those I had seen before. Wild tobacco grew in abundance below one of the caves. Japaro claimed that it was planted by the cave dwellers and added that he often ran across such plants near the old structures.

Wild turkeys thrived down here in the south and we often came upon large flocks of them. Sometimes the birds would take off in the air but other times they scattered and darted in all directions into the brush. They were easily spooked and difficult to get a shot at.

One evening we made camp in the snow far up in the dusky pines. Far away, the sun was setting in glowing red and yellow behind the endless realm of mountains that stretched below us. It was cold and I enjoyed the fire and my sleeping bag. Japaro didn't seem to be the least bit bothered about the cold, despite his lack of clothing. All he had on was some worn-out sandals, a thin pair of trousers, a shirt that let the air in from all directions, and a frayed straw hat that amusingly sat crocked on his head. He slept on the ground using his saddle as a pillow and a small Indian blanket slung over his shoulders and was quite happy with that. He was up early in the morning completely rested and already chattering away and laughing. This fellow was pure entertainment. In the evenings when we sat around the fire he would tell all sorts of amazing stories about Indian superstitions, cave dwellers, lost Spanish treasures, and the marvelous Sierra Madre.

After a while we arrived at some large rock formations that sloped down some very steep cliffs in the west. A short way down in one of them we finally found the cave dwelling where the "three little men" were supposed to be. Everything corresponded with the description: the number of rooms and location and the small chamber between them, but we didn't find any mummies. Japaro desperately searched around, then sat on the ground and miserably shook his head. But I took the whole thing calmly and said that after such a long time he shouldn't be too surprised that someone might have gotten there before us. He contemplated this a while, then cheered up a bit and smiled. Shortly after he prattled away about something else and forgot the gloom over his "three little men."

We then made our way down to the Aros River, and from snow and cold we were suddenly in palm trees and bamboo in a semitropical climate. The river's current was quite strong but Japaro found one of the few places to wade across and we were able to ride over without too much difficulty. It was beautiful and rugged down there by the rushing river, where cliffs rose to about twenty-four hundred feet in the air.

We made our way home along the western banks of the river through some of the most rugged country ever seen. According to Japaro there were quite a lot of fish in the river such as trout, suckers, and catfish, and wild pigs in the foothills. One day I caught a glimpse of a jaguar, which slunk away and disappeared into a small grove of palm trees.

At a bend in the river we found remnants of a Spanish melting furnace about nine feet long and three feet high made of a mixture of yellow clay and wood ashes. Here the ore was melted together with lead and limestone. The lead absorbed the precious metals, which were later removed in intense heat and with forced air.

The earliest Spanish mining was just as basic as their smelting. Instead of mining drills they used what they called a *pulseta*, a spear-like tool with which they pierced the rocks by hand. This was how they made deep holes, about two inches in diameter, in the rocks. The holes were then plugged up with limestone and water. When the limestone dried and expanded, the rock cracked. They could also burst the rocks by heating the rock wall with fire and then throwing water on it.

The poor *peoner* were the ones who worked in the mines for a day's salary of a handful of corn. They carried the ore and recovered metals by using a tumpline across their foreheads to support and balance the leather pouches on their backs. These people were masters in carrying and for days could haul a load of about two hundred pounds across rugged mountains.

Spanish mining was incredibly extensive, and even in faraway corners in the wilderness there are traces of it. Close to where we were traveling were supposedly two of their richest gold and silver mines— Guaynopa and Rodrigues. Old documents report that the Indians, most likely the Apaches, killed the miners. The mines were abandoned and have never been reclaimed since. It could very well be that great finds of gold, silver, copper, lead, nickel, bismuth, mercury, and so forth exist up there in the mountains. When this country becomes better explored and the problematic transportation is overcome, the Sierra Madre may be one of America's richest treasure chests.

The rest of our trip continued without anything too exciting happening other than my moody mule, Dolores del Rio, deciding to suddenly lay on her stomach in the middle of the Aros River, giving me a cold plunge, and Japaro sharing some of his most robust lice with me. One dark evening we rode up through the valley toward our humble abode in the cave. A campfire burned like a red eye up on the cliff wall, casting a faded reflection across old Farnsworth who sat leaning toward the fire.

# 14

# Prisoners from the Wilderness

In previous chapters I mentioned that I wanted to locate the Indians who in recent years had been captured during encounters with the mountain Apaches. By talking with them I hoped to gather information that, together with my own experiences, might give me an idea of the life and history of these people.

I headed east through the Sierra Madre and finally ended up in the small American Mormon settlement of Garcia, high up on a mountain slope facing the Chihuahua plains. Somewhere around here, the Apache woman Lupe supposedly lived.

In Garcia I met John Becroft, an older Mormon who told me many a tale about the wild ones. He first told me the story of Apache Kid, once the most notorious renegade Indian in the Southwest and northern Mexico. His fate had been a matter of speculation, but now I was getting the facts. It turned out that up until the turn of the century, Apache Kid was the leader of the mountain Apaches but died fighting in the Sierra Madre. Furthermore, I was told that Lupe was his daughter. A few words about Apache Kid are therefore relevant when discussing the captured Indians and the band that still struggles for survival in the Sierra Madre.

Apache Kid was a six-foot fellow, smart, adept, and hard as a rock. In the 1880s, he was stationed as an Indian scout at San Carlos and led American troops to the Sierra Madre during the pursuit of Geronimo. He was reputed as being especially sharp and was promoted to sergeant of the scouts. However, he and a few other Indians caused a small ruckus in San Carlos during a drunken spree. It all ended with a well-known white man, Al Sieber, who was the leader of the scouts, getting wounded. The troublemakers were arrested and sentenced to seven years in prison in 1889. They were handcuffed and the sheriff and two other white men drove off with them. On the way, the Indians jumped the guards, killed two, and seriously wounded the third. They then fled into the mountains.

From then on Apache Kid was a constantly pursued renegade. His permanent hiding place was presumed to be in the Sierra Madre, but little was known about how he moved about there. However, his constant raids in northern Arizona were well known. There his hostilities evolved and grew until Apache Kid was considered the most dangerous man in the territory. He had no scruples, and if he saw there was an advantage to murder, he would spare neither whites nor Indians. His weakness was women, and time and again he rode to San Carlos, where he would capture a girl and bring her back with him to the Sierra Madre. When he got tired of the girl, he would either kill her or send her back. Then he would take off again in search of another.

During his life as a renegade, Apache Kid revealed a remarkably cold-blooded, sly streak. He would roam as a "lone wolf" in Arizona where the enemy was most prevalent and indiscriminately kill them. Occasionally he would casually walk into a tent in San Carlos, shoot down the Indian who lived there, and kidnap his wife. His victims probably numbered close to a hundred. He was like the plague and his name spelled fear. He was constantly pursued, and a high price was put on his head in the Southwest as well as in northern Mexico, but he was never captured.

This was what people generally used to know about Apache Kid. Now close sources tell me that this was the man who led the Apaches in the Sierra Madre. The attacks and raids that he and his people carried out in Mexico were at least as many as those he committed alone in Arizona. He often roamed in the vicinity of the Mormon farms, stealing and being a constant threat. In the early 1890s he attacked the Thompson family, killing a woman and a child. This happened in Cave Valley, not far from Garcia.

In 1899, the Mormons Martin Harris and Tom Allen lived with their families in the isolated Cave Valley. One night in November the dogs made an awful racket outside the houses, and in the morning it turned out that a band of thieves had been there and had stolen a lot of corn, potatoes, and other things, fleeing into the mountains. Harris and Allen followed the trail on foot. They took their guns along but had no intention of starting a fight with the band. They just wanted to find out whether the thieves were Indians or Mexicans. They cut off from the trail and as they were walking slowly along, they suddenly came upon the thieves: nine Apaches. They had obviously just taken a siesta and were now in the process of loading up their horses. Harris and Allen immediately dived behind some rocks without being seen. They hoped intensely that the Indians would take off to the side, but here they were, riding straight toward them. When they were about sixty feet away, the two white men raised their guns. The front rider was a woman dressed in hide pants like the rest. She screamed, turned her horse and took off. The others followed, except for one. He was a huge fellow with a bunch of feathers on his head. He quickly reached for his rifle, but it was stuck in its holster and he desperately tried to loosen it. He had a fierce look in his eyes and showed no fear even though he had two gun barrels pointed straight at him. Two shots rang out and one of the fleeing Indians, who turned out to be a woman, tumbled dead from her horse. The huge fellow was also seriously wounded, but he wasn't about to give in: he swung his horse toward the enemy and struggled frantically to loosen his rifle. Another round of shots, and then he fell to the ground. It turned out that he had a child on his back, and it also had been killed.[1]

Later several of the Mexican officials and a few Mormons, among them Bishop A. W. Ivans, went out to view the corpse. Some of them had met Apache Kid when he was a scout for the American troops, and others had seen his photograph. They all agreed that this was his body. This is how Apache Kid died. He was one of the most notorious Indians of the Southwest, and though he was a heartless and cruel man, the people he terrorized gave him credit for being fearless and dying like a man.

Lupe was the daughter of Apache Kid. She was captured in 1910 in the Sierra Madre west of Chichupa by some Mexican cowboys. By accident they had came across the renegades' camp, which made the Natives all run off in a flash. In the confusion Lupe got separated from the others and rode up a steep slope, where she came to a dead end. She jumped off her horse, laid flat on the ground, and hid in the grass. When the Mexican Pedro Fimbres grabbed her, she fought like a wildcat until she couldn't fight any longer. She was later taken down to the area around Nacori Chico, where a childless Mexican couple named Fuentes took her in as their foster daughter. She lived with them for years but moved elsewhere as an adult.

I found the Fuenteses in a small stone cabin on the slopes of the Sierra Madre. This old couple, gentle and friendly people, lived here all alone. They willingly told me what they remembered about their foster daughter.

Lupe was brought to them just after she had been captured. At first she was not very happy. The Fuenteses let her know that she could go into the mountains and look for her kinfolk if she wished to. They gave her provisions, and the little fourteen-year-old girl took off alone into the wild Sierra Madre. After eight days she returned disheartened; all her searching had been for nothing. She now stayed for three months with her foster parents, but she longed for the mountains and her family, so she set off again for the Sierra Madre. This time she was gone much longer, wandering around from place to place, living on roots and berries. She returned, exhausted, and starved, and this time she gave up hope of finding her people. After some time she adapted to her new conditions and acquired a great affection for her foster parents. But the past continued to have a strong hold on her, and it was obvious that she feared punishment from her people because she had settled down with the enemy.

She quickly learned Spanish, and through the years she told her foster parents many a tale from her life in the wilderness. In the stories she told, there was also mention of a treasure in a mountain cave that she knew about. At one time she even brought Fuentes along to show him the place, but when they got a little way into the mountains a tremendous fear suddenly swept over her; without a word she turned and rushed back.

Now she had long since moved to Chihuahua, where she was married to a Mexican. The Mormons in Garcia told me that the couple had their cabin somewhere near there. I sent a messenger along with word that I had greetings to Lupe from her foster parents, and got an answer back that she would come to Garcia the next morning. I looked forward to meeting Apache Kid's daughter.

A rider comes into view at the edge of the forest, trotting toward the Mormon farms of Garcia, and smoothly hops off the saddle. It is a woman dressed like a Mexican, but I can clearly see that she is an Indian. She is around forty, large and strongly built, almost like a man, though her long, supple fingers soften this impression. Her hair is pitch black and swept back, her face finely featured with skin taut over protruding cheekbones. She looks tough and aggressive, but at the same time intelligent. What first catches my attention, however, are her eyes, which reflect a certain intense fierceness beneath her narrow eyebrows. This is Lupe.

One of Lupe's good friends is a Mormon woman, and with her help I soon get the conversation going. First I bring greetings from her foster parents and then talk of this and that about the Apaches on the reservation in Arizona. I must tread carefully because it is well known that Lupe is reluctant to talk about the time when she lived as an Indian. After a while, however, we become good friends, and when I start asking my questions, she has no objections to answering them. She speaks fluent Spanish.

"Do you know anything about your parents?" I ask.

"My father was a scout for the American soldiers at San Carlos, but was arrested and then killed two men. After that he fled into the Sierra Madre. He was a great warrior. He and my mother were both killed before I was caught by the Mexicans. I was an orphan."

"How did you live in the Sierra Madre?"

"I was among ten, or maybe it was fifteen Indians. Quite a few were women. Once we lived for a long time in a huge cave and during that period we grew corn. At other times we wandered, living in caves or tents made out of grass. The tents were quite low, perhaps three feet high, so that we had to crawl in. The roof support rested on each end of two stakes that were tied together like a cross. The sides were made of smaller posts that leaned up against the roof support and were covered by bear grass. We had horses. Our saddles were made from bear grass. We often sewed leather moccasins for the horses' hooves so that their tracks could not be seen."

"What type of weapons did you have and what did you live on?"

"A few of the men had old rifles, but very little ammunition. Most of them used a bow and arrows. We lived on deer meat, mescal that we cooked in the ground, the top of an onion-shaped plant that grows in the mountains, and roots and berries. We had corn for a while, too, and found honey in the cliffs. Sometimes we stole cattle from the Mexicans. We had no matches, but we made fire by rubbing two pieces of wood together. We had to find everything in the mountains, we had to make everything by hand and we owned almost nothing."

"How were you dressed?"

"We made clothes from buckskin, sometimes rawhide, and we used high moccasins that reached way up the leg. The women often used skirts, but some wore trousers like the men."

"When you sat in the cave or the tent up in the mountains, and you did not have any work to do, how did you spend your time?"

"We sang a lot and told stories, but we did not dare to sing very loud for fear that someone would discover us. For the same reason, we did not dare use our drums."

I then ask her if her band ever had any connection with the Apaches on the San Carlos Reservation. But this is the only question she is reluctant to answer, and she gives an elusive reply. I tell her that there has been a change in San Carlos since the old days, and that today the Apaches are happy there.

"No, not in San Carlos", Lupe answers bitterly, and in her voice I can detect the Apaches' old fear of this detested place in the desert where the tribe had endured so much pain through the years.

"How many Apaches would you say were in the Sierra Madre at the time you lived there with your family?" I continue.

"There were other bands, but I don't know how large they were, and we seldom met. The mountains were vast and we had enough to do just taking care of ourselves. We were always in fear of being attacked."

"Were you often involved in fights?"

"Sometimes the Mexicans came upon us. Then somebody had to fight and once in a while they were shot. Other times a man would take off to steal cattle, never to return. We waited for a long time, but then knew that he must have been killed. Our weapons were poor, and therefore we always had to be very careful. We lived high up in the cliffs where it was difficult to track us down. When we moved, we used our eyes well and kept out of view. We made small fires at dusk or in the morning, because then the fire could not be seen. We never felt safe."

"Were there only Indians among you?"

"A white man, an American, also lived with us. He had lived with my family for a long time, but finally he disappeared. He was old and had red hair."

Finally I mention that her foster parents had told me that she knew of a treasure in a cave in the Sierra Madre. I ask her if she would guide me through the mountains and show me this place if adequately compensated. Confronted with this question, Lupe suddenly becomes nervous. She wrings her hands and looks to all sides to avoid any eye contact. Then she suddenly says that she is willing to show me the cave if her husband agrees. She will give me an answer the next day. This is surprising because it is well known among the Mormons that nobody gets anywhere with Lupe when it comes to the treasure. Whenever the conversation touches upon this, she becomes agitated and implacable, perhaps out of superstition or fear of her relatives.

After a while she relaxes again. She sits there staring off into the distance with big, dark eyes. Her thoughts are probably up there in the mountains, which were once her home and where she roamed like a renegade with her people. Suddenly she snaps out of it, walks to her horse, and gallops off toward the forest and her home.

The next morning she comes riding back to Garcia, this time together with her husband, a feeble-looking Mexican. Both are riding the same horse, with him sitting behind. They dismount, and I walk over to her. She becomes very nervous. Her hands move frantically and she does not look at me. Then she says rapidly like a pupil being tested, "It was wrong what I said yesterday. I do not know of any cave with a treasure." Then she jumps in the saddle, holds the horse back for a moment while the man climbs on behind, digs her spurs into the horse, and disappears in through the trees.

In order to find two other Apaches who had been captured in the Sierra Madre, I set out on a new journey after returning to Arizona. In the small village of Cumpas in Sonora, Mexico, I find one of the captives. This is the boy who escaped injury in the battle of 1932 when

Mora, the Yaqui Indian, slaughtered a group of Indians in the westerly Sierra Madre. The child is now an adopted son of a prosperous Mexican, Cheno Medina.

As I approach Medina's house, I see a group of children playing over on the hill. I notice a small, sturdy seven-year-old among them who, in many ways, differs from the others. He has a stronger build, stands straight, and is quick and determined, like someone accustomed to being a leader. I walk a little closer and get a glimpse of his face. Without a doubt, it is the Apache boy. Medina is very hospitable and tells me a few things about the child, who we then walk toward. The boy stops playing and approaches us. He stands in front of me looking straight at me without being the least bit sheepish, only slightly puzzled. I have a small, brave figure of a chief before me with a pensive, distinguished-looking face. He carries himself with a solemn dignity seldom seen in someone so young, but behind his seriousness a child's smile shines through every now and then.

I take some pictures of the boy, which is easy to do because he is quick to understand and follow what I ask him to do. Then I talk to him a bit about his people in the Sierra Madre. It can't really be expected of him to remember anything from the time he lived in the mountains, being such a tiny boy as he was when he was captured, but I still try a few questions on him. He doesn't answer, but stares off in the distance with the same wide, dark look Lupe had when she talked about her people. Perhaps a flash of jumbled memories went through his mind from the time he lived high up in the Sierra Madre's dark forests, at one with the wilderness.

In one of the larger cities in the western part of the United States, where multitudes of cars tear along and crowds fill the streets, I meet a small twelve-year-old Apache girl, Bui, or Owl Eye. She was captured in May 1932 in the "eagle's nest," high up in the westerly Sierra Madre after the old woman who had been taking care of her was killed. By chance she was later taken north and adopted by an American family. Bui now goes to school with little American girls and has no problem keeping up with them. She is a nature child who has made a leap into twentieth-century culture.

The first time I meet Bui, she is playing with a blond American girl; the Indian girl with the jet-black hair and brown skin is a startling contrast. She might not be radiant, but she has her own quiet charm. She is reluctant to talk about her life in the Sierra Madre, but after a while she loosens up and talks about the days when she lived like a renegade up in the mountains together with her people. She remembers only those things that a child could remember. Groping for thoughts, she starts to talk:

*They named me Bui. There were only women and children in our camp. First there was Nana (grandmother), then four younger women and three children besides me. Nana was the one who decided everything and she was terribly stern. We lived in caves and small huts made out of grass. We were always afraid that somebody would come to get us, and we often moved from one place to the other. One time when Nana took me along on her horse, we rode quickly through the dark forest and I got hit by a branch, straight across my face. I got a big sore that hurt a lot and I started to cry. Nana got angry and hid me in a pit so narrow that I could not move. I stayed there for a whole day, crying, and only when it became dark did Nana come to fetch me.*

"Were there other Apaches in the mountains?" I ask.

"We visited Indians who lived in other places farther up. Sometimes some men called on us and I remember that one of them had a bunch of feathers on his head."

"Were you only together with other Indians?"

"Yes, but they often talked about a white man who had lived with the others up there."

"What did you live on and what other belongings did you have in the camp?"

"We ate a lot of mescal and dried meat and also some green grass. We did not have many things, only a few large hides, a knife, and iron needle and a cup. That was probably all. We all used the same cup."

"How were you dressed?"

"We made clothes out of hides and we had high moccasins. They were really bad when they got wet because they shrank and then I had to take them off and go barefoot". She now runs off and fetches the leather dress and the moccasins she had worn at the time she was captured, now two old and shabby garments. Then she adds, almost complaining, "Nana had just sewn a brand-new beautiful dress of buckskin for me, but then I was captured."

"Was there any singing or dancing going on when you were together in the camp?"

"No. We dared not make any noise. But once in a while, I remember that a woman sang me to sleep. I have forgotten her name. But I don't think it was my mother. I don't believe I had a mother or father."

"Did you enjoy your life in the mountains among the Indians?"

"I was often afraid and I do not want to return. Nana was so strict and we were not allowed to do anything. Once there was another small child who cried a lot. Nana strangled her until she died."

"Did you believe in God?"

"Every evening we knelt and lifted our hands toward the sky. Everybody was quiet, not a word was said. But I don't know which god we prayed to."

The captured Apaches confirmed something I had heard before from the Mexicans: that for years a white man had lived with the Apaches in the mountains. He was redheaded and lived to be quite old. In addition to this information, we also have the account referred to earlier: in 1883 the well-known Judge H. McComas and his family were killed by the Apaches in New Mexico, all except their six-year-old boy Charley. The boy was taken to the Sierra Madre, where he lived with Geronimo's people. The last time the whites ever saw him was when, as previously mentioned, General Crook's men stormed an Apache camp in the Sierra Madre that same year. A few women were then seen escaping through the forest carrying Charley with them. No one has seen him since.

Could the white man who had lived with the mountain Apaches up to our time have been Charley? They both had reddish hair and their ages matched up. It would be otherwise difficult to understand how the Apaches, timid as they were, could have been on such close terms with a white man who hadn't been raised with them. All in all, there are numerous, fascinating arguments that indicate that the son of one of the most prominent judges of the Southwest lived and died among the Apaches in the Sierra Madre.

It is impossible to know exactly how many Apaches remain there today. The mountains are so vast and the hiding places so numerous, that there could just as well be fifty as there could be ten. The fact that they still exist is certain enough.

As far as I can determine, during the last ten years the Mexicans have killed or captured about twenty-five Apaches, only five of whom were men, the rest women and children. Most of the men were probably shot down during the first years because they were the ones who had to take the most desperate chances. Everything indicates that today there are mostly women who remain.

My journey to Mexico is over, and I now make my way down from the Sierra Madre to the Chihuahua plains. I continue northward across the vast prairie surrounded by blue mountains. A jagged range rises to the east, the place where the two great chiefs, Mangas Coloradas and later Victorio, roamed with their warriors. In the west looms the Sierra Madre, Geronimo's hunting grounds. On the plains, far off on the horizon, I barely see the contours of a small Mexican village, a small community of people who for centuries have been the Apache's bitter enemies.

The sun sets behind the Sierra Madre, the crimson glow across the sky slowly fades, and a chill seeps through the mountains. A small herd of antelope quietly stands far off on the prairie.

This is the time of day when the mountain Apaches usually light their fires far up in the cliffs. In the gray of dusk, their smoke is difficult to see. A small group of people dressed in hides gather around the fire, sit and look out across the land as they talk about their world. Surrounding them is the vast wilderness that once belonged to their forefathers. Now they are fugitives. Their families have been killed and they themselves are doomed, and they know it. Yet there is still one thing they possess: freedom.

# Notes

## 1. THE LONG MIGRATION

1. According to language experts, there is a connection between the Apache language and that of the Indian tribes in Northern Canada and Alaska. They all belong to the same Athapascan linguistic group.

## 2. SAN CARLOS

1. Translation of text: "It is said that once, a long time ago, Coyote threw his eyes into the air. His eyes came back."

2. Translation of text: "I'm coming, I'm coming again, i yu-u. I'm coming, I'm coming, i yu-u. I'm coming, I'm coming, i yu-u, hi-hi-hi e-ya. Tomorrow we will surely find you again, wherever you go we'll see you again. I am coming, I am coming, i yu-u, hi-hi-hi, e-ya."

## 3. WHITE MOUNTAIN

1. Animal related to the deer family about the same size of a moose.

2. General Crook had given all the Apaches a number, and since then the numbers were often used as names.

3. As mentioned before, the Chipewyan Indians and the Apaches belong to the same linguistic group, Athapascan.

4. See author's book Land of Feast and Famine. Similar practices were earlier observed among the Apaches by Albert B. Reagan. Refer to Notes on the Indians of the Fort Apache Region, Anthropological Papers of the American Museum of Natural History, vol. 30, part 5, p. 309.

5. This could possibly be Victorio

6. A brother of the aforementioned John Taipa.

## 4. GLIMPSE OF THE OLD AND NEW

1. See History of Arizona, by James H. McClintock.

2. White Mountain Apaches seldom marry Indians who are not of the Apache tribe, and marriage to an Anglo is even more rare.

3. In the book Life Among the Apaches (New York, 1886, p. 264), John C. Cremony writes, "The Apaches believe in the immortality of the soul,

but they also place credence in two divinities, the one of Good and the other of Evil."

4. The numbers are taken from the book *The Rainmakers* by Mary Coolidge.

5. This information has been collected from the Office of Indian Affairs, Washington DC.

## 5. DANCE AND PRAYER

1. Direct translation is: woman-again-becomes-she-who, or, in other words, "she who becomes renewed by the sun."

2. This refers to Isdzann-nadlae-hae. As mentioned before, it was she who was impregnated by the sun and became mother to Nayenaezghani.

3. Actually, this means "blood relation."

## 6. APACHE COWBOY LIFE

1. Chaps: Two wide, leather leg protectors made of thick leather that are tied to a belt that hangs on the hips.

2. According to the Office of Indian Affairs, there were 25,341 head of cattle on the entire White Mountain Reservation at the end of 1938. These were divided between 700 Indians out of a total population of 2,811.

## 7. AN EXPEDITION IS PLANNED

1. *On the Border with Crook*, by John G. Bourke, p. 484.

## 9. THROUGH THE WESTERN SIERRA MADRE

1. The Sierra Madre's westerly range.

## 11. THROUGH THE HEART OF SIERRA MADRE

1. Without a doubt, the boy Charley McComas was in his time captured by the Apaches and taken to the Sierra Madre. This was not only confirmed by Yahnozah's reports, which seemed utterly trustworthy, but also by the accounts given by participants in General Crook's campaign. As examples see *An Apache Campaign*, by John G. Bourke (New York, 1886) and *The Truth about Geronimo*, by Lieutenant Britton Davis (New Haven, 1929). The boy's fate, on the other hand, was never known.

## 13. CAVE COUNTRY

1. Altogether, these various reports were so credible that when my expedition was over, I traveled several hundred miles to try to find the old Aztec Indian. In the end I tracked him down and was told he lived in the village of Granados in Sonora. But when I arrived I learned that he had died only a short time before. With his passing also disappeared perhaps the last Indian who knew the secret of the Aztecs: the art of tempering copper.

## 14. PRISONERS FROM THE WILDERNESS

1. This information was related to me by the Mormons in Garcia and was later confirmed by Apache Kid's slayer, Martin Harris, who now lives in Duncan, Arizona.

# Bibliography

Bancroft, Hubert Howe. *History of the Pacific States of North America*. San Francisco, 1888.

———. *History of Arizona and New Mexico*. San Francisco, 1889.

Bandelier, A. F. *Final Report on Investigations in the Southwest*. Papers of the Archaeological Institute of America. American Series III. 1890.

Barrett, S. M. *Geronimo's Own Story of His Life*. New York, 1906.

Bartlett, J. R. *Personal Narrative of Explorations*. New York, 1854.

Bourke, Captain John G. *An Apache Campaign in the Sierra Madre*. New York, 1886.

———. *Medicine Men of the Apache*. Bureau of Ethnology Report.

———. *Ninth Annual of the Bureau of Ethnology*. 1887–1888.

———. *On the Border with Crook*. New York, 1891.

Brand, Donald D. *The Natural Landscape of Northwestern Chihuahua*. The University of New Mexico Bulletin. Albuquerque, 1937.

Castenada, De Nagera, Pedro. *The Journey of Coronado*. By George Parker Winthrop. Chicago: Laidlaw.

Clum, Woodworth. *Apache Agent*. Boston, 1936.

Colyer, Vincent. *Peace with the Apaches*. Report to the Board of Indian Commissioners. Washington, DC, 1872.

Coolidge, Mary Roberts. *The Rainmakers*. Boston, 1929.

Cremony, Captain John C. *Life among the Apaches*. San Francisco, 1886.

Crook, George. *Résumé of Operations against Apache Indians from 1882 to 1886*. Washington, DC, 1886.

Curtis, E. S. "Vanishing Indian Types: The Tribes of the Southwest." *Scribners Magazine*, May 1906.

Davis, Lieutenant Britton. *The Truth about Geronimo*. New Haven, 1929.

De Long, S. R. *The History of Arizona*. 1905.

Dunn, J. P. *Massacres of the Mountains*. New York, 1886.

Farish, Thomas Edwin. *History of Arizona*. Phoenix, 1930.

Goddard, Pliny Earle. *Indians of the Southwest*. New York, 1927.

Goodwin, Grenville. "Clans of the Western Apaches." *New Mexico Historical Review*, July 1933.

———. "The Social Division and Economic Life of the Western Apache." *American Anthropologist*, vol. 37, no. 1.

Hodge, Frederick W. "The Early Navajo and Apache." *The American Anthropologist*, old series, July 1895.

———. *Handbook of American Indians*. Bureau of American Ethnology, Washington, DC, 1912.

Howard, General O. O. *My Life and Experiences among Our Hostile Indians*. Hartford, 1907.

Hrdlicka, Ales. "Notes on the San Carlos Apache." *American Anthropologist*, new series, 1905.

Irwin, General B. J. D. "The Apache Pass Fights." *Infantry Journal*, April 1928.

Lockwood, Frank C. *Pioneer Days in Arizona*. New York, 1932.

———. *The Apache Indians*. New York, 1938.

Lumholtz, Carl. *Blandt Mexicos Indianere*. Kristiana, 1903.

Lummis, Charles F. *Land of Poco Tiempo*. New York, 1893.

Mazzanovitch, Anton. *Trailing Geronimo*. Los Angeles, 1926.

Miles, General Nelson A. *Personal Recollections*. Chicago, 1896.

Morice, A. G. "The Great Déné Race." *Anthropos*, Band I, 1906.

———. "The Great Déné Race." *Anthropos*, Band II, 1907.

———. "The Unity of Speech among the Northern and Southern Déné." *American Anthropologist*, new series, vol. 9, 1907.

Opler, M. E. "An Interpretation of Ambivalence of Two American Indian Tribes." *The Journal of Social Pathology*, vol. VII, no. 1.

Regan, Albert B. *Notes on the Indians of the Fort Apache Region*. The American Museum of Natural History. New York, 1930.

Smith, Dana Margaret. *Indian Tribes of the Southwest*. Stanford University Press, 1933.

Thomas, Alfred B. *Forgotten Frontiers*. Norman: University of Oklahoma Press, 1932.

War Department. *Annual Reports of the Secretary of War, 1846–1886*.

———. *Record of Engagements with Hostile Indians. Official Compilation 1868–1882*.

Wellmann, Paul I. *Death in the Desert*. New York, 1935.